# A Moon TO Follow

# A Moon to Follow

## TO

# Follow

*A Novel*

Stephanie Lisa Tara

# A Moon to Follow

Preserve. Conserve. Inspire. Teach.

Stephanie Lisa Tara
CHILDREN'S BOOKS

Stephanie Lisa Tara Children's Books
San Francisco, California

Preserve. Conserve. Inspire. Teach.

ISBN Paperback: 978-0-9985060-0-5
ISBN E-book: 978-0-9985060-1-2

Printed in the United States.
10 9 8 7 6 5 4 3 2 1

For more information about the author, or the book, please visit: www.stephanielisatara.com.

# Preface

❦

*Hawaiian legend tells the story of a mystical Honu, or sea turtle, named Kauila.*

*As aumakua, or guardian spirit, she watches over the people of Hawaii as any mother would of her children.*

*Owing to a special relationship with Hina, the moon, Kauila is an expert navigator—even leading the ancient Polynesians to her islands, in the beginning.*

*There is great comfort in knowing Kauila is always watching.*

*Unless, of course, you don't want to be seen.*

# Introduction

❧

*"Mothers hold their children's hands for just a little while . . .
And their hearts forever."*

*"A n-Máithreacha shealbhú lámha leanaí le haghaidh ach ar
feadh tamaill beag . . . Agus a gcuid croí go deo."*

—Irish Blessing

# Tess

## 2016

### Hana, Maui
### December 24

Three hard knocks.

John!

I fling open the door. Christmas bells jingle.

On my steps is a stranger dressed in blue. A sharp Maui wind sails over his shoulder, into my house from the sea.

"Mrs. McAdams . . . there's been . . . an accident . . ."

His mouth is moving, but suddenly I can't hear him.

My mind transports me to Marama, I am with her in the bamboo forest. The steady ocean wind is with us there as well, its strength thuds millions of bamboo trunks together. *Click-click-click-thud-thud-thud.*

I can hear nothing else.

The man in blue still appears to be speaking.

Bamboo percussion is thunderous now . . . low thuds from wide bamboo trunks, staccato, higher notes from thinner stalks.

Then, Hina, the moon goddess interrupts the man in blue. She looks down, drenching him in light.

She extends a finger, pointing at the sea. How it sparkles in her sheen. The waves wink at me.

"Mrs. McAdams . . . ?"

I can hear him now.

"Ma'am . . . ?"

I look at him.

His head is fair, it catches the moonlight. I am reminded of my husband. John.

"Please ma'am . . ." the man on my steps says to me.

But Hina's glowing arms are around me, tight. I look to the sea, a silent flicker of diamonds.

**Nana ka maka;**
**ho`olohe ka pepeiao;**
**pa`a ka waha . . .**

*Observe with the eyes;*
*listen with the ears;*
*shut the mouth.*
*Thus one learns.*

Polynesian words echo in my mind. I do as Hina commands.

# John

How I will miss you, Tess, my love.

I am suddenly, incomprehensibly sad.

*Clarity.*

As I die, it comes.

# PART 1

# Tess

## 2016

### Stanford University; Palo Alto, California
### December 24

*"An áit a bhuil do chroí is ann a thabharfas do chosa thú!"*

*"Your feet will bring you to where your heart is!"*

The young man at the podium has the crowd's absolute attention.

"My Irish father taught me those words folks, he was a proud Irishman who lived by their wisdom, every day of his life."

The crowd is silent.

*"Look at your feet!"* he cries suddenly, startling everyone.

*"Now—place your hand on your heart!"* he continues, loudly.

*"Okay, now walk to your neighbor. Shake their hand,"* he says.

We do as he commands. I shake the hand of a girl my age, we smile.

*'So, how d'ya feel?"* he asks to us. His voice is commanding, loud and clear.

7

"Your feet brought you into *connection* with a stranger. That's what ya did. All of you. And something else too, you have started *the revolution*. You may not have known it—but that's exactly what you just did. The revolution of *caring*. You just declared, *I care*."

A few stunned claps trickle out of the audience. They morph into thunderous applause. The young man leaves the podium. A minute later, he returns . . . with . . . a sea turtle.

*But this sea turtle has no flippers*. It is maimed. Horribly. A gasp—erupts from the audience. I feel a lump rising in my throat. Tears fill my eyes.

"This is *Alani*, everyone," the man says. He holds the sea turtle tightly and raises her up to the audience.

*"Hello Alani,"* I say softly, my chest hurting.

"She was hit by a fishing boat," the speaker says, solemnly. He places Alani on the podium. He turns and takes an oddly shaped piece of what looks like plastic, from another person behind him.

*I recognize it from my studies, it is a prosthetic*. It is elaborate. The young man very gently fits Alani with her prosthetic, *her man-made flippers*.

People are gasping, pointing, looking at one another.

But then, Alani begins to move . . . with her new flippers! The young man turns to place Alani in a glass tank next to the podium. *She swims the moment she touches the water. She is fast!*

Thunderous applause resumes.

*"Atta girl, Alani!"*

*"You go girl!"*

*"Woohoo!"*

The speaker smiles and theatrically places his elbow at the edge of her tank, and his head on his palm, and nods back and forth in time with her swimming.

Cheers and tears from the crowd.

"Yep. She's happy folks. Good as new," he says.

He's right. The handicapped turtle is swimming in her tank, happy, free. He walks away from her tank and to the podium microphone again. His voice is soft.

He leans into the microphone and whispers in a language I recognize as Gaelic because I am Irish . . .

**"Is binn béal ina thost,** *it's a sweet mouth that is quiet,"* he says in Gaelic and English too.

"Quiet acts of kindness . . . like the handshake you just experienced, this is the change we need on our planet, everyone."

Then he leaves the podium.

"My God, who is he?" I ask the person on my left, whose hand I had just shaken.

"John McAdams," she answers. "Marine biologist. PhD. Here to lecture about his activism in Hawaii."

John McAdams.

*My heart turns over.*

# John

I feel the power. It is exquisite.

I have them! They are with me. I have reached them. I know it, and they know it. I have stirred their souls today. They are on their feet, cheering.

I look at Alani.

She is swimming with her prosthetic flipper as if she had been born with it. Her limb, taken from her by a heartless boat, was given back to her by my medical team.

I've been so angry. Deep down in my heart. Anger. Our planet needs a voice. Today, I was its voice!

*"Cha tèid nì sam bith san dòrn dùinte, nothing can get into a closed fist,"* Pa used to say. "John Kennedy. James Joyce. Ireland needs its sons to make it proud, John."

His words were a cloak upon my back. Keeping me warm, At times, too warm. But today, I made my father proud.

Then, I think of John Muir, my other father. *"When one tugs at a single thing in nature, he finds it attached to the rest of the world,"* he wrote.

I look out at the crowd.

*"Eiridh tonn air uisge balbh!"* I say to them. *"A wave will rise on quiet water, folks,"* do what you can, in quiet purposeful

ways. Small things. Open your hearts.

They are on their feet clapping. I raise a victory fist in the air. "Do your part! Change the world!" I cry out.

I go and pick up Alani. The turtle looks into my eyes. I kiss her. I look out at the crowd and give a small salute, from me, and Alani.

Then, I see her. Front row. Slight figure. Blue eyes. Staring. At me, and the turtle. I am stunned for a moment. Her eyes are almost too big.

Alani flicks her flipper at me. The crowd laughs.

"You want to go back in your aquarium, don't you Alani?" I ask her. I turn to place her back in the water. I look again at my audience.

"I'd like to leave you with some fine words from the inimitable John Muir . . ." I say in a deep voice.

**"When one tugs at a single thing in nature, he finds it attached to the rest of the world."**

Thank you! Good night.

The applause follows me as I depart.

# Tess

John McAdams.

His name has such a pleasant bounce to it.

John McAdams.

Irish! Like me.

I see him holding Alani in my mind. The gentle way he held her just right, beneath her carapace, so that she felt free to waves her flippers. She looked at him with trust. I saw it.

I must find this man. I must speak to him. I search the quad. Where did he go after the speech?

A warm feeling fills my chest. I can't stop smiling. What is this? This gooey, taffy feeling?

Love?

I laugh hard, aloud. A group of girls look at me. I once asked mother about love.

**"Níl aon leigheas ar an ngrá ach pósadh!"** she'd said in her matter of fact way, *"the only cure for love is marriage."*

Warm California sun warms the university buildings around me to gold, as I continue my search for John McAdams. Stanford is so beautiful. It was my first choice school. Their marine biology department is the best.

There, I see a person I recognize from the event in front of the library.

"Do you know where I can find the speaker, John McAdams?" I ask the girl with a clipboard.

"He left," she says, not looking up.

"Left? He lives . . . in town?

"He lives on the beach. Santa Cruz." The girl looks at me quickly above enormous square glasses. Her tee shirt says, *Save the Ocean.*

"Aha," I say.

My flip flops sound off a determined rhythm, as I race to find my car.

# John

Santa Cruz, California
December 24

My toes find a comfortable spot in the cool evening sand. I settle into my towel.

Love it here. Love the sea. I can never be far from the sea. Never. I must go to sleep with it in view, it must be there when I awake.

California or Hawaii. The latter being my own version of paradise.

*Hawaii.* The island of Maui. Hana, the unspoiled tip of it, raw and natural. *Old Polynesia.* There—was my spiritual awakening. *In Hana.*

I stretch languidly . . . the air is warm, still. The waves are lapping against the sand. A rocky protrusion that is a small reef has a seal hiding beneath it. My expert eye sees him.

I miss Maui. The turquoise sea. The freedom of life beneath it, unmatched anywhere in the world A freedom, unrivaled.

It's been almost a month here, on the mainland. Too long. I awakened there, I feel alive there.

Every man has an epiphany in life, a moment when his eyes open for the first time. The moment his heart falls in love with purpose. His reason. *Why he is here.*

Hana.

Raw. Real. Untamed. Ancient.

And Hawaii's oldest resident? The *Honu.* Sacred green sea turtle. It's DNA, back to the dinosaurs. Two hundred million years old.

*TWO HUNDRED MILLION YEARS.*

I ponder this. It always stuns me.

My scientific mind sees the Honu swimming through Triassic seas. Kiluaua erupting. Islands starting to form. Earth in its infancy.

As the Honu watched. *Watched.*

When I look into a Honu's eyes . . . I know I am looking back in time. I am looking back to the beginning. The inky blackness of the turtle's deep, calm gaze has held me, transfixed.

Honu don't look away—they love to hold a stare. They hold a stare, they stay, they visit. For hours. As if to say—*here, this is your home too.* Stay with me, under the waves, in this primordial soup from whence we all come. The sea.

A *memory* visits me as the sun sets.

A trip. With Pa, Jake. We were boys. That was the first time to Hawaii, with Pa. Or, Dr. Joe McAdams, Stanford professor of marine biology, as he was known to others. But to Jake and I, he was Pa, and he was taking us on an exciting adventure. To his favorite island, Maui.

*"To know a thing you must first feel it. Taste it. You cannot imagine it. You must be in it. 'Aye, then ye can see the truth,"* he'd said.

In life there is always a before, and an *after*. Before a thing, then after it. Who we were, before, who we are after.

I think about this. I remember a before . . . *Jake and I, holding hands, in our scuba suits. Flippered feet on the boat deck. Breathing our last gulps of ocean breeze.*

*Then, we jump.*

*Beneath the waves our tanks take over the distraction of breathing. All at once we are immobile. We move like any other sea creature.*

*We hold hands tightly, and propel deeper, deeper down.*

*Sunlight illuminates a world before us. Alive with teeming life in colors that defy a rainbow.*

*For me—it is their eyes. Eyes—everywhere. Looking at me. Fish. Dolphins. Sharks. Stingrays. Eels.*

*And then I see them.*

*A group of sea turtles.*

*Enormous, heavy, spherical beings that neither race nor dart.*

*Two small boys and five large green sea turtles spend an hour staring at one another.*

*Black-brown eyes with heavy lids come so close to our masks, we think they will suddenly introduce themselves as long lost relatives that now, found, want to know us well. As if they want to see a possible resemblance.*

Then I think about later, back on the boat's deck, when Jake and I are in our . . . *after. After the experience.*

We are changed. Forever. We had tasted another world. That taste now shapes us. It shapes our views. And it would shape every decision I made going forward from that moment—though at ten years old, I didn't know it yet.

"When this foot—this foot right here my boys, when it stepped on American soil . . . 'aye then I knew me' own heart's desire," Pa had said as we removed our scuba flippers that day. "Then I knew the truth. My truth."

Pa had looked at his naked foot. And then, at the sea. When he spoke again, his eyes were filled with tears.

*"But I, being poor, have only my dreams;*
*I have spread my dreams beneath your feet;*
*Tread softly because you tread on my dreams."*

Pa looked at me directly, as he spoke Yeats' lines. He never looked at Jake, it was to me that he directed his wisdom.

"I understand, Pa," I'd said, trying to stand up taller than my ten years. Pa's eyes glittered like the sea turtles we'd seen that morning beneath Maui's waves. Pa looked like he really wanted to know me, he wanted to see our resemblance.

*It would be twenty years before I'd understand how profound those lines from Yeats really were.*

I'd felt my right hand squeeze after Pa finished speaking. It was Jake, my twin brother. Letting me know he was there. He had heard Pa too. And, that was all Jake would do, squeeze my hand.

*Being simple—didn't keep Jake from feeling things.*

He'd learned to hold his twin brother's hand, and send me hand signals when he was pleased. It was a silent language we'd devised, from a very young age.

He was able to avoid Pa's eyes this way.

Pa. *A deep sigh escapes my throat.* Pa was proud. Pa was Irish. He'd left Ireland for a new life. America.

He'd also had his, *before*, and his, *after*.

His foot on soil that had the promise of a dream. Oh, how I understood that. Promise of dreams.

Pa worked hard at Stanford. And our polished American mother was a perfect wife for him, an educated philanthropist, as kind as a saint. And, the greatest supporter of his dreams.

Dreams. Pa was inside his glorious *after*. He'd tasted it here in America. The nectar. The promise. He was forever changed by the experience. His truth, here in America.

What wasn't part of his *after*, was Jake.

The official reason, the one doctors gave, was a twist of fate before we were born. Now, fate and the Irish are old friends. Fate is something that happens in relation to something else.

Jake's fate was to be deprived of oxygen. Simply put, I'd gotten more air than Jake. It was after all, two in the womb, not one.

Fate.

So I had air, and Jake did not. Jake wasn't deprived enough to kill him—no, fate is coy. Fate decided to give Jake just enough air so that he would live. *He would forever live in his brother's shadow with a dim understanding of what had happened.*

Fate. Irish fate. And Jake was the victim if it. But Jake was a topic not spoken of at home. Ireland, however, was.

"We must make Ireland proud," Pa would insist to us.

"Yes, Pa," I'd say dutifully. "We both will," I would add, for both my brother and I, feeling the responsibility even as a child to make Ireland proud, times-two.

An ocean breeze blows wet across my face bringing me back to the present moment. My eyes adjust to my surroundings. I see the tide coming in and decide to back up from the surf a bit.

I look at the fiery sun going down over the Pacific. Waves wash up over my feet. Seaweed between my toes.

And—a tickle!

I look at my toe, a tiny crab appears through soft ribbons of red and orange light. His body is so chubby—ah, a baby. I sit up without moving my toe where he is perched. He pauses and looks up at me. I see his eyes sparkle in this breathtaking twilight. I close my eyes.

"*John—buddy*—there's a girl here asking for you," my house-mate interrupts loudly.

His voice makes me jump badly, and the baby crab falls. But, I watch, amazed, as he crawls right back up again to the top of my toe. I am flooded with irritation.

"Tell her I'm out," I say, closing my eyes.

My toe tickles. The little guy is still there. The tickles feel like squeezes. My thoughts turn to Jake again.

"John—look man, she came all the way from campus. A bit of a drive, buddy."

I open my eyes and watch the sun go down with the tiny crab.

"A minute . . . a minute . . ." I say.

The sky is a watercolor tapestry of reds and purples and oranges and yellows and browns and blacks and blues. The sea beneath is a perfect mirror.

Large darkened silhouettes are boulders in the surf, they

glitter under the magical light. The black rocks trigger another memory. Yesterday. Leatherbacks. *With Jake.*

We'd gone out on a boat, he's loved boats since we were kids. Monterey bay was where he wanted to go. He was silent as always, until suddenly, he pulled on my arm, "here, drop anchor," he'd said.

He pointed, and there, in a multitude—were enormous, massive, circular black bodies. Hundreds. With deeply-gored backs.

LEATHERBACKS!

"Here? Impossible!" I cried aloud, grabbing my twin's arm.

"Jake . . . extraordinary," I whispered to him.

"*EXCUSE ME*—Hello—John McAdams—it is John, yes?"

Jolted, interrupted; again, I instinctively leap a foot in the air. The crab is jettisoned somewhere.

"What the—?" I sputtered.

The voice comes from a skinny, young woman who now stands before me.

Her eyes are enormous. Too big.

"Woah . . . you scared me!" I say.

The woman looks afraid.

I feel a tickle—again—on my toe—I look down, it's the baby crab.

"There you are!" I yell at his quivering head.

"I can see you have company . . . I beg your pardon," the woman says.

"Wait—" I cry out, then trip like a fool, falling flat on my face, directly in front of the crab. I see his impish glittering eyes, and once again I pounce to save him. He is pleased! He jumps onto my shoulder.

I look around—the woman is gone.

I shrug my shoulders and settle down onto the sand with my new charge. We watch the colors melt from sky to sea.

# Tess

*Where is my blue VW?*

Then, I see it in the darkness, under a street lamp. I stumble inside, stubbing my toe hard.

*Ouch! Dammit. Why am I so stupid?* I say to myself. The old car starts after two tries.

A bed & breakfast. I must find one. It is a beach town after all. I seem to remember one along the coastal highway. Signs flip by rapidly as I drive.

*So stupid!* I think to myself.

*"Ye are not stupid, darling lass,"* Mother says in my mind. "It's ye heart. 'Tis too big," she adds, her words flavored with Irish.

"Hmmm," I remember replying to her, I was a child of four.

"That's why I cried when Lulu died?" I asked, about the butterfly we rescued.

"Yes. 'Tis why," she said.

"Tess, ye have an affliction, ye do." Mother had sighed. "'Tis called; *Big Heart Affliction.* Through no fault o'yer own, in fact, 'tis the fault o'yer Irish genes, genes that go back, way, way back to Cork . . . 'tis where your affliction hails from."

"Will I get better, Mother?" I asked, horrified.

"No. Not at all child. 'Tis a lifelong affliction."

"Will I die of it!"

"'Aye . . . ye might. Ye might yet, child. *But, let us be clever.* 'Aye? Let us be clever, my Tess. We shall face the troll that smote you with this affliction and we shall call up all our fairy powers to defeat him!"

"Okay, Mother," I said, "but . . . what shall we do?"

"Well, child, when you see someone that needs your help, someone in need, and 'aye it can be a someone with wings— it can! Or feathers. Or fur. Or scales. If you see this soul, and it asks you for help, you must deny it. You must turn your eyes away and say, no."

"Oh . . ." I say. "I . . . um, Mother, I don't think I can do that?"

"'Aye . . . I doubt ye could child. I never could, either . . . God be saved."

"So . . . then . . . what will happen to me!" I cry to her.

"Well . . . 'tis a sad tale, my girl. For those like you—*those with big, big hearts, hearts that see inside others* . . . well . . . they are destined to carry the pain of the world."

"No!" I start to sob.

"Hang on, hang on there Tessie, let me have a look at ye . . ." Mother peers at me, she zooms in close to my face with hers. She wrinkles her forehead. She makes her eyes squinty. She looks intently into my eyes.

*"AHHHHHHH!"* she cries loudly, all of a sudden.

"WHAT????" I cry.

*"Briseann an dúchais tri shúile an chat!"* she cries.

'I see it in your eyes Tess! Ahhh. Your true nature! Your character! Tis revealed through your eyes," she cried.

*"You are a magical girl, and you will save the world, ye will, 'aye ye will,"* Mother declares.

"Even though my heart is too big?" I asked her.

"'Aye, *because it is too big,* 'tis that very *reason* that you will be able to save it," she replied.

Smiling at the recollection, I drive on through the California night.

Big-hearted, *I did it for love.* I did it for his words. For him.

Then, I think of an article I'd read that morning . . . it said something about rare leatherback sightings in Monterey. Two-thousand pound ancient sea turtles. Mothers.

It is nesting season. Maybe? I smile.

My heart begins to swell again.

# John

I dream in blue.

Such peace, here in my dream . . . the sea around me. Cool, with rivulets of warmth. Ocean currents like a soft lullaby, soothe me as I propel forward.

The weight of the water is on my back, the sharp taste of salt in my mouth as I breathe. I wish to never return to the land. Never. Here, under the waves, in this blue vastness is where I find my quiet place. I can think here. I have so many thoughts . . . such plans. So much to do.

There, ahead I see a flicker. A shadow. I push forward . . . I look to see my hands that are flippers, driving hard.

Who is that?

Here in my dream, I wait for a cue. She is coming. She approaches slowly.

Her eyes—catch me first. Luminescent. Too-large. Way, way too large.

I hear something . . . it is her heart beating. It gets louder. Louder. *Boom-boom-boom.*

Suddenly—I am awake.

My blue dream melts to black and I am in my bedroom. Jesus. I curse softly and get up.

I walk outside the beach house to find a velvet black sky,

strewn with glittering stars, above me. A million diamonds.
Winking.

I decide to go back to Monterey Bay at dawn. Maybe Jake's
leatherbacks might return?

# Tess

## 2016

### Monterey Bay, California
### December 24

I love to get up early. I always have. Mother always shared my energy.

"Best to make the most of every day, Tessie," she'd declare. She'd rise with the sun every day.

At first, when I was very small, I had thought the sun was a special friend of Mother's. It felt like we were sun's first stop, on her way to the top of the sky. Our little house on a cliff above the sea blazed yellow every morning around six.

But the moon was also a special visitor in Mother's magical house.

"Come now, Tessie. There's someone you need to be meeting," Mother said, as she took me from my bed. I was surprised because it was after my bedtime. We went, hand in hand, outside.

Gleaming down was a blue-white round sun! Except that its

light was cooling, and felt like a kiss.

"The *moon*, my Tess," Mother pointed upward.

"She comes in different shapes, as per her mood, 'aye she does. Not the same, every day like her sister the sun. No, this lass is mysterious. *But, always there, nonetheless.*"

"Ohhh," I'd said to her, looking up. The moon was easy to look at. I studied her. Her light didn't hurt my eyes like the sun. I liked to look at the moon. White. Blue. White. It kept changing colors.

"Mother . . . ?"

"Yes, Tess?"

"What is that . . . next to the moon . . . see there . . . the sparkles?" I pointed at the stars in the night sky.

"'Aye," said Mother. Her voice had changed. It sounded like she had drank a cup of moonlight . . . as if the moon cooled her voice down.

"Those there, are the folks that were here before us, dearest Tess. They used to live here, they did. Then, they left, to go and live up there. Near the moon. They like it up there, the moon watches over them. Those folks keep an eye on all o' us, they do."

"Oh," I'd said. "Mother, why did they leave?"

"Well, well now Tessie, *sometimes it's time to stay . . . and sometimes it's time to go.* It was just . . . their time to go, is all."

This made sense to me. And look, they are so beautiful now! Twinkling.

"I want to twinkle too, Mother."

"Oh Tessie girl, ye will, ye will, but not for a long, long, long time . . . yet, me' love." She hugged me tightly.

I am suddenly back, in my bed & breakfast inn. Standing, I walk to the window, and draw the curtains. There she is, I see Mother. She is now a third star in the sparkling night sky.

I check my watch, 4:30 a.m. I zip up into my running suit and pull the hood around my face. Quietly, so as not to wake anyone in the inn, I step outside and shut the door. The wet beach sand feels reassuring under my feet.

At this hour, the full moon still rules the sky. Her long white fingers touch the sand softly. It illumes in silvery glow. But, not for long.

As the minutes pass . . . the muted blacks and blues of the sky canvas melt into a watercolor wash of red and yellow and orange.

Minutes more and the colorful stain spreads, absorbing the darkness completely.

I lift my arms to catch the fading moonbeams.

*The beach stirs another memory.* Maui. The western tip. A sacred place, called Hana. My first trip to the islands. And, my first meeting with—her.

She came with her sisters across the sea.

The tops of their wet shells shining like opalescent pearls under a fat Hawaiian moon. Thousands traveled slowly, in a magnificent silent army.

Ancient mothers. As old as time. Mothers, who watched over the earth, as it grew. Time keepers they were, the story of the world recorded in their lined faces. Ancient, glittering eyes that saw civilizations rise, and fall.

Yes, she and her sisters knew this journey well. They remembered it. The journey was in their souls. To this very beach they returned year after year after year to lay their eggs.

I remember watching the multitude in a trance. All I'd studied evaporated into this real moment. Here, on a Hawaiian beach. I was not disappointed. One by one they came out of the sea and up onto the sand.

Slowly, carefully, one flipper after another. Their heads, and eyes, gazing forward. To the sand, to the dunes. To the place they would make their nests.

Then, one stopped. She turned her head to look at me. Her heart-shaped form was completely illuminated by the magnificent moon above her.

Her eyes. A mother's eyes. Looking right at me. I don't know how much time passed. But time seemed different when I was with her.

She, a creature from the beginning of history, *seemed to direct time itself*. As if time was stamped in her footprints and *as she paused—so did time*. I fully expected an epoch to pass as we locked our eyes in a gaze.

"Honu . . . " I whispered. The word for green sea turtle was yet new to me then.

SQUAWK—the scream of a seagull snaps my mind away from Hawaii and back to California. I am on another beach, at the crack of dawn. My eyes scan the Monterey Bay. Dark lumps, on the water. There—to the east.

*Leatherbacks.*

How different they are from their cousins, the greens of Hawaii. These shells are riveted, like helmets for battle.

My hand instinctively reaches to my shoulder—my camera— no! I've forgotten it. It's okay. I narrow my eyes and snap pictures, instead.

# John

It's her.

On the beach. A slim, slight form outlined in moon glow. How can this be? I check my watch, 4:45am. Everyone is sleeping in Monterey—everyone, except for the two of us. She is watching the water. My gaze follows hers.

There, on the surface of the sea, dark shapes emerge, disrupting the even line of horizon. The sea is bumpy, now.

I breathe in sharply. There, the silent army. The moon picks up the bodies now, and thousands of riveted shells gleam white on the waves. They float, a battalion, toward the shore, I can see heads now, bobbing. They are swimming. Fast.

*Jake's leatherbacks have returned.* The oldest and rarest of all sea turtles, these leatherback mothers are returning to the beach where they were born in an eon-old ritual, to nest.

They start to come ashore, legs moving slowly, as they are carrying two-thousand pound bodies, now out of the buoyant sea. They are the size of small cars, I instinctively step back.

Then, my heart lurches. She is there—next to the army, brave, unafraid. I've never ventured that close, not to nesting leatherbacks!

She . . . loves the turtles. This is love. I see this. She is unafraid because she loves them. And they know this too. They are undisturbed. They walk within inches of her, on either side. Turtles the size of cars. She is . . . communicating with them. When I realize this, *my heart turns over.*

No—I tell myself. Stop.

I've no time for this. I have too much work to do. My project in Maui. I have no time for this.

Then suddenly, I feel sand spraying all over me, it flies into my face, stinging my eyes . . . I blink to see a turtle mother, several feet away, using her back flippers to dig a hole for her eggs. Her enormous, powerful size was able to send sand hurtling two-dozen feet.

Now I am a witness too, like the girl. I drop to my knees and watch in awe. A two hundred million year old ritual, the cycle of life. Tears drop from my eyes.

I'm melting in emotion.

And, a little afraid.

# Tess

The mothers are here.

My heart pounds crazily. I have to kneel and hold my hands in my lap to still them.

My mind races back and forth from Hawaii to here. The same silhouetted lumps, slow-swimming dinosaurs, under their ancient sister, the moon.

"*Mother . . . look,*" I whisper aloud. "'*Aye, child . . . open your heart now, let it all in . . .*'" I hear her voice inside my head whisper back.

The turtles are enormous.

One by one, their black tank-shapes arrive at the shore. They walk through the surf, no break in their stride. As they approach, I see that these turtles are the size of my Volkswagen bug.

Their action is fluid, they simply don't stop, which is incredible given their size. They segue from swimming to walking, as they parade through the surf, onto the beach. Their feet make deep grooves in the wet sand, like heavy vehicles leaving sharp tire marks behind.

I crouch to my knees and crawl now on all fours. I inch closer. I can hear the sound of water splashing over their huge backs as they journey through the surf. From my low vantage point, here on the ground, they appear absolutely gigantic.

They seem to come from a vortex—a wormhole in time—*a doorway where long ago creatures found a tunnel from the past to the present.*

These mothers are stepping from the pages of earth's history itself. *As if the sea opened up to its very first chapter, written hundreds of millions of years ago.*

I remember now—time standing still—with ... *she.* In Hawaii. *She,* is not here, but her sisters are. And with them, as it was with her, *I am frozen in time.*

Huge moon shadows fall upon me, as the gigantic turtles lunge forward. Silently. One heavy-footed flipper, after another. A mission, as old as the story of the earth. It is written on their stern, angular faces. Their faces. Expressions. It's all there. In those deeply grooved lines, in the scaled flat brows, in the glittering black eyes *that see everything.*

Earth's oldest story. *The manifesto that made the universe.* Our planet. And us. The manifesto that marries ocean to land.

Then, I see that one mother on the far left appears slower than the others. She pauses, wearily. I strain my neck, I think her foot may be damaged. It looks twisted. It is at an unnatural angle.

My heart opens. I want to rise and go help her. But the scientist in me holds up a firm hand. I must not interfere. Yet my heart starts to hurt. I see, now. This mother is too tired to go on. Her swim must have been hard. Currents. Predators. She is exhausted. My hands are shaking.

Instinctively, I look up and see stars twinkling down at me about to fade out in the early morning light.

No!

# John

This, is my church. I kneel. Thousands of leatherback mothers are arriving under the blaze of the moon. I watch them come ashore, on their two-hundred-million-year old migration.

*It is, as it always was.* My heart thumps, I place a hand on my chest to quiet it.

**Is binn béal ina thost**, I think to myself. *Silence is golden.* The old Gaelic words whisper to me. *I am a witness here.* I honor this moment, as I peer into the old, prehistoric faces. Angular, placid, intense. Flat brows, straight noses, stern jaws. Dinosaurs.

I imagine the eggs that these mothers are about to lay, here on this beach, under this moon. Inside each egg, DNA that traces back to the beginning. *The beginning of earth's calendar.*

The notion strikes me so deeply I am suddenly dizzy. I place my hands in the sand in front of me to steady myself. It is so stunning to be here. To see this.

I look up and watch the turtles tracing a clear moonlit path, an uninterrupted blue line from the sea to the sand. They seek out and find their nesting spots. They settle into the task. Light coming from the enormous blue orb above plays on the ancient black leatherback bodies in a surreal, dramatic way as sand sprays, and holes are dug.

My mind plays tricks on me—where just a few moments ago, I was kneeling in the sand of a modern day California beach—the place is now utterly transformed into a *Triassic age* beach, newly birthed from a young earth in its infancy.

Then, I see something that doesn't fit the scene. An upright, thin form, next to the nesting mothers. It's her, again. How can this be? That close? They trust her that much? Impossible. My scientific mind rattles loudly.

Yet, it is true. She is there, alongside the mothers. She looks from one to another, as if to offer help. Two-thousand pound black bodies millions of years old, and a wisp of a human girl in the middle of them.

My heart turns over again. This time, I am no longer afraid.

# Tess

Halleluja! The ailing mother is now moving.

I look up to see the morning sky is lighter now, the sparkling stars are receding. I wave goodbye to them.

I watch the tired mother find a comfortable spot on the sand and settle down to nest. It's as if she knows she has triumphed! Sand sprays everywhere as she digs her nest, like confetti in celebration. She takes her time. There is no rush. She alternates her hind flippers to dig her nest deeper. A large hill of sand forms beside her.

Time passes. The egg laying begins. It is a quiet time. A reflective time. The mothers gaze at the sea, at the sand, at the moon. I am sure they are thinking about the great duty they fulfill, the obligation they have to create more generations. To leave their magnificent genetic footprints behind. As all the ancient mothers before them have done. The awesome responsibility in that is daunting, and satisfying. Yes, I'm sure they ponder all of this, as they rest.

Then, slowly, gently . . . the sun starts to extend her think pink arms outward as the moon quietly tiptoes to her sleeping space.

My eyes have not left the mothers. Their eggs laid, they cover their nests with sand as carefully as they can. They know the precious cargo they leave on this beach. They pause, and appear to take big, glorious breaths, and bathe in the dazzling colors of sunrise . . . the hues soak the sky, awakening it.

The mothers are moving now, away from their nests. They begin to flipper toward the rising sun. It's time to go home. A lump rises in my throat.

The mothers finally reach the sea. They slip under the waves.

I wait for the last mother to disappear. Then, I rise slowly, I unzip my hood a bit. I turn to go.

And, there he is.

It's John. John McAdams.

The soft expression on his face is like that of the leather-back mothers.

I step into his open arms.

# John

She slips into my arms as the new day's sun rises.

# Tess

His warm kiss is like morning sun.

# John

Love.

# Tess

Love.

# Jake

## 2006

### South China Sea
### December 24

The ship lurches. I giggle as my stomach lurches too.

*"Seas at sixty feet! Get outta there, man!"* a sailor screams into the wind.

I stay my post. I'm not missing this! Sheets of rain throw me to the floor. I laugh.

Lightning cracks the sky open! My laughter explodes too. What a game this is! I'm so happy I joined up to play!

Smiling, I pull myself up by the railing—the wind hits me hard, smacking me to the ground again. *Ha ha ha!*

There—some rope. I grab it and tie my waist to the masthead.

The storm is playing hard! A wave of water smashes the ship—cracking my head against the wood. I hear the sound of bone breaking and I taste blood. *I laugh and laugh and laugh.*

Waves are rising higher and higher, I see. Their shadows make my face dark. They crash—and the ship turns almost all the way to the side! *Yes, more, more, more!*

But no, the ship bounces back up. *No! Come on ship, play better.*

But then, I see it. A black mountain of water rising in the distance. Now the whole ship is black! I throw my arms out to the sides. *Yessssss!*

The wave gets bigger. And bigger, and bigger. Its shape is outlined by the big moon above us.

*"She will sink! It is certain,"* a sailor screams from below.

*"Come on! COME ON! It's your turn now!!!"* I scream . . . watching the black wave. It's so angry! We're gonna have big fun now . . .

I am alone on deck. *My ship, now!*

*I'm the captain!* It's me! It's me!

*It is finally me!* Captain Jake McAdams!

I am happier than I have ever been in my life.

# PART 2

# Jake

## 2015

❧ ⁓⁕⁜✦⁜⁕⁓ ❧

### Hana, Maui
### December 24

❧ ⁓⁕⁜✦⁜⁕⁓ ❧

Ouch.

My head hurts. I rub my temples to make it stop. The sun is hot. I wipe sweat from my face. Sand burns my feet. I feel nervous.

"Jake—is that you—glad you could make it."

"Yep," I say. I am too warm. I am sweating too much.

"Jake . . . look at this. It's finished. I finished it yesterday. I wanted you to be the first to see her," my brother says to me. I look, a large boat is bouncing in the water.

"Forty-three feet . . . my new cruiser," he says.

I wade out to the boat, and take my hat off. I dunk it in the sea and splash my face.

"Thirty knots . . . v-hull," he says.

John wades out and stands next to me. He touches the

boat gently.

"Sixteen foot beam . . . two large emergency rooms, Jake, amazing, huh."

I wonder if the boat is fun in storms.

"Oh, and 480-hp diesels," he says. John's fingers stop at the lettering. He smiles, touching each one.

## *The Tess*
*Turtle Rescue, Rehabilitation, Release*

It's for her. He built this for her.
Not me.

# Tess

Only John would give me such a gift like this. John, my *twin flame.*

I look at it again. Beautiful, shining. Perfect. Tears fill my eyes, again. He knows. He just knows exactly how my heart beats. Why it beats. What it beats for. Why it opens too wide. His opens too, we'd discovered together. Our cure for this? Love.

There she is. My boat. My boat dedicated to love.

## The Tess
### *Turtle Rescue, Rehabilitation, Release*

She is rolling gently on the sparkling water, waving . . . she is inviting me aboard.

Then I see him. Jake.

Jake is here. John must have called him. I sigh, and put my sunglasses on. I pull my sun hat down on my head.

John's twin brother scares me. He has never spoken a word to me. He doesn't look at me.

John tells me to accept him. I have. It is strange, a twin. A twin of a husband. Until one has experienced this—it is indescribable. Jake is an exact replica of my husband. Yet, in all other ways, *not my husband.*

I wanted to love him. I tried. John loves him. I opened up my heart, as I know how to do. I tried. But then came the day of the beached hawksbill.

She had floated to our shores, tangled in a fishing net. She had washed up on our Hana beach, unable to move. Jake found her.

And he sat, on the beach next to her, and watched her die. It had taken several hours. When she was dead, he went and found John. He told him exactly what had happened.

John's temper gave way that day. Usually, he reserved an innate patience with Jake. But, not that day. It may have been my tears that triggered John's anger.

I knew Jake was simple . . . I knew he was deficient. But . . . how? How could he do this? His brain was deprived oxygen, not his heart? It was impossible for me to grasp.

All I could imagine, was the hawksbill, struggling, looking at Jake, struggling, slowly dying. As Jake watched.

"She wanted to die," he'd said to John.

"No! You let her die!" John yelled. "You watched it happen."

"It was what she wanted," Jake said.

It was incomprehensible to me. It is still incomprehensible to me. I walk across the sand and wade out in the surf in my hat and sunglasses. I touch my boat . . . my fingers linger on the letters.

*The Tess.* Me.

*Rescue, Rehabilitation, Release.* What I do.

I see my turtle children in my mind. My babies, my hatchlings. The painted words recall images.

*Rescue.* Heads smashed by speedboats. Fishing tackle swallowed so deep inside a tummy that insides come out with the extraction. Cracked, smashed shells. Plastic bags choking throats, swallowed because they look like jellyfish.

An image of John, then . . . hoisting the victims aboard, one by one, onto our old trawler boat. John assessing damage. Me, holding flippers gently. And the helpless stare from their scared, luminous black eyes.

*Rehabilitation.* Honu Hospital. Our hospital. The one we founded nine years ago. Each tank labeled with love, with each patient's new name.

Hubert, for his lopsided, darling head. Samson, for his courage in overcoming a severe case of *fibropapillomatosis.* Mary, for bravery in guarding her eggs, in spite of her flippers and shell crushed by poachers. Jonah, for living deformed because of a plastic can holder since birth, his shell a painful eight-shape after years of suffering.

And, my eggs, the orphans. Rescued from ravaged, unsafe nests. My babies. Transported, cozy and warm in my nursery.

*Release.* Homeward bound, healthy and able. One by one, down the beach they crawl, flippering fast in a blur of excitement. Instinct drives them into the foamy surf, where they start their brand new amazing lives. I know they feel our love. It is a beautiful thing.

I look at *The Tess*, again. Yes, for all of my children, I am glad for this *ship of hope, of life, of love.* Above her is a pale, serene day moon, translucently beautiful against the blue sky. Hina is happy.

Then, my eyes fall onto Tess's captain.

"Thank you my love, " I say, walking toward John. "Merry Christmas darling."

Jake looks at the ground.

# John

*The Tess* shimmers in the sun. I see my twin gazing at her. I know he loves boats. I want to make him happy. I hope he is happy with our new boat.

They say twins have a bond, but my bond with Jake has always been weighted.

Weighted to me. He relies on me. It is a responsibility I took on as a small child. My brother needed help.

I was the other half, I was the helper. I taught him to speak. I taught him to read. I taught him to read signals. To the best of my ability, for I was a child, myself.

I guess I had a fantasy of saving him. Of rescuing him. *Rescuing him.* I turn those words over in my mind.

My twin. My identical twin.

We have the same face, eyes, nose, mouth, hair. We share the same hands, feet, legs, arms.

When I look at Jake, *I look in the mirror.*

Except his eyes—his eyes give him away. They are vacant. The blue that they are is a watery blue. Like rain-on-a-cloudy-day-blue.

I look in the mirror and I see fiery blue eyes blazing back at me. Cerulean even, when passion flares my soul.

I think of Jake and what he must think when he looks in the mirror of me. He has to see—all that he is. *And, all that he is not.*

Does he comprehend this, I wonder? This thought haunts me.

"Give her a spin, Jake?" I ask him. He is watching *The Tess* intently. I let a few moments go by.

"Let's take her out, buddy," I say, patting Jake on the back.

# Tess

## 2016

### Pipiwai Trail; Hana, Maui
### January

*It sounds like a tropical breeze, her singing.*

It is a surprising sound, low and bouncy, all vowels . . . dipthongs and glottal stops. I know a bit of the old Hawaiian language, and though I can speak a little, my voice isn't music like Marama's.

*I recognize the song . . .*
*'O ka hali'a aloha i hiki mai*
*Ke hone a'e nei i ku'u manawa*
*'O 'oe nō ka'u ipo aloha*
*A loko e hana nei . . .*

*Sweet memories come back to me*
*Bringing fresh remembrances of the past*
*Dearest one, yes, you are mine own*
*From you, true love shall never depart . . .*

My hips sway in an unconscious hula and my heart is immediately light. The song words bounce from the floor of the rainforest to its canopy, lingering on ferns and moss until they trip and spill back down through the dense green again . . . *A loko e hana nei* . . . "Marama!" I cry, happily.

A tiny, singing woman emerges from a wooden hut, her eyes are two flecks of sparkling volcanic glass. She lifts her hands to me. I always marvel at her size, no more than four and a half feet. Her form is solid muscle. Stunning for a woman of her eighty years. She walks many miles each day. It is her passion. Walking. Walking meditation, she calls it. It balances her, she says.

Marama believes in balance. The balance of all things. A lack of balance, is when problems arise. Getting back into balance is the key to happiness. Being in balance with all things in nature. Honoring all things in nature. And . . . giving thanks. Gratitude.

I have learned much from Marama, whose name means *moon*, from ancient Polynesian lore.

"All you need to know can be seen, *keiki*," she would teach me, using the Hawaiian word for child. "In the flowers. In the sea. Look—see the faces in the rocks?" she'd ask.

And indeed it was true. In the lava that had cooled thousands of years ago, were faces. Some smiling, some scowling, depending on the shadows. I looked, I learned.

Marama taught me to, *be*. To be inside a moment and not wish for more than that. She taught me to reflect. To pause. To breathe deeply. To see not only with my eyes, but also with my ears. My nose.

"I already see with my heart, a lot," I'd told her when we first met.

"Oh, I know, *keiki* . . . I knew from the moment I saw you and looked into your eyes."

"You did?" I'd said, remembering Mother who had said the same. My too big heart that wanted to save the world.

*"Hoʻolaʻi na manu i ke aheahe . . . my child,"* she'd say, *"the birds poise quietly in the gentle breezes,"* meaning peace within is most important.

My love for this old Hawaiian woman had grown like the flora around us on our walks. It took root, deep in the fertile soil beneath our feet. It bloomed high to the sky in glorious pastels. Its seeds taught me patience. Her glittery black eyes would lock with mine in total understanding. Such a comfort when she squeezed my hand in hers.

*"E komo mai . . . ke aloha,"* she says to me today, *"welcome, beloved."*

Then, she stops to inspect my feet.

"Mmmhmm," she says. She approves. Bare feet only. Walking with Marama was always without shoes.

She takes my hand and leads me behind the hut. She has a smile on her face that can only be described as a child seeing a lollipop for the first time. It is always this way with her.

Her old gnarled hand fans out in front of her to show me the rupturing wild ferns that have achieved the height of her house. Their fronds dip low, almost touching pink kokiʻo flowers that have a found a peaceful spot to bloom.

Marama pauses here and touches my nose. I am suddenly dizzy with an overpowering scent—kokiʻo blooms have a potent fragrance that has the power to send purveyors into a spell.

We walk on in silence. No more lessons from Marama. Time passes. I know she will tell me something of importance soon.

"Hina . . . has been active . . ." she says, then.

"Oh . . . ?" I reply.

"Yes. Tonight is *Hoku*, my child . . . night of the *full moon*."

Ah, I understand. She has read my mind. She knows I have been wanting a child. She knows. I haven't had to say a word to her. She read my mind.

"Tonight then . . ." I start to say.

"Perhaps," Marama squeezes my hand. "Hina will show you the way when the time is right."

I nod.

"But remember . . . Tess, you have been charged with your other babies, you have Kauila's children to look after, child . . . imagine! *To be entrusted with her babies.*"

Oh, I know the deep honor. To be selected by a goddess. To look after her children. It is the culmination of my life's work, to have Kauila, sea turtle goddess choose me. A tear slips down my cheek. I think of my hospital. The work we do there for Kauila.

"Yes . . . Marama, I know . . ." I say softly, wiping the tear away.

Her voice trails off as she looks toward the sky. The slight outline of a white day moon hovers above. She is looking hard. My eyes follow hers. We are quiet and in that space the rainforest becomes louder.

Sounds of creatures all around us are like a chorus, I think because we are focused so intently on listening. Slithers and chirps and crunches and whooshes. I close my eyes to take it in. *Yes, I can hear you . . . I can hear you all*, I say to myself.

Then—I hear Marama gasp.

My eyes fly open. I turn to look at her quickly. Her hands are on her cheeks, her eyes are wide. She is staring upward.

"Marama—?" I exclaim, I look up to see what has upset her so much.

*An immense owl, a pueo—in a perilous nose dive!* It is falling directly across the silhouette of the moon.

Then— in a surprise shift—the peuo jettisons upward, just as fast, retracing its perilous flight.

The owl repeats this pattern, zigzagging against the outline of the full moon, each time more perilously than the time before.

"Hina is Peuo's mother," whispers Marama.

"The moon goddess, Hina, is mother to the owl?" I ask, surprised. I did not know this.

"Yes," she replies.

"Peuo's father is Maui, this island. The land upon which we stand," she said.

She looks into my eyes. *Fear.* That is what I see in her eyes.

"Peuo sends us a signal, now, Tess. A sign. It is a warning," Marama says, her voice flat.

After a while, she stands and takes my hand again. We are silent as the forest around us speaks. We listen intently to clicks and hiss's and drips and whooshes and brays.

"*Ka `ohe . . .*" she says, then. She turns onto a higher path, cutting through a paddock of white flowers.

I know where she is taking me.

*Ka `ohe* is bamboo.

Yet, my head is still filled with visions of the diving owl.

A warning. Of what? Who is the warning for? John. Our hospital. What is going to happen? Chills fill me in the rainforest heat.

We walk.

Soft earth under my feet feels cool and comforting, like carpet. My strides are long and slow. The pace starts to calm me.

Then, I hear it. Distant, at the very outside edge of my hearing.

**Click, clack, thud.**

The sound intensifies. It is a curious sound. Rhythmic.

**Click, click, clack-clack-clack, thud-thud-thud.**

Soft percussion notes.

The thinner ones click and clack a resonant baritone, the wide heavier ones thud in deep base. A soothing hollow echo picks up the beat then, as a swift ocean breeze blasts over my shoulders.

Then I see them. *Bamboo. The bamboo forest.*

Rising from the jungle floor, is a soaring cathedral of green watercolor columns that are *millions and millions* of bamboo trunks.

Their hues are divided into variegated tones of every conceivable green imaginable. It is overwhelming to take in all the color variations, delicately arranged by a master of shading.

*Only nature could have painted this.*

The breeze has changed now and the bamboo trunks hit one another in a new way, creating a musical tenor that is softer, it is the most soothing sound in the world.

Then the wind changes again, causing the trunks to swing and sway and bang into each other harder, and a dramatic new magical, thudding resonance happens . . . a thousand wind chimes playing a mystical symphony.

My heart lightens completely.

Instinctively, Marama squeezes my hand. I close my eyes and listen. I can hardly feel my feet, my heart opens and flies high up to the tops of the bamboo trees. It stays there, floating free.

The thuds and clicks change again, as the ocean breeze shifts. Marama squeezes my hand again and I hear her giggle.

I am instantly transported back in time . . . *and it is John now, squeezing my hand, here in the bamboo forest.* The first time he brought me here.

"Will you marry me, my darling Tess," he'd said that day.

Bamboo played its lovely low cacophony of sound around us. Angel's trumpets, in the middle of the paradise.

"Yes, my darling John," I'd said. And, our love was made complete. *Two healers had healed each other.*

"Tess, sit," Marama is speaking to me now. The forest floor is cool here, I am feeling happy again.

She starts to sing . . .

**Me he lau no ke Koʻolau ke aloha . . .**

*Love is like a zephyr, gentle and invisible but present nevertheless.*

She finishes, and looks down. Long moments pass.

She looks up at me. Directly in my eyes.

"Heed Peuo's warning."

I nod.

"Next week we will have a *blood moon.* A full orb, the color of *fire,*" she says.

I stare at her.

"It's best to make a sacrifice to Pele soon."

She looks at the piece of bamboo she is holding in her hands. She hands it to me, kissing my cheek. Then she stands, and turns to leave. She doesn't turn back. I watch her form shrink and disappear into the green bamboo.

I must tell John we have to visit Kilauea.

# John

## 2016

### Ahihi Bay, Maui
### January

"I'm glad Tess isn't here." My voice cracks with anger. The pit in my stomach twists and widens as I stare into the red water. I will never get used to these sights. Never.

The turtle's head is split open. A blood pool grows around her bobbing body. Her carapace—shell, or what is left of it, is shattered.

The agonizing pain this creature must have felt!

This visual image, the movie, of a boat slamming into a turtle, slays me. My stomach twists again. Tears don't come though, white-hot anger has replaced them.

The turtle's blood reaches *The Tess*. Red waves wash over the starboard side, leaving a pink sheen on the new white paint.

My hands have instinctively balled themselves into fists—I

knife my head around to find the killers responsible. A boat, there has to be a boat nearby. My eyes search the horizon. Then I scan the shore. I study the surface of the water for a clue.

Nothing. *Dammit.*

I grab my snorkel mask and dive. The turtle's blood splashes my face. I pump my arms full strength. I slap the water hard, I kick, converting rage to speed.

But as I approach, I see that her eyes are closing. I hold her broken body to me. Her head is in my hands. I press my cheek to hers.

She shudders. Then she looks at me weakly. And then, her body is still.

I hold her to my chest, treading to stay afloat. Her body is light, in the water. She is cold, slippery. Her flippers fold over my back. *Like, a child.*

"John."

Jake's voice from the boat.

I continue to tread water. I am covered in blood. I blink back red drops out of my eyes. I stay. The dead turtle in my arms stays with me.

The scientist in me starts to whisper. Protocol. Disengagement. Protocol. But I remain, paddling. The weight of the dead turtle is the weight of a child. I hug its lifeless body. I am crying.

A splash, then. It's Jake.

He swims to me. He takes the turtle in one arm, and me in the other. He hauls us both into the boat.

With a hose, he washes us both down. His face is impassive. He hoses the red blood off the turtle, off the deck. His hose pools a red puddle, then he switches the hose to high, and wipes away all evidence of the death.

He moves methodically. In silence.

I stare at my twin.

It is *me*, my face, my hands, my legs, it is *me*—holding the hose, cleaning the blood. But it is a *macabre version of me. A soulless, me. A, me,* I might meet in a nightmare.

I feel anger rising, and I know this isn't good. Yet, I can't . . . seem to stop it. Rage in the form of hot salty tears forms in my eyes.

*This freak of nature!* This monster. What hell I have been given, that I must look upon an exact version of myself—and see a mindless robot, *devoid of all feeling?*

It is a monstrous thing to do to me! The horror of it slaps me in the face, *I flinch.* My eyes are wild. Incredulous. I stare as Jake continues to hose the deck.

My shirt is soaked in red, but I cross my arms to protect it from Jake's hose. *I want to remember the turtle!* Her death has meaning for me. I want to remember this day, and redouble my efforts to right this atrocity. To save these creatures from mankind's greed!

But not Jake, *Jake cleans the evidence away.*

He finishes with the deck, and goes below. He fetches a bag from the hull.

I watch him put on rubber gloves, carefully. He approaches the body of the lifeless turtle. His face is deadpan. There is nothing there.

I watch in continued horror. The turtle is stiff now. Frozen in death. My twin brother yanks her up by a flipper that makes a cracking bone sound—*I wince and cover my ears.*

He hoists her like a sack of ice, flinging her into the black plastic bag. Her weight makes a loud thud noise. He seals the bag with an elastic tie.

His face, emotionless. Devoid. Empty. It is the face of nothingness.

I look at the black bag, and the creature I'd just held in my arms—inside. If Tess were here, she'd have named her. She names all the turtles. In life and in death.

I will name her, in my wife's absence. *Grace.*

I close my eyes and say the Lord's prayer, and I make the sign of the cross. Grace will not die in vain, I promise myself.

And then in Gaelic, I whisper aloud . . . "**Eiridh tonn air uisge balbh**, *a wave will rise on quiet water.*" Our work—Tess's and mine, will redeem this lost life.

My thoughts are cut short by he shriek of something above the boat.

It is an owl. Strange. The owl is diving. Is it falling?

A nose-dive. Death spiral. I stand up and see it continue to go down. Straight down.

Then, incredibly it sails straight up again.

Then—down—again.

A light outline that is the moon is behind it.

Jake, doesn't notice.

# Tess

## 2016

Molokini Crater, Maui
February

"Ready, darling?"

My husband nods at me in my scuba suit, I check my tank, and give him a thumbs up.

I take a last look at the surface. The aqua green waves, the sunshine sparkling their tips. And the thin strip of horizonline of green that is the shore.

I breathe in the crisp ocean air, and close my eyes, hot sun on my cheeks.

Then—I flip backwards off my boat.

I fly through the air, my arms and legs close to my torso in a trained reversed somersault.

My body hits the water hard.

An overwhelming sensation that always reminds me of a

heavy blanket suddenly happens—and I sink down, down, down into the deep ocean water.

It only takes me a minute to adjust. I adore this feeling of heaviness from the water. *It is like a hug.* It is soothing. I feel safe and free.

I stretch all my limbs outward, as far as I can.

Then, as my body retracts back into itself something magical happens.

Being *below*, is different from being *above*. To move with ease and grace, *I have to change.*

I look at my arms, they must be my *front flippers.*

I change the curve of my legs, and they stretch outward into *hind flippers.*

Then, I find my central weight . . . in the center of my back. Yes, there it is. *Much like a shell.*

Now, I feel right. I move slowly, carefully. I feel for the current. I have it. Then, I ease into it, it is running north.

Easy.

I use the current to my advantage. I float with it, propelling gently with my flippers. I move my head up and around very slowly so as not to disturb my glide.

My energy evenly distributed, *I conserve . . . then jettison, with the movement of the sea.*

As I move forward, I feel the current change a little, a surge of water tells me something is ahead. Soon, the influx brings three young hawksbills into view. We flipper in place, holding our spots and observe each other. I feel their eyes scrutinizing me. I gently tread, and lob my head slowly from side to side. They seem satisfied with this and swim away. Then, I tilt, and kick hard, propelling my legs outward.

*I descend.*

A dense city of life abounds before me. Reefs are bursting, teeming and alive in robust activity. The spellbinding explosion of coral color dazzles my eyes as I swim close to the bumpy, sometimes jagged edges. In one glance, I see lobsters, octopus, crabs, sponges, groupers, clown fish, eels, parrotfish, snapper, jellyfish, anemones, sea stars, shrimp, snails, and clams, who have come out to say hello.

Algae grows wildly here, a constant food extravaganza as well as the very breath of the ocean, as it breathes life-sustaining oxygen into the sea. Happy gills move in and out with the plentiful air, as I float through torrents of bubbles. I touch some algae with my fingers carefully, feeling its malleable surface. Bubbles escape the rubbery leaves and float upwards as I do. I know that more oxygen is produced by undersea algae than all land plants worldwide combined.

Being respectful to the inhabitants here, I propel extra gently, in and around the bulging reefs. Goosebumps of green rice coral spill onto lower beds of protruding finger coral that seems to beckon me to come, come closer. I glide over the coral easily by centering my weight and propelling with my limbs that are flippers.

Brain coral holds fascination for several sleek Moray eels, their sinuous bodies undulate with the current over and under the formations. I adore their expressive faces that always look surprised, as well as their beautiful coloration of red, yellow and orange speckling. I see some at five feet and others at two, they are all

71

fat and happy munching away as they love to feed constantly.

My flippers softly jettison me forward, and I see my favorite . . . lace coral. It does remind me of Mother's Irish lace that covered almost every surface in our home . . . the same intricate interlocking designs are woven in this living rock that attracts flame angelfish by the hundreds. I have to blink back the fiery color.

Out of nowhere—a snow white eel slides over my mask, I see a dozen more eyeing me from the lace, I turn slowly to see a barracuda patrolling, nearby. I acquiesce to form and glide very gently, not wanting to disturb sediment and block the eels' view.

I am feeling at home in this magnificent reef, and I think the sentiment is returned as rainbow runners pass by my face, followed by a blackfin tilapia who is chasing him. He rounds on the tilapia and uses my body as a blockade. I don't mind at all. When he departs, I dive low with my powerful hind flippers and immediately bump into a longjaw squirrelfish. He reels—but rights himself and quickly burrows into an inviting anemone bed.

Time to rest, I stop moving entirely and just paddle softly in place. The weight of the water around me is utterly soothing, it is both cool and comforting. I breathe deeply from my tank. I look up and see light streaming in from the surface in neverending ribbons of yellow. I look beneath my feet and see the quiet beauty of tranquil reef life. And the sand, like grains of pearls, iridescent, rolling and light. Above all, beautiful, lovely, silence.

**Mai ho'oni i ka wai lana mâlie**, I think to myself, *do not disturb the water that is tranquil.*

Then, the peace is suddenly disturbed. Ripples awaken me,

and bubbles explode. Another diver is in the water. I shrink back, drawing my flippers in close. The diver's form comes into view. It is large. Enormous. I see he is grotesquely fat.

His fat legs are kicking hard and haphazardly, his flabby arms are flailing wildly. His movements are upsetting everything—stinging columns of sand kick up from the sea floor blinding me, and everyone else.

*Marama is right . . . these haoles are different.* I see the tank on his back is dented and rusted. My instincts flash red flag warnings. Instinctively I pull upward, into my tank, again. It feels like a shell.

I allow my weight to descend on its own, as I watch the new haphazard diver. My body finds and settles into a welcoming school of *lau hau*, threadfin butterfly fish, I am grateful for their presence. I can still see a little of the diver from inside their yellow, white and blue body-camouflage.

But then, the *lau hau* start to spin their familiar dance around me and I am rendered blind inside a swirling funnel of color. I feel the edges of their fins and bodies tickle me through my suit. Faster, faster, faster! The bodies spin around me. Ha ha, I laugh. My head starts to spin with them and I feel dizzy as if on an amusement park ride!

Then—all at once—their column of color *freezes*. Thousands of lau hau eyes look into mine. I try to count them, it is impossible. Maybe . . . ten thousand eyes? I smile.

Then, I extend a hand, and gently place it between their bodies. They look at me and those closest to my hand, part a little. I can now see outside.

*My heart stops.*

I see the fat diver from earlier—he has a *large knife* and he is *stabbing a stingray* in what looks to be a rage. His grotesque form is shaking blubbery fat as he battles this poor fish. The look on his face is deranged. Blood is spurting from the ray's side as he twitches uncontrollably. I realize, in horror, that I am watching a murder.

Rage fills me—I use all my flipper-strength to propel madly toward him, I scatter all the *lau hau* fish in my wake.

As I approach, I see the diver is lunging at the ray's head, now. He hits it squarely with the knife. Blood fills the water. The attacked fish stops, reels in pain. My plan is to put myself between the ray and the diver.

The diver sees me. He is surprised. *I move in between his knife and the stingray.* The diver's fat face is contorted with rage.

Suddenly—John is in front of me.

He shoves me aside roughly—and nods his head upward, signaling for me to ascend. His other hand is on his hip. It's holding an *Archangelo UWS stun gun.*

I ascend, but with my head looking down. I watch John, through my flippers. He has pointed the stun gun at the diver's face. Then he snatches the knife from the diver.

I stop ascending and tread to watch. The diver fights—he hits at John's hand, and John, my husband—*fires the gun.* The diver slumps immediately, I watch John place the knife in his belt, and then turn, to find the stingray.

The poor ray is spiraling downward, in its final death spiral. Its grey and white body blurring into the blue. I imagine it floating to the bottom of the sea, to its final resting place. I close my eyes and say a prayer. John dives after it, but soon returns, I see that he knows it is too deep to follow. *Some depths are to be taken, but once.*

Sighing, I paddle upward, until I am at the surface. I climb onto *The Tess*. I grab the radio, and I hold it at the ready. I wait.

Then John emerges—in his left arm is the unconscious diver.

"He's out cold," John spits. "He may be on drugs . . . or drunk . . . or crazy . . . I don't know."

I look at the unconscious man. Unshaven. Obese. He smells horribly. Even after being beneath the sea.

"The ray is dead," John says, his voice, ice.

I shake my head. I look at the grotesque diver. The *Haole*. (Hawaiian for white man.)

"Let's put him in the back," John says.

We take his arms and legs and haul him into our rescue room. We leave him on the cot.

Then we go up to the deck, grateful for the fresh clean air.

"Do you know him," I ask.

"Nope," John answers.

"He's Hawaiian," I say.

We pull up the anchor, and set sail for Hana.

About an hour later, we hear noise from below. We find the diver sitting on the cot.

"So. Who the hell are you?" John says to him. "Not that it matters, I'm dropping you off at the police station."

"What charge?" the man slurs.

"Animal cruelty," says John. "Felony. Animal cruelty."

"*Kanapapiki*," he says, swearing in Hawaiian. "*Son of a bitch.*"

He waddles off the cot and up the stairs to the deck. The stairs creak as he steps on them. He looks about three hundred fifty pounds. We follow him as I hand John the radio.

I watch the diver light a cigarette. He turns to stare out at the sea. Smoke spirals up and around his balding head.

Then—I see a strange thing, he has a scar, a deep scar, behind his jaw. It looks like a *bite* mark.

The diver's cigarette smoke lingers at the deep scar, as if trying to cover it up. I point to it, showing John. His eyes catch mine, and narrow.

Then, abruptly, the diver turns to look at John.

"I'd put that radio down, if I were you," he says, quietly. He flicks cigarette ash onto our deck. His stomach jiggles as he does.

John glares at him. Then he dials the coast guard.

"I'm in business with your brother Jake."

John stops dialing.

He stares hard at the diver, who now smiles.

"Bullshit," John spits, and continues dialing.

"I'm in business—with your brother," he says again, spitting. "We do this, n'that."

"Right. Tell it to the police," John says, holding the phone to his ear now.

"Yes, this is John McAdams. Can I speak with officer Stanton, please?"

"Name's Kaholo," the diver says. "You'll be wanting to tell 'em dat. Oh, and here's some ID too," Kaholo fumbles with his wallet, it is inside a sealed plastic bag. He takes out a license and a small photograph. The photo is of he and Jake.

John looks at the photo.

"John—it's Jim Stanton here." The voice rings out from John's phone.

John is staring at the photo of his brother and the fat diver. They are at a small café in Hana. Two beers are on a table in front of them.

He pauses.

"Hi Jim, yes, it's John here. Hey buddy. Sorry—false alarm. Tess thought she saw a poacher. She was mistaken. Righto. Yep. See ya this weekend buddy. Hello to Lily."

John hangs up.

"Ask your brother 'bout me," Kaholo said, smiling. His teeth are black.

# Jake

## 2016

❦

### Pipiwai Trail, Hana
### March

❦

I can't breathe.

I fight.

I still can't breathe.

I fight harder.

But my arms won't move. My legs won't move. I try again—I kick. Hard.

I can't move. Nothing. I am still in the same place.

What is happening? I try once again. I need air. I need to surface. I need air. I fight—as hard as I've ever fought in my life.

Nothing. Noooooooooooooo!

I scream. But no sound comes out of my mouth.

Suddenly—I am sitting in my bed.

A *nightmare*.

My head aches. I look at the floor of my hut.

A black snake is staring at me. I stare back. The door—I look at the front door. It is open.

The snake looks at the door now, then back at me. I look over the black snake's head. Outside. The jungle.

I hear it hissing. Slithering. Crunching. Buzzing. Clicking. Crackling.

A wail. A grunt. A whimper.

The snake is still looking at me. I get up and walk to the snake. I sit down in front of it.

Its head starts to sway. My head sways.

It is watching me. It darts its tongue. I dart my tongue.

Its head strikes—moonlight from the window drenches the snake's fangs bone-white. My head strikes—I bare my teeth at the snake.

*Our heads hit—hard.*

But—I have limbs. The snake does not. I take my arms and the hands attached to them and I grab the snake's throat.

I squeeze. I squeeze until the snake's eyes bulge. And burst. It drops dead in my hands. I let it go in a thud on my floor.

*Thud.*

I look at the window. I am covered in moonlight. I look down. At me, at the dead snake, at my bloody hands.

I get up to go to the bathroom. I need to wash myself clean.

# John

Honu Hospital; Hana, Maui
March

I look around our emergency room. I take great pride in this hospital, our hospital. The one my wife and I built together.

My eyes sweep over the tanks. The patients look peaceful.

In the middle of the room is my Tess, her back is bent to her work. She is very thin. She looks so small and frail to me—astonishing when I think of her enormous heart. Inside that tiny frame is a heart as big as the ocean.

My heart swells. This happens with my wife. Regularly. She is more than a wife. She is my Tess. My other half. My partner, in saving sea turtles. In saving our oceans. In preserving our planet.

Two human souls dedicated to saving ourselves . . . from ourselves. From other humans. Humanity, per se, has a lot to learn. It's hard work. It goes slowly, for we are only two people.

*"Meileann muilte Dé go mall ach meileann siad go mín . . ."*
I say to myself, *"The mills of God grind slowly but they grind finely"*.

Loud creaking noises interrupt my thoughts. It's Tess's sharpie pen. I laugh—Tess is making name cards.

Twenty-five tanks are scattered around this room, our emergency room. I watch as she finishes a card and attaches it to a tank.

### HANNAH.

She's naming her children. I sigh. We've been trying for a child. The doctors can find nothing wrong with either of us. Marama tells Tess that when the time is right, we will be blessed. I never question Marama. It is good wisdom. I walk around the room. Most patients are asleep. I look at a chart.

"John, could you help me with this one," my Tess asks then. She is preparing Hannah's tank. Soft sand, algae, seawater.

"Sure, doll," I say.

Hannah is our latest patient. Tess is arranging her algae carefully, to the side. She creates a mound of sand and a depression where the water will pool.

"Some sea water, John . . ." Tess directs me to a bucket.

I carry the bucket to Hannah's new tank, and pour some water into it. It fills, covering a lot of the sand. I leave a small space for Hannah to rest upon.

I lift the tank and place it on the floor. Tess attaches Hannah's name tag. Then she goes to do her admittance paperwork.

I turn and leave. Outside the sun is hot and the heavy humid air is full. I rub my eyes hard. I look at the glittering azure blue sea. At the prodigious flowers hanging over my head. The ferns exploding at the foot of our hospital grounds. The fertile black soil that grows everything to extremes.

*When the time is right.* I hear Marama's words in my head. *When the time is right.*

They say Marama is descended from Polynesian mystics. They say she knows things. Sees things. I drag my hands through my hair roughly.

"I think I'm ready, John." Tess is calling me back into the ER. "John . . . ?"

"Okay love, lets do this," I call out, walking inside. We put on surgical gloves. Hannah is resting on a temporary gurney.

"Hello darling," I croon at her, I see her eyes are half closed and that the heavy antibiotics I gave her are working.

"She's gained a little weight, John," Tess says smiling.

We lift the large hawksbill turtle. Her hundred-pound-weight challenges us for a moment, but we find our balance. It's a few steps to her tank.

"She's a good girl. A brave girl," Tess says softly.

Hannah opens her eyes.

"In you go, sweetheart . . ." Tess says, lowering her hind flippers, I lower her front flippers as she looks at her new home.

"You're gonna be fine my darling . . ." I whisper.

The turtle looks at Tess. "Hannah," says Tess. She strokes her head gently. Hannah closes her eyes and seems to smile.

It had been touch and go with this one, I hadn't expected Hannah to survive. We'd found her off the coast of Wailea. It wasn't good. She was floating. The last stage, before death. But I saw her. I got her. It was her dazzling shell shining in the tropical sun that saved her.

Mistakenly called tortoise shell, these Hawksbills have jeweled mosaic shells of brown and orange coloration outlined in black line patterns.

Poachers consider them gold. So, they're hunted.

These murders for profit—*otherwise known as poaching*—of Hawksbills specifically, has reached all-time highs. It's outlawed of course, and that seems to drive the poachers harder—a shell can fetch thousands of dollars on the black market.

Hannah wasn't the victim of poachers, however. Surgery revealed that she'd eaten a *plastic bag*, thinking it a *jellyfish*. It had blocked off her intestines. She was literally starving from within. Gas backed up and formed an air bubble. Hence . . . she floated to the surface.

*Floating in agony, waiting to die.* Until I found her. We gave her antibiotics and put her on a drip, to hydrate her.

And now, in her new tank, she looks peaceful. Tess is rubbing her flippers to help her sleep. Only my Tess would hold a patient while she slept. She doesn't want Hannah to be alone.

My girl. My Tess.

I make a decision. I know what I need to do.

"She'll be okay doll," I say, but Tess can't hear me.

She's sitting in Hannah's tank, holding her flippers while she sleeps.

# Marama

## 2016

### Pipiwai Trail; Hana, Maui
### March

Mother knew I was different, right from the start.

"*Ka ua,* Mama" . . . I said . . . looking at the cloudless blue sky.
Rain.

And it rained, that evening.

"*Kai . . .*" I said, once, standing in a dry river bed.
Flood.

The river flooded soonafter.

"Koni will die."

And when my little brother died that spring, of dengue hemorrhagic fever, my mother brought me to the Kahuna, the priest. In secret, for it was illegal, forbidden to worship the old religion.

"Your little *moon* has been chosen, he said, referring to my namesake meaning the moon, *"she has the gift,"* he whispered, for it was forbidden to say such things, *"ua i waeia. Ua i ka makana."*

*"Ua he hookahi o kakou,"* he said to mother in the old tongue. *"She is one of us."*

*"Kahuna lapa'au,"* he added, in a solemn voice. I knew this phrase. Kahuna, priest. *Lapa'au*, future. Priest who divines the future.

*Me.*

"Keep this quiet," the Kahuna directed her. *"E mālama i kēia mālie."*

"She will see *qaitu,*" he said. *"Ghosts."*

*"The dead? She will see the dead?"* Mother's face was white.

"Yes, she will see *qaitu*. She will know them when she sees them. She will know they are of the *Po-Milu*, the dark spirit-world."

Mother nodded, frozen.

"She will know *ghost sickness* too. She will see when a ghost or evil spirit inhabits a person. *She will be able to reason with the ghost."*

Mother stared, nodded. Mother was a child of the ancient world. She took in what the Kahuna said to her.

Later, at home, she treated me exactly as she always had. She had me help in the house. She had me help with my sister. I cooked, I cleaned, I sewed, I gardened.

But I would catch Mother watching me. This was different from before. *She would watch me, watching things.* Especially the rocks. There were faces in the rocks. I would spend long hours looking at them, trying to hear them. Sometimes they would tell of a coming storm. Other times they would signal to me about Pele, and new lava flows from Kiluaeah. Sometimes they just wanted company. And I would sit by them and listen.

Mother never asked me to tell the future. *She knew the gods didn't work that way.* She knew they would speak through me when it was their will. If I had something to divine, then I would speak. And, only to mother.

"Don't tell anyone else about this," she'd warn me. Everyone in our village had joined the new church and attended every Sunday. But mother had not given up the old ways.

*"He mea weliweli e huli ae ko kakou lākou kua i nā kūpuna o kākou!" It is dangerous to turn our backs on our ancestors,"* she said.

It had been over a hundred years since our ancient ways had been stifled.

Still, mother insisted we honor the old ways. She would teach me in secret, of the *Akua, the Gods.* She taught me to honor Kane, god of the sky and creation. And Ku, god of war; Lono, god of peace, rain, and fertility. And of Kanaloa, god of the ocean.

In a part of the rainforest that only mother and a few others knew about, stood *heiau, shrines.* Thatched triangle roofs and mud walls, these temples grew out of the earth they were made from.

*Inside, fearsome images carved of wood ruled.* They stood on flexed knees, arms and hands with mouths open in a teeth-bared expression. Tiki gods, scared all—but me. I felt comforted in front of their bared teeth and aggressive stances. Evil magic was to be feared. *The gods were our protectors.*

In the days of the ancient ones, the Polynesians, human sacrifice was common, it was what these gods demanded. No, they were not to be trifled with, that was clear. They were to be obeyed.

Mother would recite to me from the **Kumulipo**, the bible of truths. The lessons were easy to understand. Darkness from light. Land from sea. Life. Men.

*"Marama, it is important you know the tale of the beginning,"* mother would whisper on our late evening walks. *"Our sky father Wakea and earth mother Papa gave birth to the islands. The gods Kane and Kanaloa, their children. And, the priests, Marama, you— are their offspring. You are from the stars. We are all tied together."*

"I am, mother?" I'd ask.

"Yes . . . you are my little Marama, we have been blessed . . . you have been chosen." Mother's eyes were glittering black glass. I felt so proud to have made her so happy.

"Marama, listen to me. **Mana**, spiritual energy, it is what drives us. *Mana* is inside us all. *Mana* is inside flowers, stones, beasts, rivers. It is the essence of all beings. Our intelligence, skills. We must pray to nurture our *Mana*," Mother warned.

"I will, mother, I will . . ."

"And above all else, Marama, my little moon," mother loved to refer to my namesake of the moon, "our **aumakua**, our ancestors, are always with us . . . they are the most powerful. *Aumakua* links us from the *present—to the past*. To the very beginnings of the world! We are all one story, new chapters unfolding. Our ancestors will appear to us in an earthly form, Marama, so always be watching . . . which I know you do! I see you. I watch you," mother said.

I grew up hearing of **polo**—*right living*. Living in respect of other things. *Balance*. Always balance. Honor. Tradition.

Respect for our land. Our sea. Ourselves. Plants, animals. Always balance, unity.

Mother taught me *healing*, how to make **la ʻau lapa ʻau**, secret potions, herbs from the forest to treat ailments.

We healed together, often children, for very often the haole's medicine didn't work on our bodies, our special bodies that were of the gods, of the stars, as mother said. The haole medicine, the white people from the mainland, gave us poison potions that sickened us. Some died. But our own healing always worked.

"*Restoring balance,*" mother would say. "That is all that is needed to heal sick bodies, sick bodies are sick because they *have fallen out of balance.*" She used prayers and chants at every stage of an illness, from the gathering of plants to the final **pani**, or ritual end of the treatment.

I followed mother, I was her shadow. I studied her and learned. Time passed.

I grew.

I used my powers sparingly.

I practiced **nana ka maka;**

**hoʻolohe ka pepeiao;**

**paʻa ka waha,** *I observed with my eyes;*

*and I listened with the ears;*

*and with my mouth closed.*

This is how I learned.

My mother always praised me for honoring the family with the special Kahuna blessing I had. My special powers to *see.* A blessing.

It was later, that I realized it was also a curse.

# She

Pacific Ocean; Hana, Maui
March

I move slowly.

I rise.

I fall.

I let the current take me.

I always have.

I always will.

There is such peace in this.

A letting go.

My mind is clear.

My thoughts are free.

I am here.

Where I am supposed to be.

My dreams are in blue.

They shimmer yellow.

And turquoise too.

I open my mouth to feed.

I am satisfied.

I float.

I sway.

Here in my dream, I stay.

Then, a vibration.

Water around me pools.

My body tenses.

Then, relaxes.

Then . . .

Into the deep,

I go.

# Tess

## 2016
❦❦❦❦

### Bubble Cave; Makena, Maui
### April Morning
❦❦❦❦

My eyes are glued to John's flippers. He is looking for the cave entrance.

It is a clear, perfect day, visibility is over a hundred feet. I watch his flippers stop, then tread.

I know he is looking for the rocks that lead to Bubble Cave. They are easily missed, I know. I have had trouble finding the entrance, myself.

There—he's found it. A rush of his flippers alerts me to follow.

We are at fifteen feet, at the sandy bottom of Makena beach at Maui's most southern point. The slope of the sea is different here, it deepens unexpectedly.

I watch as my husband's fair blonde head seems a bright light bulb here at the entrance of the lava tube which leads to a magnificent underwater cave. My heartbeat quickens.

He enters.

I follow.

The wide opening soon narrows as we slip inside this ancient space. I flip on my diving lantern and follow John's flippers. We swim about fifty feet into the tube, John turns his flashlight on, and we finally reach the end, a large cave area.

He is signaling to me to surface. Both our heads pop up together. I remove my mask.

"Darling, it looks different in here . . ." I breathe, looking around the twenty-foot cave. About six feet exist between us, and the cave's ceiling.

John removes his mask. "The air pocket is smaller, Tess," he says, eyeing the ceiling. "The water has risen."

"A storm?" I ask.

"Not sure," he replies.

"Just a sec," he says, diving down to the bottom. It is usually a shallow fifteen feet.

He surfaces. "It's about twenty feet to the bottom . . . the water has risen five feet. Could be storm surge."

My ears are popping . . . this is certainly new. Air pressure is different.

"Has there been any volcanic activity? Mt. Haleakala's dormant, yes?" I ask.

"Yes, she sleeps."

John looks perplexed. I watch him studying my face.

His face changes suddenly.

"John? What is it," I say.

His mouth has dropped open. He is staring over my shoulder. I turn. As I do, I hear it. A strange sound. A gushing, sucking-air noise.

At once, John is next to me. He thrusts his hand against the wall. It crumbles. The wall crumbles like charcoal under his fingers.

"John!" I cry, my voice ricochets off all the walls.

"It's a tunnel," he says.

He shines his flashlight into the opening.

"My God," he says.

I go to see.

Under the light, inside this new tunnel, are dozens . . . hundreds . . . of bright orange bags. They are shiny. 5678, 5679, 5680, 5681, 5682. The bags are numbered.

"Someone dug this tunnel," John says in a low voice that chills me. He swims inside and drags a bag out. 5678. I watch him open it. I already know. John already knows.

When his flashlight illuminates the contents, it isn't a surprise to either of us.

Hawksbill shells.

No bodies, just shells. The bodies, have presumably been disbanded with. Sold, eaten.

But the prized shells, are here. Hidden. Bubble Cave is being used as a poacher's den. A pirate's den.

*"Dammit!"* cries John, then.

I find, I cannot not draw a breath.

John turns to look into the cave again. Then he disappears inside. I follow.

# John

Under my nose.

On my island.

My hands touch the sides of the walls of this new tunnel. I keep my flashlight at my waist as I swim.

Fifty feet more. Endless orange bags beneath me.

A hundred feet, now. The orange bags continue. A funerary line. I feel the souls of the dead crying here in this tunnel at the bottom of the sea.

I am so angry, so upset.

The dead beneath me are growing to a number that my heart cannot take in. I estimate five hundred bags. A thousand murdered turtles.

Murdered for these, their shells. Their bodies.

I close my eyes and cover my ears so I can drown out the *screams of them dying*—for I hear them all. Every one. As it was butchered, *some still alive as its shell being ripped from its back.*

My wife is next to me now.

"John, John, John my love," she says to me.

"Please . . . we are so far inside, let us return . . ." she pleads.

I look to the ceiling of the tunnel, I see it has closed in on us . . . Only a few inches of air space. I have not been paying attention. This is indeed a risk. Should the sea rise . . . should the water rise higher in the big cave way behind us . . . I have put Tess in danger.

"Tess, you are right," I say.

Then—as if out of a nightmare more terrifying than the one we are presently in—we hear a muffled noise.

It comes from the very far end of the tunnel.

# Tess

We are in trouble. Every instinct in my being tells me this. John has taken us too far. His passion has overcome his prudence.

I look down at the flashlights we are carrying. I look down to the end of the tunnel. I know we don't have much time. Whatever is at the other end of the tunnel, knows this too.

"John—now—go!" I say to him. I turn and start swimming. I look back—incredibly he is still stalled.

"JOHN!" I yell. I shouldn't have, but I did.

He moves. He starts to follow me.

Truth is I do not like small spaces. I much prefer wide-open skies, and stars and sunrises that paint the horizon in endless miles of openness. And seas that spill endlessly beneath me, forever.

Cramped tight spaces, are not my thing.

Then—a scraping, crunching sound. It gets louder. My heart is now thumping very loudly.

I feel a yank on my ankle, I look back—my husband is motioning for me to let him go ahead of me. He has his hand on his stun gun, at his hip.

The crunching noise is very loud now. My God, I understand. Something, someone is trying to *seal this tunnel.* They are trying to bury us inside this cave.

*Poachers.*

Poachers returned to check on their bounty.

# John

I hate myself. I have brought Tess into this mess, I took her into the tunnel. Will I never learn? My Irish passion will be the death of me. Of us, both.

I take my gun out, I turn it to the highest level. I pull the safety. *Whomever is trying to kill us will have to deal with me first.*

I see up ahead, in the water, a large cloud has formed. Sediment has been stirred up. Someone has frantically tried to fill in this tunnel opening.

They had to have heard us. They know now—that we know.

This is no small operation. This isn't a local job.

No.

To have amassed thousands of shells, each expertly bagged and numbered—*this is an organized crime operation.*

And whomever is in charge knows, that we know.

I will fight, to the death if I have to. I make this decision easily. I will do all I can to save Tess.

# Tess

Here it is, good versus evil. We are now facing the enemy. Straight on, here he is.

I know my John will protect me if he is able. I am content in this fact. I feel no real fear. I marvel at this, I feel no fear other than leaving my husband. In death, that is.

It is a strange thing to face a situation like this and know inside of it that *I still feel the greatest love.*

I watch as John approaches the sediment-filled area where the opening used to be.

I look up, to the ceiling of this larger end of the tunnel. The twelve or so inches we had a few minutes ago, has now shifted to about six.

And, the water is still rising, I realize.

# John

I push my mask over my face hard and ram the mouthpiece into my mouth. I sink to the bottom of the opening as fast as I can.

*Got him!* My flashlight reveals billows of sediment from movement on the other side. *Smack-smack-smack.* Someone is hitting the sand. *Someone is forming this wall!*

*Bastard!* In full fury I step back a pace, extend my right leg, remove my flipper, flex—and then kick as hard as I have ever kicked in my life.

*My foot hits him*—I know it the moment of impact. It's not sand, not mud, it's *a body*. I feel it. I know it. I let no time go by—I kick again, harder. I quickly remove my other flipper and I begin a rampage of kicking with both legs.

The wall gives way, and the body I had connected with moments earlier—*is gone*. It is hard, impossible, to see through the thick sediment that has filled the water.

I pop up to the surface and find Tess waiting—in horror I see she has her head pressed to the ceiling of the tunnel. The water has risen—is rising—*fast.*

An outside storm must be doing this.

I grab at her wildly and dive us down through the muck, through the sediment. We are blinded, but I catapult us forward and out of the tunnel.

We surface inside Bubble Cave.

"John . . ." Tess sputters, spitting mud out of her mouth.

"John—*look*—!" My wife points the water behind me. A hat is floating there. I pick it up, a faded cap.

"Time to get out of here," I say to Tess.

We swim the fifty feet to the opening. The water is becoming colder, and choppier, even here inside the lava tube. Soon we reach the entrance.

We emerge—torrents of rain batter us.

"Freedom," I whisper, taking her in my arms. The rain, which has become monsoon strength, pelts our bodies. We stay like this for long moments.

*Then my wife screams.*

My head knifes hard in the direction she's looking. It is unmistakable. A tall figure is getting out of a raft at the far end of the pier. A hundred yards down.

I squint hard to see. The rain is pelting, the wind is screaming, we are exhausted from our trauma.

A man. My height. My physique. My hands. My legs. Mop of blonde hair my mother used to try and tame with a comb.

If only I could see his eyes. But no matter.

It's Jake. He was here.

Was he fishing? Was he boating? Was he swimming? Before the storm picked up?

My wife's scream has already accused him. My brother tried to kill me? It is not possible. It is simply not possible.

I remember the numbered orange bags in the cave. I need to call the police.

# Tess

Bubble Cave; Makena, Maui
April Midday

"*Nothing here, Mr. McAdams,*" the officer, in a diver's suit stands in front of my husband, hands on his hips.

John and I stare at each other.

We look over the officer's shoulders to see a dozen more officers in diving suits emerging from Bubble Cave. They are swimming back to the shore.

"Nuthin, sir," one says as he steps out of the water.

Another comes ashore. "About two hundred feet of lava tube . . . empty. Found some crabs, lobsters, a sea snake. But that's it."

"*Impossible!*" John cried. "Let me go inside!" he barks at the Sargent in charge.

"Police investigation, Mr. McAdams. Can't have you disturbing evidence."

"But you just said there's nothing there! I am telling you—my wife and I were here two hours ago! We found hundreds and hundreds of orange, tagged bags of contraband! Sea turtle shells! Massive! It's an organized operation!" John's face is blood red.

"Do you have photos?" asks the Sargent.

"No. We didn't bring a camera."

My heart sinks at this. It is my fault. I often forget cameras. I have since I was in school. They have never been important to me. "Look hard and remember," Mother would tell me. "You're best camera is here," she'd say tapping my head and heart.

The officer walks to a dozen others. They talk quietly.

"What difference does a camera make? I saw hundreds . . . thousands of bags of contraband! They have to be in there somewhere! My wife and I were almost walled in by the criminals!" John checks his watch, "It's been less than two hours. You must have the wrong tunnel."

"Mr. McAdams, there is only one tunnel as you described. One. It's a small cave. One tunnel at the far end of a small, fifteen-foot cave."

"Impossible, " John says.

"Look. We found zero. Nothing. But you may escort Bill here, into the cave and show him what you think is there." The Sargent nods at a large, burly diver.

John puts his mask on and dives into the water as gracefully as a dolphin. The burly officer stumbles and then follows.

*The poachers were tipped off,* I think to myself. I am certain it was Jake on the pier. John is not certain it was. I am certain it was Jake.

But a disturbing question remains.

Is it possible . . . that a mentally retarded man, a simple man, could be involved in something like this?

Is it?

I watch John disappear into the cave.

# John

It's empty.

I shine my flashlight into the lava tube. Fish. A crab. Rocks. Sand.

I dive down, twenty feet. I propel hard with my legs kicking up sediment I know I shouldn't.

I feel for the floor, the walls, with my hands, wildly. I wait. One minute. Three. Five. The sediment settles. I swim farther down. I hit a back wall. This is even farther than Tess and I swam. How did they get several hundred utility-sized enormous bags of contraband sea turtle shells out of here in two hours?

Several men couldn't have done so. Ten couldn't have. Twenty, perhaps.

No. *God, no.* The scope of the operation blinds me. I put my face in my hands.

# Tess

## 2016

### Honu Hospital; Hana, Maui
### April

"It's a *what*? A *drone*?" I pick up a large metallic spider and inspect it carefully.

"A drone . . . ? I ask the young woman.

"Yes, a DRONE. Or Small Unmanned Aerial Systems, SUAS." The woman is smiling, her nose ring glitters.

"And . . . you are telling this thing works . . . like my cell phone? My Smart phone?"

"Yes, ma'am. YES!" The woman has streaks of blue in her hair.

I turn the drone over in my hands. It is large, three and a half feet of microprocessor technology.

I glance at the business card on the table; *Sasha Goodwin, Ocean Tech Industries.*

"Ms. Goodwin—"

"Call me Sasha . . ."

"Sasha . . . I like it. I like the drone. I do. I'm a Silicon Valley escapee, you may know . . . I glance up at the black-clad woman with the blue hair, nose ring, and bookish library glasses.

"This is . . . kinda . . . *cool*," I say, setting the drone onto the table. "Tell me more, Sasha . . ."

"Dr. McAdams, drones *are* cool," she begins.

"Call me Tess," I interrupt.

Sasha looks at me. "Tess," she says.

She looks like a cross between a rock star and a librarian. I like her. She has sparkle, spunk. She's fun. She also looks like she doesn't take any crap from anyone, I think, giggling aloud.

"Tess?" she asks me.

I shake my head at her. "Please go on—" I say.

She is encouraged now, and leaps to her feet, throwing her arms out.

"Tess. Imagine . . . you could send out trusted little minion soldiers to do all your turtle tracking? And I mean, 24/7."

"Mmmm . . ." I say.

"Imagine you had a little turtle army at your disposal. A battalion of turtle crusaders that never tired, never faltered, worked round the clock for you?"

"*Turtle crusaders . . .*" I smile.

"Imagine all the time you would then have freed up to care for your patients?"

I'm nodding at her.

"To rescue new patients? To, watch over your eggs? To conduct releases? Think of the time saved. Think of the efficiency your entire operation here would enjoy!"

The girl is crackling with electricity.

Then Sasha grabs the drone off the table and flings it recklessly from one hand to the other. Her nail polish is the same blue as her hair.

"Meet *Joanna*. She is powered by a high performance single board microprocessor."

"Oh . . . Joanna," I say. I'm gripping the table. Joanna is three feet across, and a mass of silver metal wires. She looks like an enormous robot-spider.

Then—Sasha leaps onto the table top with Joanna.

"Joanna is eager to begin her task Tess! She is programmed to do what you do. Just better."

Sasha winks at me. She pulls a remote control from her pocket and touches a button on it.

*Two red lights that are Joanna's eyes*—turn on and glow at me.

"Jesus!" I scream, jumping away from the table now.

Sasha is speaking from the table. Joanna is leering at me.

"Joanna is eager to be dispatched, she will fly out and scour the beaches, Tess. She will locate turtle tracks. She will follow these tracks to the nests. She will observe nests. She will report back to you their location and their condition. She will do all of this aerially, silently, efficiently."

I'm cowering on the ground now beneath Joanna's red eyes.

"Joanna will perform her duties day and night, in all weather. She can stream video to you Tess."

My face is aglow in red.

"I mean, you could try to match Joanna's effectiveness . . .

but honestly Tess . . . Joanna has the bonus of *secrecy* too. She can see everything. She can see everyone. She can even report . . . *poachers.*"

My eyes narrow. "Tell me more," I whisper.

Sasha's eyebrows rise. "*Joanna can see where we . . . cannot.*"

I'm convinced. "I'll take her. And any of her friends too," I tell Sasha.

"Terrific. You will not be sorry!" Sasha says, eyeing me closely.

"You will stay on here and help us set this up?" I ask the blue haired girl, from the floor.

"Yes, indeed. I can stay as long as you like!" she replies, grinning.

# Kaholo

## 2016

### Makena, Maui
### April

"How m—?" I rasp. The high winds hijack my words. "How many," I repeat.

"'Bout four hundred, 'aye, ye know—I'd say 'bout five hundred, tho' I'll be a gimp, I will, if it ain't six hundred," he says, his cigarette is a red glow in the darkness.

"Hawksbills?" I ask, incredulous at the large number.

"'Aye. Mostly. Few greens. A leatherback as well, I'm told tho' ye never can be sure o'these things, ye can't."

"No! Leatherback? Yer kiddin' me?" My heart is racing now. My mind, the cash register, is making *cha-ching- cha-ching-cha-ching* noises. Thirty-five hundred a turtle, but a leatherback . . . it's triple what the others bring.

"Cash—we only take cash," I say excitedly.

"'Aye," he tells me.

"When?" I can hardly contain my excitement.

"End o' month."

"That's just great. *Great. Great. Great.* I'll schedule the trucks." I am stammering with giddiness.

"Oh, I can deliver to ye, direct, I can," he says, drawing hard on the cigarette. "No pick-up required."

"Direct—oh—really?" I ask, thinking of the money I won't have to pay drivers and haulers and divers.

"'Aye. I know where da drop is at, I do."

"You do?" I ask. *How would he know?* One of my guys slipped up. *Dammit.*

"'Aye. I hear things. I do. Ye know. Things. I'm no *gowl*, ye know. No *tool* either. *Stupid—tool means stupid.*"

I'm stunned. *Stupid?* Did he just say that? The boss just said this? *He sounds five years old.*

"Ah . . . no . . . no you're not, boss . . . not at all. You're a smart dude," I say slowly, feeling a little wary of the man who controls all the money in this operation.

"'Aye, I am, dat's da truth, it is. And don't ye forget it. I do da *killin'*. You do da *storin'. I kill. You store.*"

I stare at the red glow of his cigarette in the darkness. I am speechless. Suddenly I feel the need to *test* him. Criminal instinct calls me. *I'm not gonna give up the drop.* He's gonna have to tell me. He's gonna have to show me he knows where it is.

"Might you need help at the drop, boss? I ask him, "that's a lot of product."

"Nah," he says. His cigarette is burning low.

"Okay . . . cuz ya know, it's a lotta work . . . even finding it. Not a job for just one man . . ." I say.

"'Aye, ye may be right. Ye may. Big gale last week too, stirred up da *cave*," he says.

My eyes open wide.

"Yeah . . . that's right boss. The *cave* gets stirred up. Could be dangerous."

"Specially, dat dere cave," he says.

"Right . . ." I say slowly.

"*Ssss-tttt-iiii-rrr-eee-dddd it on up, it did, it did, stirred it on up it did*," he declares, sounding out all the letters as a child might do and then singing them as if in a nursery rhyme.

I am dumbfounded. Silence hangs like a fat full moon between us, silent, burning bright. My mind races to the hundreds of thousands of dollars I'm slotted to take home after this drop. From this dude, who is sounding out words in a song.

Then—he starts to laugh. Giggle.

"Somethin' funny, boss?" I say, feeling dizzy. He's crazy, I realize. But he keeps laughing. Then he is laughing so hard he is on his knees. Now he's choking, and still laughing. It's not normal laughing either. It's crazy laughing.

He finally stops.

My legs start walking backwards instinctively. Away from him.

"'Aye. Okay, send me three of your best blokes. Have 'em meet me at Spitting Cave on Oaha in seven days, no more, mind ya. An hour before dawn," he says in a commanding voice again.

*Oaha? Honolulu?* "Boss. It's right here on Maui. Bubble Cave," I say.

"No."

I look at him. No trace of the laughing child now.

"'Tis changed, it has. Bubble Cave infiltrated."

I'm astonished.

"'Aye, so here's da deal now, listen up: tell yer people to take da boat to Oaha, nice n'quiet, too. It's near Honolulu, but be careful, all o'you. Be discreet! All of ye blokes, I ain't sayin' dis twice. Spitting Cave. 'Bout an hour's ride."

"Okay," I say, my voice trembling, "I need a cigarette."

He steps out of the shadows. He cups his palm around my cigarette to light it. The moon catches his blonde hair glowing it an eerie bone white.

These haoles are so strange looking.

"Thanks, " I say. His blue eyes are ice. I glance away quickly.

# Jake

Makena, Maui
April

*There's a race of men that don't fit in*
*A race that can't stay still*
*So they break the hearts of kith and kin*
*And they roam the world at will.*
*They range the field and they rove the flood*
*And they climb the mountain's crest*
*Theirs is the curse of the gypsy blood*
*And they don't know how to rest.*

I like saying these words.

I like singing these words, even better.

I've learned them. They are in my head. They are stuck in there. No getting them out now.

The sailors taught me. On the ship. They sang these words over and over.

I listened.

I learned.

Now I sing them too.

I like to sing them. Over and over. And over and over. And over and over.

I sing them all day.

I sing them all night.

# Tess

## 2016

### Panalúu Beach; Kilauea, Big Island
### May

*"Darling—look!"*

My husband tucks me into his arms, both our hands rest upon the steering wheel of *The Tess*. He has become very protective since the Bubble Cave incident.

I look. There, straight ahead of us, is a beach of *black sparkle*. Black sparkle, where white sparkle should be. *But this sand is volcanic!*

It was once exploding chunks of three thousand-degree-lava. When lava hits the ocean, it sizzles, then cools to millions of black volcanic glass grains, obsidian glass from the stomach of the volcano.

*It becomes a black sand beach.*

Like no other in the world, these are earth's first beaches. They are from the time when earth was born. They are the very guts of the earth, they are *new earth.*

"Oh John . . ." I breathe. Hundreds of happy, sunbathing sea turtles stretch across the hot black sand beach. *My charges,* Kauila's turtle children.

Greens and hawksbills are strewn like polished gems gleaming in the sun. *They take my breath away.* The hawksbills' heart-shaped shells are a feast for the eyes in intricate patterns of orange, black and gold. The greens' shells explode in a labyrinth of reddish hues, catching fire in the blinding sunshine.

Behind the sleeping turtles, Kilauea smokes, the clear, steam-like plume, while not dangerous, fills the air with her heavy sulfur breath. It is the breath of the earth itself. Sulfur fills my lungs and eyes as we steer closer to Punalu'u black sand beach.

"John . . . they love it!" I breathe. Flippers sprawl languidly across the soothing heated black sand that was once lava.

*"Pele is jealous, yes, but very loyal to those she loves,"* I hear Marama's voice in my head.

The amazing sight of the smoking volcano in the near distance is always soul-affirming for me. Our planet is alive! Its fiery heart burns hot, deep down inside. I gaze at the steady stream snaking skyward. Pele, goddess of fire, *is sleeping.*

"John, let's hike the summit," I whisper. He nods, and follows my eyes to the smoking peak. "We can make an offering of branches," I whisper in his ear. *"E Pele, eia ka 'ohelo 'au;*

*(Oh, Pele, here are your branches) e taumaha aku wau 'ia 'oe (I offer some to you) e 'ai ho'i au tetahi (some I also eat),"* I add. He hugs me tighter, listening to the Pele prayer.

We drop anchor and prepare our gear. We flip backwards

into the water and quietly paddle to the glittery black shore.

"Like this," John whispers to me, as he floats silently, barely moving, closer and closer to the shore, upon the current. He wants to approach the sleeping turtles as quietly as possible.

We float to the dark embankment. We wait, on our bellies, unmoving. *Then . . . the turtles awaken.* One by one, they venture toward us. The greens are first. John turns his head very slightly, smiling at me.

They are bold . . . fearless . . . coming very close to my face! I look into their eyes, deep brown and expressive. I don't speak, or move, now. Several hawksbills follow behind the greens, I feel them brush their flippers over my hands and my feet. It tickles, but I swallow my giggle.

John tries to swallow his giggles too, so as to remain as still as possible, but he fails. He giggles aloud. And so do I. It is just remarkable that these wonderful ancient creatures are visiting with us.

A few propel away from the vibration of our laughter, but others stay, still curious. Dozens and dozens of luminous turtle eyes are fixed on us. I float, my front and hind flippers tread water as I greet my guests.

An hour later, I have started to recognize certain turtles who have been circling us, making second and third passes. In the bright island sun I am easily able to discern their faces, their eyes, their expressions.

I try to lock a gaze with as many as I can. John reaches slowly underneath the water and takes my hand. We are surrounded by several hundred turtles. They are many layers deep, forming a huge circle. They are inspecting us, checking us out. It is extraordinary, this friendly visit between species. We haven't succumbed to our sense of time . . . no. We have allowed the turtles to determine the length of the visit. And, they have taken their time. We are, essentially . . . on *turtle-time*, now.

Then, the peace ends as a *deep menacing grumble* explodes beneath us—the land is all at once moving, shaking. *The turtles freeze.*

Shocked, John and I look up at Kilauea. Something has changed.

"JOHN!" I say too loudly, in the middle of several hundred stunned turtles. He doesn't quiet me. He is staring at the crater, at the orange glow now coming from it. It is no longer clear steam.

"Tess—back to the boat. NOW."

We both turn hard—dive—and swim. Our toned bodies are trained for this, quick escapes.

Kilauea is an active volcano and lava is a daily occurrence but Pele vacillates between her slow and fast moving flows. It is deadly to be caught unaware, of which type it is.

The turtles—whose instincts are tied to Pele, are moving away from the black sand beach and disappearing under the waves. The ones, already in their watery home have made good progress, the ones farther up on the black sand dunes are flippering down clumsily.

My heart hurts as I watch this. When lava hits the water, it boils it instantly, anything unfortunate enough to be caught, is boiled too.

We arrive at *The Tess*—lift anchor, and power away from black sand beach. John flips on the radio.

"Hi, we're aboard *The Tess* here and just wanted to report

a burp from Kilauea . . ." John's voice was thin, as he waited.

"Roger that . . . okay our reports here indicate lava is currently erupting from two places, the summit's Halema'uma'u crater and from Pu'u 'O'o on Kilauea's eastern rift. Pu'u 'O'o is flowing into the ocean, we are asking all boats to be aware . . ."

"Roger that."

John looks into my eyes and turns the boat . . . I know what he is doing. He wants to see the flows.

# She

I am awakened.

I am warm.

Too warm.

I shift . . .

Ripples.

My warmed flippers move,

I surface, to see.

Fire.

Pele.

I submerge.

# John

## 2016

### Kilauea, Big Island
### May

Sulfur is heavy here. My head starts to ache. Instinct tells me to be careful, very careful. I remember my mistakes in Bubble Cave.

Yet I am impetuous. My Celtic blood races. Just a look. That's all. I turn my boat toward Kilauea's eastern shore.

*"John—LOOK OUT!"* my wife yells as a white bloated body pops—then slams our bow.

Alabaster white. Its eyes gone, mouth wrenched open in an agonizing cry. It smells like cooked flesh. The boiled-alive flounder bobs silently.

A harbinger. I pull hard back on the wheel. My eyes glaze over. Then, there ahead.

Pele.

Red, orange, black explode upward from the crater, puncturing the blue sky. It's a steady explosion. Kilauea is erupting.

*My God.*

In the faraway distance, I can see a river of red is charging down the side of the mountain. It slows as it nears the bottom, above the sea.

"John, turn back . . . please . . ."

"*Steady on . . .*" I whisper, as lumpy, molten rock crooks its dripping finger at me. It is beckoning to me, *come . . . come here . . .*

I am back in Bubble Cave, swimming farther and farther into the abyss. *I can't stop myself.*

The lava river widens. It is racing down the eastern slope. It begins to pool at the bottom.

As it hits, it clumps up—and crashes into the sea, exploding into scalding deadly steam. Two-thousand degree temperatures.

It kills everything in its wake. Yet—it also birth's new land. *It kills and creates.* I am mesmerized by the duality.

Mesmerized.

*Pele, the destroyer, Pele the creator.*

**Pa`a Ka Waha** . . . *Observe, Be Silent and Learn.*

"*John! No!*" Tess is trying to pull at the wheel. But, I am stronger. Creation. Genesis.

**IKE LOA!** *To seek knowledge and wisdom . . . to grow and expand into greater aloha, harmony . . . as we walk up the mountain of life.*

I just can't tear my eyes away. I am looking into the face of God.

Enormous lava hunks fall into the sea causing explosions of steam. I feel my face burning.

Death. Life. Death. Life.

**KA LĀ HIKI OLA!** *The dawning of a new day . . . hope and promise.*

Suddenly, burning plastic fills my nose. The toxic vapors slap me awake. My boat has begun to melt.

Then, the radio yells:

"***EMERGENCY SOS***—*situation with Kīlauea as it continues to erupt at its summit and from its East Rift Zone.*

*Summit lava lake rising at alarming rate.*

*Feeding from Pu'u 'Ō'ō in the East Rift Zone—entering the ocean at Kamokuna: flying debris is being shot out by exploding interactions between lava and water; breakouts pose dangerous threat to all nearby communities!*

*Acidic plume laden with fine volcanic particles will burn eyes and lungs; Mandatory evacuation—NOW!*

*All units on alert, all units on alert!*"

"Johnnnnn!" I suddenly hear my wife's cries.

I wrench *The Tess* hard. We are powering away from the shoreline now. My heart is pounding crazily.

I take the boat around, hard again, thirty knots by my reckoning. We are approaching the black sand beach that just an hour ago was peaceful.

My wife feebly points at the black sand shores. Boiled turtle bodies are starting to float past us. I breathe deeply, my scorched lungs ache.

Tess is crying. I am crying. Pele has spoken. *Create, destroy, create, destroy.*

But. *I have vowed to save.* That is my vow. Even now. Even here. I must. *Kuleana. I accept my responsibilities and Reason for Being, and I will be held accountable.*

"Tess?" I turn to my wife, asking the question silently. She nods at me. Again, I wrench the wheel hard, in the *opposite direction*. It screeches. It doesn't want to obey. I wrench harder. We head back to black sand beach. To the lava-boiled waters.

To save those than can be saved.

# Tess

*Marama—HELP!* My mind screams out for my muse.

***E aloha kekahi i kekahi,*** *love one another,* I hear her say to me.

If only I had been able to honor Pele with the visit. Time ran out. I know Pele is impetuous. Impatient. Now, however, I must save Kauila's children. There may still be time for that. There is no choice for me, there is no question or hesitation.

Like in Bubble Cave, I know John will protect me. I have no other belief.

I race down to the boat's hull, near the stern are large canvas bags, tethered to the wall. I yank them all onto my back, and race back up to the deck.

Floating white turtle bodies are surrounding the boat. In horror, I recognize some of them as the friends we'd made earlier. I power my legs to go faster.

John is dropping anchor.

Here, the water is warm, but still swimmable, my toe tells me as I dip it. I try to narrow my concentration from distractions. It is hard.

*Explosions. Lava. Sulfur. Steam. Screams.*

I hear the screams. Most people cannot. But I hear their low frequency cries. *Turtle chirps, are now screams.* The turtles are screaming. My children.

John and I dive into the water. I paddle hard behind my athletic husband. He cautiously moves forward.

*Lava is crashing. Water is vaporizing to steam.*

As I swim, I see it all. The dying, the dead, the victims.

A young hawksbill bumps my shoulder, she's floating sideways—but still breathing. I push her into my sack. Bubbles indicate life, and show the way in the seawater. I follow them, a trail of desperation.

Underwater, I see them coming. Some are able to swim feebly, others are floating in the hot water. I have become a lobster and I use my long arms to scoop them all up into my sack. *Over and over and over.*

There are more, stranded, helpless. Overheated—unable to swim. I propel into the hot water. I start to collect the unconscious. I swim on.

*"Tessss!"*

But my limbs do not listen to John. There is still some room left in my life sack.

**OHANA,** *my family.*

I hear my name screamed behind me. My boiled, seared arms hoist a heavier green sea turtle. I am almost at the shore. I see the hot surf breaking. Soon, I am on my feet. Hot lava debris rains down on my back. But I must search now . . . this beach. It is hard to see under the smoke and steam.

There! *TRACKS.* Turtle tracks.

I follow them. I see where they stop. I'm on my burned knees, my bloodied hands now dig. I ache. But I dig. I hear their screams. The chirps. The chirps that are screams are in my ears as I sob and sob and sob—and dig.

*Success!* My babies—eggs, here they are! I scoop them into another smaller bag I have on my burned shoulder.

*"Tessssss! What the hell are you doing????"* a voice screams from the sea.

*More tracks.* I follow them. I see where Mama made her nest. I dig again.

Burning skin smell. Burning hair smell. *I dig. I dig. I dig.* More nests. More eggs. I continue. The sack on my back is very heavy now. I can't see very well. I keep on.

*Ash. Sulfer. Steam.* I continue.

Kauila's babies cry out to me form inside their shells. "Yes, I hear you," I say aloud. "I hear you all." More eggs now, the sack grows heavier.

*THEN*—a strong arm on my shoulder. It pulls down hard and I fall over immediately.

All fades to black.

# Marama

*Ike aku, 'ike mai. Kōkua aku, kōkua mai. Pēlā ka nohona 'ohana...*
Ah! Her face moves. She hears me. I smile.

**HO'OMAU!** I say the word I love, *to persist, to never give up.*

"What did you say, Marama?" It is the haole husband speaking to me. I don't answer. Instead take the child's hands. He studies me and walks away.

"Tess . . . can you hear me?" I peer at her face hard.

Her blue eyes open! **Wakea**, color of the sky.

"I . . . I . . . I tried, Marama . . . I tried . . ." Her voice is lighter than ash.

*"Kauila knows, child,"* I tell her. I rub her cheeks with my old brown hands. She needs **koko** to rise, *blood.*

"Yes . . . she is pleased . . ." I say, "very pleased child."

"And Pele, *Pele saw your courage* . . . to save Kauila's children. She knows. She is pleased." I tell her, "pleased with *you*," I finish.

"With *me?*" Tess asks weakly.

"Yes, with you."

Tess looks at me. She understands.

"Pele is . . . still angry . . ." she says to me. "I didn't have time to hike . . . to see her . . . she gave her warning so fast . . ."

"It is her way, *alas, it has always been her way* . . . she is

130

impetuous. But it is wise to heed her warning," I say. "Pele's power can both destroy and create life. It is her way, her will. She is easily vexed. But she has taken note of *you*, Tess."

Tess looks at me and I see she is pleased with my words. Color is rising in her face. Good.

"You showed great courage. Your scars show your strength." I smile and point to her burned and bandaged arms.

"You showed great **malama** child, *service, protection, caring.*"

This child named Tess, birthed far from our sacred isles, has always astonished me. I am reminded that there is hope for **aloha** even beyond our Polynesian world.

"Sleep now . . ." I whisper as she closes her eyes.

The potion I have with me today is a greenish liquid, one of the first I learned to make with my mother. I quickly smear it all over her wounds. Her scars, which are her triumphs, are many. I soon use up all my liquid.

I look out the window, the moon is in its half phase. Suddenly the owl cuts across its silhouette.

Yes, Pele is still angry.

I rub the last of my balm into Tess's burns and nod silently. These scars will serve her well in the coming months.

# Sasha

## 2016

⸙

### Hana, Maui
### June

⸙

My staff of five, reporting for duty. Right on time!

*Joanna. Timothy. Alexis. Cole. Madeline. Colin.*

Lookin' good . . . lookin' good.

"We're doing some great work here . . . yes we are," I say clapping my hands together. I press a button on the remote . . . *six sets of red eyes light up in front of me.*

"Okay, Joanna," I say . . . pressing another button.

Joanna rises slowly into the air. Her metallic arms reach out, then in, then out, then in.

I press another button and she settles back onto the table with a little click noise as her feet touch down.

"Very good Joanna . . ." I say.

"Timothy. You're next."

Timothy follows the same drill. Then I test Alexis. Alexis has a problem with landing, her feet smash too hard onto the table. This will definitely be an issue with nesting turtles. I make a note on my pad.

Cole, Madeline and Colin pass their tests perfectly.

I press a few other buttons. Various lights and antennae flash, whir, spin and vibrate. Next to the specs for each of my gang, I check off all six boxes.

I've programmed each one. Each is coded uniquely—with his or her own personality.

Joanna prefers to fly at night, she has a special nighttime microprocessor.

Cole loves the reefs, the hidden beaches where no human foot has ever stepped.

Madeline is a dunes girl, she flies low and easy at dawn, and is specially programmed for nesting hawksbills.

Timothy has sensors for heat, the volcanic beaches are his specialty.

Alexis is a green girl . . . she tracks the Honu, she is programmed to follow the moon in its cycles and when full shining orbs are at their height, she patrols the beaches.

Colin is a turtle-of-all-trades and assists the others in their tasks. His microchip is universal and programmed to pick up the others' signals.

Tess is going to love the new staff. I know she names all her patients. I love my new bungalow in Hana too. I've never been happier. I feel . . . I've come home. For a while at least. I certainly don't miss Los Angeles.

I take a deep breath. The island air is so sweet. Fragrant. Always fragrant with a zillion different floral scents. Hawaiian flowers, they are just *different*. They permeate every oxygen molecule. Things are just . . . divergent here. Special. Magical.

*"Kids, it's time to fly,"* I say to my group. I go to the laptop and type in six different codes.

*"Ready . . . one . . . two . . . three . . ."* I call out.

All six drones levitate an inch off the table . . . and then, rise slowly. They turn to look at me.

"Excellent," I say, using my professional tone. "Let's go."

I jump up with my laptop and walk to the door. The drones follow me. Outside the hospital I turn toward the beach and continue to type rapidly.

One by one, my drones fly toward the sea.

I watch as Joanna, Timothy, Alexis, Cole, Madeline, Colin, *disappear into the morning.*

I go back into the hospital and sit down. My laptop registers six live stream video windows! I pour myself some coffee and watch my team go to work. The feeds are surprisingly clear.

I glance at the clock on the wall . . . 6:30. Most of the action will happen this evening. I check the moon chart, aha, half moon. *Plenty of light.* I open my calendar book to today's date. Then, I look back at the feeds.

*This is going to be amazing.*

# Kaholo

The whiskey is just hitting my bloodstream now. I take a long drag on my cigarette.

I start coughing. I end up on my knees, spewing phlegm. Five full minutes. Gotta quit, gotta quit, I think. Bad habits. Hard to break. *Cough, cough, cough.*

"Kaholo . . . truck's here," Hale says, spitting himself, tobacco chew all over his mouth. A truck approaches with its lights off. Maleko hops out.

"Maleko—ah man, you bring a horrific stench, man," Hale says. It's the stench of rotting bodies.

Strange. I'm accustomed to the smell of death. I don't notice the odor at all.

"Hale, Maleko, listen up. Boss says to bring the bodies to a new drop. On Oaha. Near Honolulu. We are to take the boat. Tomorrow. Hour before dawn," I say.

"All of them? To Oaha?" Hale says, shocked.

"Yeah. Bubble Cave—off the list. Permanently. But you gotta clean 'em. Strip off the shells." I look the two men in the eyes. I see distrust.

"You can sell the meat. Do whatever you want. Boss wants the shells only," I say.

Hale and Maleko look at eachother.

"And we keep the dough? From the bodies? The meat?" Maleko asks.

"That's right." I spit on the ground.

I am starting to smell the death stench all of a sudden. I am nauseous as hell. Vomit starts to rise in my stomach.

"Just make sure you clean them shells. Be at Spitting Cave at 4am. Don't be late. Turn off the boat motor a half mile out. Use the sails. No lights. Silent as death."

My stomach turns over again.

"And d'eggs . . . what about d'eggs, Kaholo?" Hale asks me.

Shoot, I'd forgotten about that.

"Right. Eggs too. We gotta go get the eggs. Alright. Tonight then. Midnight. Start diggin' 'em up. At three am, we load 'em into the truck. Take 'em with us at dawn. Be at Kipahulu at midnight. Same drill. No lights. Truck engines off a half mile out."

# She

## 2016

### Lahaina Coast, Maui
### June

I twitch.

Cold current.

A shift.

Death.

My eyes narrow.

I smell death.

My nostrils flare.

# Hale

## 2016

### Kipahulu, Maui
### June

"Shit," I look up at the sky. Three quarter moon. Kaholo screwed up again. We shoulda done this earlier. I squint in the blazing light.

"Aight," I call out again. "I'm getting' da eggs. Back in a minute."

My head hurts. Dammit. Home made rum. I rub my temples. OUCH—the hangover cuts my brain with a knife. I bend over my knees . . . expecting to vomit. It passes.

I stumble down the beach. Where's that goddamned sack? The moon blinds me—dammit, it's full.

My head lurches again. I trip on a dune. On my hands and knees I crawl. Dammit! *Great. Just freakin' great.* I spend seven hours digging up nests and now the freakin' sack of eggs is gone. What the f—?

"Hale—move yer ass, man . . . we got to go!" Kaholo whispers loudly from across the sand.

*Yeah, like you did any work today asshole*, I say to myself. It's always like this.

Suddenly I am overcome with a coughing fit. I'm on my back in the sand, bright white light from above. The goddamned moonlight is killin' me.

DAMMIT! I stand up and give the middle finger to the moon. Then, I stagger around . . . *where's the goddamned sack of godforsaken eggs?*

Just then I see a large shapeless lump in the distance. How the hell did it get lodged between the rocks at the shore?

"Comin'" I rail in a ragged whisper to the men waiting at the truck.

I run to the bag and grab it. It's completely stuck. *Dammit to hell!*

I tear at it wildly, it's jammed between the rocks. I wade out into the surf to get a better grip.

The moon has turned the sea into a huge floodlight on my activities. *But I have to get those eggs. Three hundred dollars each. Hundreds of eggs. Thousands of dollars.*

Waves soak me to my hips as I wade out farther. My hands close around the top of the sack. Okay—now I can rip it free! I heave as hard as I can. I hear the sound of eggs cracking inside the bag.

Then—my leg—PAIN!

*EXQUISITE SEARING PAIN.*

And—I'm underwater.

It happens so fast that I am unable to scream. The scream forming inside my throat doesn't have a chance to escape. The pain in my left leg sears through my being. It feels like teeth, but in less than a second I am simultaneously dragged under the shallow surf.

In another second—I feel my body shooting backward at a speed that feels like a submarine missile being launched. The force rips the shirt off my back. It also rips the sack from my grasp.

In a final second, I face my attacker. It lets go of my leg.

Moonbeams have penetrated the water and catch the thing's eyes—it has black eyes, I see in horror.

It looks at me. Then it disappears and the pain in my leg screams again. Teeth.

The thing has clamped down on my leg—I am being dragged down, down, down.

Water pressure builds as I descend with the monster. Deeper, deeper. I feel my body crushing inward.

Then I feel no more.

# Maleko

## 2016
*⸙⸰⸰⸙*

### Kipahulu, Maui
### June
*⸙⸰⸰⸙*

"Kaholo . . . man . . . did'ya hear that?"

"Nope." Kaholo's cigarette burns orange in the dark.

"That splash," I tell the boss. "Splash down the shore."

Kaholo drops the cigarette and grinds it into the sand.

"Maleko, all I hear is the silence of that drunk fool not getting his ass back here with my goddamned eggs."

"I think he fell into the water, man . . . I heard a splash, somethin's . . . up . . ."

"Christ! I'll go down there. Godammit. Them eggs are worth bucks man . . . at least fifty-grand."

I watch Kaholo trip down the sand unevenly. His dirty straw hat blows off head.

Suddenly, we are both distracted by an enormous dark shape

in the sky—a huge bird. It has come out of nowhere and moving quickly. Too quickly.

It's oddly shaped. Then the moonlight illuminates it and Kaholo—unbelievably—screams.

An enormous metallic spider with red eyes is bearing down toward Kaholo. It's flying at breakneck speed.

I clamp my hand over my mouth, and stumble backwards to our truck containing thousands of contraband poached sea turtles. I try to muffle my screams.

The red-eyed alien spider is circling Kahola on the beach. He's on his knees, crying like a baby.

The spider descends. Its red eyes flood Kaholo's face.

"Kōkua . . !" Kaholo screams for help in Hawaiian. The spider is just above his head.

I can't tear my eyes away, though I don't want to see.

"Arrrrrrgggghhhhhhhhhhhh!!!!" Kaholo screams and lunges his entire body upwards, grabbing the spider with his hands.

Now, I hide my eyes. It is too much to witness.

I hear screams. I hear the sound of metal breaking. More screams.

I look.

Kaholo has the spider in his clutches. His face is bloody. He is crazily smashing his head into the spider's body. The sand is drenched in blood. In horror, I watch the spider try to claw its way out of the Hawaiian's hands. I can't believe it but I am feeling sorry for it. Kaholo's face is contorted, twisted, dark. He has gone psychotic. I watch him attack the spider, but his rage looks crazy, irrational, he is screaming and smashing and destroying the spider with his own head! Blood spurts everywhere. I am reminded of what a serial killer might look like. When the spider finally breaks free . . . I am almost glad. It flies away limply, on an angle.

When I realize that I am looking at a man attacking a flying alien with red eyes, it occurs to me that I may have had too much to drink, earlier. Rubbing my eyes, I stagger to my truck.

I throw it into reverse, and floor the gas pedal.

# Tess

## 2016
❧✿❧

### Honu Hospital; Hana, Maui
### June
❧✿❧

"Sasha, can you bring the maps, sweets?"

"Got 'em right here Tess," Sasha says in a voice full of sunshine. Only the ends of her hair are blue now. It's almost grown out.

I look at her. She's awakened, she is joyous. I smile as she hands me the printouts. Her face is glowing.

"You look happy, Sasha, " I say.

"I am, Tess. I am. It's . . . the sunshine. The moonshine. The sea. The air. I've never been outside this much. I am more out-side than inside, here, more than I have ever been in my life. It makes me . . . happy," she says to me, shyly.

I don't answer her, but I know. It's like Marama always says. Sasha has simply woken up.

I hear Marama in my head . . . "we are one inside this perfect chemistry of the elements, the water, the wind, the earth, Tess. We are a small part of the greater truth, the bigger scheme of things . . ."

The greater truth. It is why John and I are so content here. Here we are free. Free to be, to care, to love. Without boundaries. Freedom is contagious. Sasha has caught it, too. She's connected now. To the greater truth. The ancient Polynesians knew this, tens of thousands of years ago. Our connection to nature is the very meaning of life.

I walk to my new hire and kiss her cheek. She smiles and hands me the reports.

"Sasha . . . oh my . . . this is incredible . . ." I am looking at her readouts from the drones' work. One hundred and thirty eight nests. It's an astronomical number. Never—ever, have I had this kind of success. Drones go where humans cannot.

It turns out Madeline is the star drone. She found ninety-seven of the nests herself.

"Amazing . . . ," I breathe.

"Thanks Tess. Here, something new for you," she hands me a small metal device.

"It's a nest sensor," she says.

I pick it up and turn it over in my hands.

"It's placed in mother turtle's nest. After she's laid her eggs. It sits there, watching the eggs. When they . . . start to change, move, vibrate . . . when they are getting ready to hatch . . . it lets us know," Sasha says, watching my every move.

Extraordinary. Another technological miracle. Chills race down my spine, I realize that this little device will help me rebuild our turtle population. I will know when Kauila's babies are going to hatch. I will know, and I will be ready to help her help her babies.

My mind races into a visual of the nest, I see the eggs. Three feet under the sand. The babies are ready, they start to stretch. They need Mama. And now, I can be there. The statistic rattles in my mind: one in ten thousand babies survive after hatching. Now, I can change this.

"Sasha . . ." I say, tears in my eyes. She comes to me and we hug like sisters.

"Sasha, our problem's always been that there's no way to know exactly when my babies are ready to hatch . . . it's impossible to predict an exact time . . . it's always been a window," I say, "they've always been on their own." Tears roll down my face.

Sasha lets me cry. I take a deep breath.

"Can you imagine the scene, Sasha," I say, shaking my head, "one hundred and fifty hatchling babies suddenly decide to hatch. They start to rattle around inside their eggs. They are stretching, flexing, pushing . . ."

"And now, you can be there for the babies Tess, you can be watching over them all . . ." Sasha says, squeezing my hand.

I shake my head in wonderment.

"So we do two things now. Our drones locate the nests, and we insert sensors into them. Then the sensors let us know when hatching begins. When the . . . boil begins," Sasha says confidently.

"Please stay with us, Sasha. Always. Stay here at Honu Hospital. With John and I. We want you to run it with us," I say, taking her hands in mine.

Sasha smiles at me. Yep, she's home.

# John

## 2016

### Hana, Maui
### July

"I'll go get the truck Tess," I call out.

I look at the new maps, the drones' work. Unprecedented. We have the locations of *hundreds of nests*. We have sensors to place inside the nests. We have . . . *nest sitters*. Babysitters. It is phenomenal. What I started here on Maui years ago has *skyrocketed* in success. I needed . . . *a woman's touch*. Tess's touch. I feel warm inside. *I love my wife so much.*

Tess's dream of personally overseeing the eggs hatch and go home, is made seamless. Her intent to rescue eggs whose nests have become unsafe, and relocate them to the Honu Hospital's hatchery, a cinch now. The improvements will triple the turtle population of Maui. *Saving sea turtles—one egg at a time.* I imagine the large federal grants we can apply for, with such prosperous data. And then I imagine poachers finding their lives impossible under the new awareness, the new scrutiny, the new eyes-everywhere for sea turtles. A win-win situation!

I pull the Jeep around the front of the hospital and load the sensors inside. It's morning—Hawaii is just waking up. I look around. *Ah, this color always ignites my soul.* Pink is not pink . . . it's a new hue. It is deeper, electric. Koki'o ke'oke'o, hibiscus . . . explodes from the ground, appearing at the top of two-foot stalks, enormous petals gush the most intense, dizzying perfume. It is as if the Paleolithic age decided to keep going here. After all, bigger is better.

Soon we are pulling into a jungle area that hides a very secluded part of Hana beach . . . the dirt road narrows and the trees grow so thick here it is almost impossible to get through. I drive very slowly now. Trees, vines, scratch at the windows. Inching along, I don't want to disturb too much. A deep ravine has formed from the recent rains and we make our way over it, with an inch of room to spare on either side of the truck.

"It's all grown in . . ." Tess whispers. "The jungle here . . . it reclaims the land."

I decide to stop a few feet from the dunes at the entrance. I find I cannot open the door for the riotous vines growing, I have to pull them hard to the sides to get out.

"What's that?" Tess asks, pointing ahead, as we take a step onto the fine white sand.

Tire tracks. *In the sand.*

We are both on our knees with our fingers in tire tracks. Tracks that shouldn't be here.

"This beach is *restricted* Tess. Nesting."

"Yes. Yes it is," she whispers.

She sits back on her feet. Then she stands and goes to the truck. I follow. We get the maps and the crates of sensors out and stack them on the ground.

"Okay . . . first nest . . . is . . . *over there* . . . Cole found this one. It's by the rocks, a few feet from the shore, far too close to the tide," my wife says, pointing.

Tess takes a sensor out of the crate and looking at the map . . . slowly crosses the sand. She steps on a hat.

"What the—?" She picks up a dirty straw hat. She turns and looks at me sharply. I grimace.

Tess turns back to continue walking, shoving the dirty hat into her back pocket.

A slight rise in the sand is one mother's nest site. I see it, but I don't smile. My heart feels heavy.

Tess stoops and reaches into her backpack for a plastic shovel, she begins to dig very gently . . . when she reaches the nest she puts on surgical gloves. They have been treated with a special agent to ensure no toxic materials touch the eggs or their nest.

"Easy . . . does . . . it," she whispers, "Mama's here . . ."

She's smiling now . . . my Tess loves her babies. The sensor inserted, Tess carefully covers the nest with sand once again. When it's time, the babies will hatch, and Tess will be there to escort them to the hatchery.

She stands and faces me.

"Wanna do the next one?" She smiles weakly. "It's over . . . okay . . . over there, down by the water."

We walk together. I rub her back.

"Hmmm . . . it should be . . . map says a few inches this way . . ."

Surf is splashing up against our calves. It feels soft and warm.

Tess suddenly freezes. I bang into her, almost toppling her with my weight. I grab her so she doesn't fall. Her face is white. I follow her stare. Then—I put my hand over her mouth, sensing she will scream. She screams anyway. It is only slightly muffled by her hand.

There—in a tiny tide pool a few inches from our feet . . . is an eye. An eyeball. Nothing else. Just a staring eyeball, with bloody filaments around it.

It is clearly—human.

# Tess

"John, we've got to alert the authorities."

I study my husband's face. It is stern.

"John. *Truck tracks. A hat. A human eyeball.* You know what this is."

I'm standing with balled fists. I feel I am going to explode.

"Where is Jake?" he asks me.

I stare blankly at John.

He rises, walks to his cellular and dials his brother. It goes to voicemail.

"I'm not calling the police until I speak to Jake."

John walks out of our bedroom.

I stare speechless.

# John

*I know he's simple.*

My twin brother's face appears in my mind. No emotion. No expression.

Then, images of him on board *The Tess*. Hosing away the turtle's red blood. In silence.

He didn't get enough oxygen. I got enough oxygen. *He did not.* More images of Jake. Sailing *The Tess*. Waxing *The Tess*. Cleaning *The Tess*.

Emotionless. Expressionless.

I look at my hand. I remember Jake's hand in mine, when we were boys. *Did he hold my hand, or did I hold his?* I turn this question over in my mind.

All I can see is Jake's blank face. I recognize it—it's mine. *It's mine, minus any human feeling.*

# Jake

The spider is sleeping tonight.

I watch her in her web. I've been watching her for hours. The black widow moved in about a year ago.

I watch her eat her prey. She traps them. Then wraps them in webbing. Then she injects them with venom. Then, she drinks their liquefied guts.

But right now, she sleeps.

I turn over.

I know there was something I was supposed to do today. I can't remember.

Sometimes, I can't remember things. But it's okay. I'll ask the spider when she wakes up.

Oh I know, I remember now. I had to call Kaholo. That's what it was.

I sit up.

A bit of the spider's webbing has fallen to the floor, I pick it up and wrap my finger in it.

I bite my finger. I start to suck on it.

# Sasha

The spider in my hands is mauled.

Cole has been attacked. But, how? Who?

I stare at him. His arms are bent into grotesque contortions. His face is smashed, there are bits of flesh and blood stuck in his circuits.

*What did this?*

I pick up the microprocessor. It is smashed. Its delicate central unit with the tiny green board and thread-thin wires is snapped in half. There are grooves in it. *Teeth marks?* This is crazy. *What the hell did this?*

I cannot read the feed, the spider's brain has been destroyed. Whatever Cole was recording is now gone forever. I get a white towel and wipe Cole's head on it. Red smears streak it. I shake my head.

I decide not to tell Tess. For now. No, I'll mull this one over myself.

# Tess

Hana, Maui
August

A trip. Away.

Sometimes wives know best. I need to be with my husband, alone. We need to rebalance. *Just John, and I.*

And, the ocean. The sun. The moon. That's it.

I am stretched out on our bed. My gaze settles on John's prized *paipo*, mounted on the wall. John only refers to the Polynesian word for surfboard.

Oahu. Waikiki.

Yes.

# John

## Waikiki, Oahu
## August

I look out of the window, the view is sublime. As magnificent as our islands are beneath the sea, so too above, way above the sea. Maui shrinks to an oblong hexagon shape . . . and Oahu grows as we approach. Primordial green velvet lumps, begging to be explored. *Hawaii.*

My thoughts carry me to an earlier trip, with Jake on a plane to Hawaii, the very first time. Looking out this same window.

"John . . ." he said, pointing. "Gum drops!"

The islands did indeed look like candy. I feel a sigh settle in between my ribs. I keep it there.

"Darling . . ."

It's my Tess, the arbiter of this holiday surprise . . . I look at her oval face, her enormous eyes. She has the delicate beauty of a medieval maiden. She is smiling at me.

"John, I want you to teach me to surf . . ." she says, breathlessly.

Ah, yes. I love to teach.

"Shall I review first . . ?" I ask her, teasing.

She squeals. I take her hand and press it to my chest. I pretend we are back at Stanford, and I am at the podium . . . when Tess tells me she first fell in love with me.

"Ahem," I clear my throat.

"Okay . . . let's see . . . well, of course it was the ancients that surfed first, the Polynesians who came to Hawaii from Tahiti. And their *paipo*—the first surfboards, were easy transportation. First on the belly . . . then later standing upright was a natural way to travel between islands . . . along the magnificent and powerful ocean waves."

Tess squeezes my hand and snuggles against me tightly.

"The boards grew longer and longer, as length made for speed. Chanting while upon the boards was common . . ."

Here I stop, I look around on the plane to see if it's crowded— yep, it is. *I'd better not chant for Tess.*

"Many chants were used . . . chants to the Gods . . . to create bigger and bigger waves, chants to give courage for surfers."

"Sir, would you care for a drink?" a stewardess interrupts me.

"Sure, we'll have two daiquiri's," I say. Tess giggles again.

"Soooooo, my love, yes . . ." I stop and drain my glass. Wow. The rum is strong. I don't usually drink.

"Yes?" Tess looks at me with those enormous blue eyes. She sips her drink.

I continue.

"As . . . Marama may have told you already . . . the chiefs . . . were allowed long, long boards . . . boards of . . . my God, Tess, twenty-four feet, imagine it, darling?"

I pause, and wave the stewardess over for another daiquiri. *I must get away more often.*

"The royalty . . . the ali'i surfed on these amazingly long boards that are inconceivable today. Boards that were fast—FAST!" My voice is a bit loud. I laugh.

"Twenty-four feet! John . . . that's . . . that's . . . two Jeeps back to back!" Tess says.

I laugh loudly.

"Mmhmm. And doll, of course, you and me . . . we'd be on the twelve-foot boards, course. For commoners."

"I'd be *royaaaaaaalty*, John . . . my board would be . . . fifty feet long!" Tess says, elongating her words. I look at her daiquiri. Half gone.

"We are beginning our descent. Please fasten your seatbelts." The announcement has us sit up. We drain our glasses.

Tess burps.

I laugh again. What a delightful wife she is.

# Tess

A-plus. That's what I give myself.

We pick up our luggage and jump into a taxi. Honolulu is as far from Hana as can possibly be. A large, in-your-face fabulous, luxurious city.

*Perfect.* I feel like patting myself on the back.

And, as for my surfer-husband? *Waikiki.* And the famous Halekulani hotel where the *best waves in the world* live, and where the top surfers have gathered since the turn of the century.

"Close your eyes dear," I say to John.

"They're almost closed hon, from two daiquri's," he slurs.

"Okay, open," I whisper.

The beautiful hotel is before us. We step out of our taxi and my heart soars.

At last!

# John

I open one eye.

Where am I? Gold and ivory furniture against a marble floor . . . silk curtains . . . is that a champagne bottle?

I sit up. Aha. I remember. My darling has brought us to Oahu. My foggy head is slowly draining of rum. I never drink, now I remember why. I stretch and stand up.

The carpet feels strangely squishy under my feet. I catch myself in the long mirror. Woah. Man. I look tired.

A piece of paper flutters on the desk by the open window. I hear ukulele music coming from below.

*My love,*

*I have gone for a massage . . . shopping . . . at the market near the hotel. Easy to find if you want to. Please rest if you like. Champagne on table. Dinner reservation tonight at 7. Alan Wong's.*

*Love you,*
*Tess*

My eyes follow the walls, covered in silk paper . . . the ceiling, finely carved marble, Grecian marble. The window is almost as tall as the ceiling. I walk to it.

I look out. I see them. *The surfers.* My heartbeat quickens.

This is why surfers call Waikiki heaven. From my window I can see *Fours,* to the east . . . *Fours* is a wave that only comes alive when the surf gets big.

I look to the east for *Threes,* nope not there. I know what I really want though, and I look for it . . . there, I see it; *Paradise.*

*Paradise* is what longboarders dream about. A surf zone with big, rolling, shifty peaks.

Well. *That's all I needed to see.* I grab my board and start for the door. I look down at my blue blazer and slacks and loafers that my wife insisted I wear for the trip.

Oops.

I retrace my steps and change quickly into shorts and flip flops. I check the window, once again. *Populars?* Nope, don't see them. Yet. My second favorite spot to surf.

I fly into the elevator. *Off to catch a wave.*

# Tess

Soft music, soft lights, soft petals under my body.

I am perfectly at peace after the best *Lomilomi* massage I have ever had in my life. Two heavenly hours.

The thing about Lomilomi is the neverending strokes that continue nonstop for the entire massage. It is an utterly blissful experience. Created here in Hawaii.

*"To knead, to rub, soothe, as the paws of a contented cat . . ."* Marama had said once of the ancient ritual. I stretch now . . . like a cat. I purr.

Then, I get dressed.

I have decided that today is *yellow* day. I put on my yellow sundress. And my yellow, floppy straw hat. And my yellow flip-flops.

Soon I am strolling through the outdoor markets.

The oversized yellow bag over my shoulder wants to be filled up with goodies. I spy freshly potted succulents in delightful re-purposed vessels.

John will love these, I think, looking at the eggshells, teacups, and tunafish cans bursting with blooms.

And there, next booth, I see the native sea salts. All of our favorites. Maui Onion. Hawaiian Chili Pepper. Kiawe Smoked. Hawaiian Ginger. Spicy Hawaiian Seaweed.

A treasure trove. John will be pleased.

I swing my big yellow bag as I walk through the market. Sunshine splashes across all the lovely items.

*So many people!* Lots and lots and lots of people, it is so different to be amidst a large crowd. Hana is a quiet paradise, but *darn
it,* it's nice to be in a *pretty dress,* shopping with a hundred people.

"*Ono lau e kuai lede, delicious vegetables to buy, lady . . .*"
A vendor calls to me in Hawaiian. His beautiful coffee colored
skin reminds me of the earth.

I reply, "*Mahalo mai kuu haku, thank you kindly, sir.*"
My vegan heart is satiated with his amazing array. Nalo Greens.
Dandelion Greens. Braising Greens. Baby Kale. Baby Swiss
Chard. Tat Soi. Purslane. Sumida Watercress. Kamiya Papaya.

I am loading the veggies onto the scale, there are too many
and I clumsily topple my huge yellow purse. It spills everywhere.
I stoop to gather the contents.

As I do—I see John!

I see his Italian loafers first, from down here on the ground.
I stand and see him, across from me at the flower stand. I see
he is picking pink and white plumeria for me! His blue blazer
looks so smart. I'm glad I made him wear it.

I throw my things into my purse and start to walk toward him.
Then I freeze.

My husband is handing the flowers to a woman. She is
standing next to him. *They kiss.*

Shoppers pass in front of me, blocking John. I feel faint.
I walk blindly toward the flower stand, bumping into people,
knocking things over.

The crowd parts and he is gone. The woman is gone. I stand in
the middle of the shopping market trying to find a way to breathe.
A strong cigarette smell overtakes me and I start to choke on it.

# John

It takes me exactly *three minutes* to go from my hotel to Sandy Beach.

Board in the air over my head, I am moving toward the water. One long, unending movement that lands me in the surf.

I stay low on my tummy and paddle out.

The sheer power of the sea here, the power that the reef waves have, here in Waikiki, is daunting. I feel it. Hundreds of years . . . men have been doing what I am doing now. I am thrilled to my core.

I paddle. *I look for a Paradise wave.*

The sun is hot on my back, its baking effect is interplayed with this gentle ovulating of the ocean current beneath me. Hypnotic. I rock gently. My mind softens.

I think of my work in Hana. I think of the turtles I love so much. I think of this ocean the turtles call home, this splendid sun above it, this superb world beneath these waves I am trying to ride.

I think of blue. Of yellow. Of turquoise. The sea.

As I wait for the wave my mind thinks *a thousand different things.* It's a meditation. I am a part of the ocean. I am ready to ride on top of the world. I am free . . . I am on an adventure that I create.

All the stress of the last few weeks drains from me . . .

I feel fresh, now.

Then, I feel it—the uplift . . . the current. I look behind me. There she is—*the Paradise wave.*

I wait . . . I wait for it.

Then I rise.

I am rising to my knees, then to my feet and the wave catches me high.

I pivot and center my gravity.

I spin like a football through the wave . . . inside the wave is a surreal blue tunnel, the one I just dreamed of.

*I am inside blue.*

The sound is rushing, clean . . . I feel the power. I harness it.

I'm riding a wave. I'm a bird riding on the wind. I have nature's energy in my hands.

*I am close to God.* I can feel it, very strongly. I am with the Creator, inside this powerful wave.

It seems to last forever. But blue melts to yellow as sunshine explodes at the exit of the rolling wave. I am out, a gliding thing of grace, still on my feet. I give myself a victory cheer.

Then I drop to my board, exhausted. Time to rest on my tummy. I float in the peaceful hot sun, as it sinks deep into my bones.

"Aloha!" A voice awakens me. I look up from my board. A small sailboat on my right, a friendly face. "Aloha . . ." I call. I notice the red tow rope attached to his transom in the back of his boat. He grins.

"Want a tow? I'm heading over to Spitting Cave for a look-see . . ." the captain says.

I think about this. The long red wakeboard rope dangles in the bright blue water.

"Haven't been there in a while . . . I remember it burps like a toad when the waves hit the cave just right," I say, laughing.

"It burps? I gotta see this. Here, I'll throw you the rope, we'll take it slow," he says. "A slow tow," he adds.

I paddle over, sit on my board, and catch the rope when he throws it. He pulls in his sails, and turns the motor on, and we are off. Very slowly.

"You've done Spitting Cave before, then . . . ?" my host asks me. "Name's George, by the way. George Hampstead."

I take a look at him, a tourist for sure, flower shirt, huge straw hat, too much sunscreen on his nose. I like him.

"John McAdams, pleased to meet you. You wont be sorry, George, Spitting Cave is fantastic, a diving must," I say, cheerfully.

"Oh . . . heh, heh, I don't dive, a little snorkeling with the wife sometimes . . . I do like a nice afternoon sail though . . . the hotel said I need to see this cave . . . whatcha know about it?" he asks.

"The hotel is right, George," I say to him, feeling my teacher's chops warming up.

"Let's see . . . well, it's *a marvel of five different sized caves,* naturally carved out from thousands of years of constant ocean pounding. Strong currents too. And . . . for the likes of me, and other divers, it's not a deep dive, the cave bottoms out around fifty feet, then gradually deepens to one hundred forty. But, yeah, after that, it plummets, ending in the great blue. It's a drift dive, imagine being transported by the water movement of the tide . . . like flying . . . sometimes bumpy."

*"No kidding, John!* Five caves. Lordy. Well, I'll be, I'll leave it to you youngsters to see it from underneath . . . I just want a

glimpse of the *burp*," George says. Then his cellular goes off and he waves to me that he has to take it.

Within fifteen minutes, we are rounding on the caves. From its face, it is prehistoric looking—a huge, smooth but layered rock wall, with the ocean pounding away at it.

George comes back around and waves to me again as he undoes the wakeboard rope. His phone is cradled in his ear. The boat is a nice, small twenty-six foot Fantail. I see a little sign on the top of the hull that says, RENT ME. I giggle. Nice guy.

"Bye George!" I call to him. He sees me and mouths the word, *goodbye,* then points to the phone and mouths the word, *wife.*

I paddle slowly, around the Fantail. The waves here, against the rocks, are treacherous, fatal. Without diving gear, I've decide to swim around the mouth. I'm careful not to get caught in the current, the wrong way. And then be bashed to bits by the waves, the rocks, and the unrelenting suction-power of the cave who likes to spit everything back out that it drinks.

"John—here—*borrow this*, it's from the hotel, just leave it over there by the rocks, I'll get it later," George yells, still on the phone. He throws a snorkel mask and tube at me, attached to an orange, flotation device.

I give him a diver's thumbs up. *Now we're talkin'!*

I paddle on my stomach to the farthest stretch of rocks, away from the suction of the cave, and I hoist the board up half-way. It sticks to the hot rocks. Then, with mask on . . . I dive.

The water is cooler here than Hana, the great depth is why. I swim hard to build body fire up, warming myself. The mask is an inexpensive hotel rental for sure but the scenery is gorgeous nonetheless.

Enormous-sized lava boulders with strange canal-like carvings snake before me, they are everywhere. They are small-scale lava tubes, I know. Molten lava from nearby Mount Koko ran down into the sea thousands of years ago here. I swim over it, pumping my arms, still trying to warm my body. Around me floating sea urchins, stars and small, darting crabs, who have all made their home inside these endless little roads.

I stop to adjust my mask, making it tighter. Then, I turn back—*and scream,* like a kid. Man, I know better, a Hawaiian monk seal isn't exactly a stranger to me. But . . . five inches from my face, is, *woah!* He's huge, a terrific specimen for sure. Several hundred pounds, at least. *Chill, John,* I say to myself, smiling. Hello buddy, I wave to the seal. The striking animal pays no attention to me whatsoever, and swims away. Small crabs, fish and sea urchins trail him, they must have been in his mouth when he was startled.

I spy white-tip reef sharks closer to the cave's opening. They look lulled by the sucking noise of the waves. Funny, they appear dazed . . . floating . . . enjoying the back and forth of the current.

Then I realize that I need air, *no tank on this dive* . . . so I gently surface and pop the snorkel tube out of my mouth. A loud burp erupts from the cave just then, as the current is roughly ejected out of the mouth. *It's a really loud belch*—I turn to see if George has caught it. There he is, on his boat! He has taken a folding chair out—but leaps up giving me a huge victory salute. *"Yeehaw!"* he yells. I laugh hard.

He looks, about twice my age. What a kind guy. Looking out for me like an uncle.

*"Great burp, John!"* he calls out.

"A *doozy!* Say, George . . . sure you don't want to join me?"
I yell back.

"Nah . . . have fun . . . I'm gonna take a siesta here."

I dive down again. Ah . . . my turtles! I see a family of
hawksbills. One, two, three, four, five, six. Good size too.
Heart-shaped shells. So beautiful. The light is hitting them
perfectly, they are moving art.

Slowly, I feel for the current, and I swim with it to the front
of the cave. I drift inside with the tide. I don't have a light of
course, but I have dove here before. Stingrays and eels greet me
in the darkness, light at the front of the cave reveals them to me,
just a few feet inside.

Then I see a plastic diving flipper—on the ground of the cave.
Five feet from the opening. I swim to grab it, and I slip into the
back of my swimsuit.

That's when I see it. *An egg.* A turtle egg in the sand.

*No turtle egg should be here.* Mother turtles do not lay their
eggs in caves. Could it have been dropped here by a predator?
Or a silly tourist . . . throwing it over the upper ledge of Spitting
Cave?

My scientific mind contemplates the situation. It also realizes
I need *air*—badly. I wish I had my tank, not this plastic device.

I jettison out, and then upward and break the surface gasping.
I push the mask up and rub my eyes. A strong, unpleasant smell
overwhelms me. *Cigarettes.*

No . . . not George? I turn my quickly to see him on his boat—
asleep in the sun. Not George. I look up. The mouth of the cave
shields me from whomever might be above.

I decide to swim out a bit. I'll get my board and rest on it.

I hoist myself to the rocks, hoping nobody sees me as I'm a professional and I know this is impossible for an amateur to do.

Again the strong smell of cigarettes. I look up the cliff above the cave. Now I can see.

Instead of the usual cluster of teenagers and binocular holding couples—I see four men in Panama hats. *One . . . is smoking.* I look back to George who is asleep. I look at the wall in front of me. The molten lava flow, now rock. I see the shape of waves, like a layer cake. It isn't jagged, it is . . . somewhat inviting.

*Ready for some rock climbing, John?* I ask myself. I leave the board and start my ascent. I'm certified as a Lead Guide . . . but . . . it has been a while. I feel along the grooves in the rock ledges and when I find the right one, I center my body, breathe deeply, and, hoist. *Pause, Feel, clamp, hoist. Pause, Feel, clamp, hoist.*

I am at the summit in a few minutes. I am really hoping that kids don't see me, I hate to send a message that this is for amateurs. Collapsing in a heap on the top ledge, I close my eyes. The rock feels smooth.

"Man, that was cool!" I hear in familiar teenage tongue. *Oh no. I've been outted.*

"Yeah, man . . . listen," I say, sitting up. "I'm a professional . . . climber and diver . . . please don't ever try this—"

I stop speaking.

Behind the kid are the four men. *The four Panama hats.* Unmistakable. Three have their backs to me. One stands in front of them, facing me, but is partially blocked by the others. I strain to see better. I am not sure why. Oahu is clogged, crawling with tourists. These are just four more. Yet, I can't stop looking. I stand up.

"Yeah, those dudes were bothering us here a while ago," the boy says to me. He looks about sixteen.

"Bothering you?" I ask.

"Yeah, me and my friend," he points behind him to another Hawaiian boy by a tree.

"We wanted to jump. Ya know, jump Spitting Cave. It's cool. Only sixty feet down."

"*You could die jumping, kid,*" I say sharply.

"Yeah, yeah . . . that's what they said. What, *he* said. The guy, smoking. But he wasn't nice about it, ya know. He was mean. He doesn't own Spitting Cave. I told him we wanted to jump. He said, yeah, you want to jump . . . *then let me help you . . .*"

"*What!*" I yell, loudly.

"Yeah, man, he made like he was gonna push me, man . . . a mean dude."

"Jesus, kid, I'm sorry. Why don't you go on with your friend. Here." I take the plastic bag out of my zippered swimsuit and retrieve my wallet.

"Get yourselves a hot dog." I hand him a ten dollar bill.

"Thanks man! My name is Ano. That's Kai . . . over there."

I look, Kai is hanging from a tree, now. I wave to him.

"You are real nice man . . . funny, you kinda look like the other *haole,* haha. No offense, man."

With that the boy runs off.

I turn back to find the four Panama hats. *Haoles.* That is what we are to the islanders.

I sigh, and start for the hotel. Need to shower and dress before dinner. Blue blazer time again.

# Tess

I look at the daiquiri glass on the table in front of me. The café is filled with laughing couples.

*I try to piece together what I saw.*

There is no question that I saw my husband, John McAdams in his blue blazer buying flowers for a woman.

Maybe I had an irrational reaction? Maybe he saw someone he used to know? Maybe it was someone from his past? Maybe she is sick? Very sick . . . and he is being the man I love, and he is buying her flowers?

I order another daiquiri.

Alcohol feels strange in my body. I don't feel myself.

Why the kiss? It was a kiss between lovers I immediately had thought.

*Wasn't it?*

A lips kiss. Longer, than is chaste.

Am I doing it again, am I giving into my life-long affliction of my too-big heart? I try to think with my head.

Maybe it wasn't a long-lips kiss. There were dozens of people in the market.

Maybe the multitude of heads that blocked my view, breaking it up—had deceived me into thinking I saw a long kiss when it was a short kiss?

I look at my yellow dress. I was happy in yellow an hour ago. John loves me in yellow. *There must be an explanation.* He is my whole world. My light. My reason. I know he loves me.

Then, I lay my head on my arms. A sob escapes from my throat. It must be the daiquiris . . . I am suddenly crying my eyes out.

Stop it—I say to myself.

This is my holiday, my romantic reconnection holiday with my beloved. There must be an explanation!

I pull my head up, wearily. Sitting across from me is a man. I jump.

He has an enormous camera—it looks like it could photograph the moon, the lens is twelve inches long.

*"Y'alright Miss?"* he asks me, looking concerned. He has an Australian accent.

"Oh . . . yes . . . just . . . a momentary lapse . . ." I stammer, wiping my eyes with the edge of my yellow dress.

"Well, I have those all right . . . all the time, here . . . take this napkin . . . don't want you to mess up your pretty dress," he hands me a tiny paper napkin.

"Coffee?" he asks me as the waitress comes by.

I nod gratefully.

"I'm Peter. Peter Sloane," he says.

"Tess McAdams."

"Nice to meet you Tess McAdams," he smiles and take the camera off his shoulder.

"That . . . is something," I say, quietly.

"*Nauticam Nikon D500 . . . rectilinear ultra wide angle lens,*" he says, lifting the enormous machine and handing it to me.

"Oh . . . no . . . I shouldn't . ." I say. He laughs.

"No need to be afraid Tess . . . this audacious little hussy is quite sturdy. She's a thief, she is, crikey! Stealing moments from nature, she does," Peter says, laughing.

I notice his black hair is in a long pony tail. Earring in his ear. I touch the camera, the lens.

"Nature," I say, slowly, "is my life. Sea turtles."

"Crikey!" Peter's green eyes open wide.

"Yes . . . I . . . ah . . . well, I run a turtle hospital in Hana. Maui."

"I know Hana . . ! I adore Hana. I've shot there many times."

"Really?" I look at him, and smile weakly.

"Yes! Really! *Sea turtle girl.* Well, I'll be darned."

I touch his camera again . . . it is gargantuan.

"My Mother . . . used to tell me to, *look hard and remember,*" I say softly, "I've never been handy with cameras."

"Aha. I see," Peter is grinning turning nobs and buttons on his D500.

"Well Tess . . . I see, what you see . . . under the sea, you know. We see the same things."

I fold my shaky hands in my lap. Peter looks at me.

"I . . . I go into the sea, into the field . . . and ah, well . . . I ah, I tell a story, a story I can bring back about what is actually going on. I witness things . . . I document them."

"I'm here in Oahu, shooting a reef that's crushed by monsoons. I discovered . . . a family of stingrays while there . . . mother, father, children . . . it was an amazing, a magnificent find . . ."

Peter stops and looks at me. I can see he is gauging if I am interested enough in this elaborate tale. He must have read, *yes,* as he takes a breath and continues.

"My story . . . kind of, then . . . became the story of the sting-rays. My pictures have to tell this story, in a beautiful, lyrical way. But photographs must do more, Tess. *I must transcend story-telling.* And, to be honest . . . this is something not taught in university, in journalism school."

My eyes are glued to him.

"And . . . with my art . . . you know, it's transient . . . I have, but a moment. I have, but the blink of an eye, to capture people's hearts and minds. And, in this instant, you know . . . it's ephem-eral . . . I must use *poetry.* The poetry we all grew up with. Pictures have power. Our job is to convince the unconvinced."

I lean toward him. "So, you . . . are invited into a story, you see it happening . . . you . . . look hard . . . and then snap the photo?" I say.

"Yes," he replies.

Our eyes lock.

"I can't change film or lenses underwater," Peter continues.

"So I'm stuck with taking different lens and film systems down. I often go down with ten underwater camera systems. Tess—a system is not just a camera. *Think of a large crab.* That's like a system. There's a housing, with one to three strobes attached. I can shoot twelve hundred pictures on a single thirty-two gig card. I can stay under forever. For a week . . ."

Peter stops and laughs raucously. I laugh a little too, then.

"Ah, I've made you laugh," he says.

"Yes . . ." I say, and look at my hands. My wedding rings sparkle.

"And where is the lucky Mr. McAdams now?" Peter asks avoiding my eyes.

I pause.

The makeup stain on my dress needs to be cleaned.

"He's buying me flowers," I say, looking at Peter as he looks down.

"Well, I say we get together for a beer, yes? All of us?"

Peter's Australian accent is very inviting.

"Here is our number," I say, handing him a business card.

I stand, and put my yellow bag on my shoulder.

"Bye . . . Tess of the turtles," he says, smiling.

I walk out of the café.

# John

## 2016

### Honolulu, Oahu
### August

Where is Alan Wong's? I have been up and down the streets . . .
I check my Honolulu map.

There. I see it. I step inside. Wow, eye candy. So Tess, I smile
to myself. A beautiful, pale room, accented with gleaming wood
and sprinkled with flowers.

"Table for two, name's McAdams," I say to the hostess.

She seats me. I stretch my legs . . . I'm sore from a day of
surfing and diving. But my soul is happy. This holiday is exactly
what I needed. What we needed.

"Wine list, please," I say to the waiter.

I scan the list. A French white, I think. I need Tess to choose.
"John."

I look up.

"Darling," I say, jumping up to hug my beloved. She looks beautiful in a white silk short dress.

I hold her close. The silk of her dress is slippery. She slips easily from my grasp. I sit down.

"What a day! Oh my dear . . . you were right about coming. I love you." I take her hand in mine across the table.

"I'm always right," she says, smiling down at her menu.

"I caught a Paradise wave Tess . . . in the channel . . . it felt sooo thrilling . . . then I met this incredible guy with a boat and he towed me to Spitting Cave . . . fabulous . . . did an impromptu snorkel, and climbed to the top, too . . ."

"Really . . ."

She is still looking at her menu.

I look at mine.

"You look beautiful darling," I say softly.

She looks up.

*Woah.* What is wrong? *Her eyes are red.*

"Tess?" I say, suddenly upset.

"Allergy. To the massage oils today," she says.

Oils? I wonder to myself, but keep quiet.

"What would you like?" the waiter asks.

"Filet mignon, potato, and . . . asparagus," I say, trying to smile.

"Ceaser salad," Tess says.

"That's all doll?" I ask, surprised.

"Yes," she answers.

I fold my hands. Then I pour the wine.

"What's up for tomorrow," I ask.

Tess nibbles on a roll. Then she answers me, chewing.

"Laniakea Beach . . . ?"

"Turtle Beach! Excellent!" I say, grabbing her hand again. "Yes."

"I know a little about it . . . can you tell me more?" I ask. Something is definitely wrong with Tess. I decide to let her tell me when she is ready.

Perhaps it is the stress of the last few months . . . releasing. Yes, I'll bet that is it.

Tess swallows the roll. She looks at me.

"John . . . ?"

"Yes?" I say. My heartbeat quickens.

"I . . . I . . ."

"Yes, dear, tell me . . . ?"

Tess puts her hair behind her ears. *I know this move.* It means she's upset.

I squeeze her hand. She is silent.

"It's been a long several months darling . . . Bubble Cave . . . then Kiluaea . . . I understand. I'm tired too . . ." I offer.

*Tess bursts into tears.*

Ah. This is it. Just a stress melt down. I jump to my feet and go to her. I don't care if people are looking. I hug her for all I'm worth.

"It's okay darling," I whisper.

When I sit back down, I refill our wine glasses.

Our meal is served.

"You know, I was reading about Turtle Beach . . . ah . . . earlier. Found a magazine in the room. What a great idea," I say.

Tess nods.

"It's right here—Oahu's north shore—Turtle Beach. Our greens will be basking in the sun . . . waiting for their mama to come visit," I wink at my wife, knowing this should make her smile.

It doesn't.

"Why were you at the market today, John?" Tess asks then, looking at her salad.

"The market? I wasn't my love. I was surfing. Then diving."

She looks at me. The sadness in her face is shocking. *What the hell is going on?*

"Tess—I was surfing at Sandy beach. Catching my Paradise waves."

"I saw you, John."

"You saw me where? The market? I don't even know where it is? Where is it? Near the hotel?"

"You bought flowers there. Please. It's okay. I forgive you. Your friend . . . with you. It's okay. Just don't lie, John."

*I am totally flabbergasted.*

"Tess. I was not at the market. I did not buy flowers. I have been surfing, and diving, all day. I had to rush to get here tonight, to meet you!"

"Not true." she says to me, quietly.

Then she jumps to her feet, knocks over the wine bottle and storms out of the restaurant.

I am more shocked than I have ever been in my life.

# Tess

I can't see. Everything is blurry. My face feels wet. My body is numb.

Suddenly, I long for Mother. Our quiet house, on the cliff.

The boardwalk feels stiff under my ballet flats. I see the ocean surf, white and foamy. I slip off my shoes. To cool my feet, yes.

I stumble across the sand. It is completely dark. I look up at the sky. It's new moon. *"Hina, where are you?"* I sputter.

But, she's sleeping this night. She cannot help me. I am alone in the dark.

A lamppost suddenly comes on. At least I have electric light.

I collapse onto the sand and thrust my feet into the foam. The surf washes up over my waist. I don't care. I'm not in the mood for this silk dress, anyway.

*He lied.*

The weight of this settles.

A good and decent man of honor—*lied.*

*Why?* It means . . . the woman must mean something to him. A great deal.

*He could have made something up.* But he is too honorable.

And if it were nothing, *why not tell me?* If she were, say, *ill,* and he was being kind, well then, the truth is easy to tell me, *isn't it?* Yet he didn't do that.

I cannot grasp it. I cannot.

My John could not deceive for deceit's sake. No, he is protecting someone. Maybe he fell in love, once before. *Perhaps a long time ago?* My head spins.

*"Why did I come here?"* I say aloud to the sea.

*"Marama . . .* you are an island away from me. *Hina . . .* you are sleeping in your quiet phase," I say. I am utterly alone.

I suddenly stand up. *I see a hatchling!* There, in the surf! I run to it . . . I see it has flipped itself onto its back. Accidentally.

"Darling . . . hello," I say. I crouch down next to it and look into its eyes. *"You can do it . . . push hard with your hind flippers . . ."* I whisper. It looks at me and continues to struggle. A wave crests and then crashes onto the beach, the hatchling looks at me and uses the billowy foam to flip! Soon it is right side up, on the waves. I see it looking at the lamppost and then at the sea . . . the sparkle from the lamp's light works as the moon, and I watch the hatchling turn to swim away, on top of the sparkling water.

I watch the baby turtle go. I feel better to have helped it. *I suddenly feel my power, my strength.* Kauila needs me! I have purpose. I have a greater purpose.

I take a very deep breath. I will deal with this situation, somehow. I turn to go.

I see that John is running toward me, across the sand. This is the first time in my life that I do not wish to see him.

# John

"Tess. Stop. Now."

Tears are spilling down my cheeks. I grab my wife.

"Tess. *You saw someone else.*"

This is the first time in my life I see that my wife doesn't want to see me. It strikes me like a lightening bolt.

*"TESS! It was not me!"*

"It was you. Blue blazer. Loafers. It was you John. At the flower stand. Buying flowers for your friend. Then you kissed her. Please. Admit it and just tell me the story. I will be okay. I am calm now."

*Am I living in an alternate reality here?* I think to myself. Do I have a clone following me around?

I stop. I stop speaking. I stop breathing.

*Jake? Is Jake here? Is Jake here in a blue blazer and loafers buying flowers for a woman?*

How could it be possible? It is not possible. Yet, how many times have I said that sentence in the last five months? *It is not possible.* That sentence right there.

"It's okay John, please talk to me. I will understand. You had a life before you met me."

"Tess." I say her name and sit on the sand. She kneels next to me.

"Tess . . . is it possible . . . that you . . . saw . . . *Jake?* Today?"

Tess looks at me, blankly.

*Then, her face changes.* Her eyes enlarge. Her mouth drops open.

# Tess

John's arms are around me.

Here we are, in our hotel bed, our first night here. And Jake . . . has managed to ruin our happiness.

It had to have been Jake.

Jake is not what he seems. No, he is playing a game. He may be simple. But there is another side to Jake.

He has learned how to *mimic*. That's it. He mimics. He copies. *He copies John.*

He doesn't plan, scheme, plot. No, the facts are the facts, he was born deficient.

*But he learned how to adapt.*

He has been watching John for years. He watches and he copies. Of course he does. What twin doesn't do that? *It is what twins do.*

Jake learned by copying. By pretending to be John.

Yes, pretending to be John. Smart, dapper, handsome, caring . . . and so he copied John and followed us on holiday.

He must have snuck aboard a boat or a plane and tracked our activities. He wore the clothes John wears. He is here, pretending to be John. *And I saw him.* Today, at the market.

I hug John to me. It is a crazy situation.

I think . . . what if there was another Tess? *An evil Tess.* Following me around. Tricking John. I hug my husband tighter.

Exhausted, I drift off to sleep.

# John

I awaken. I look at my watch. Three in the morning. Tess is asleep.

*Jake.*

My minds turns over and over and over.

It occurs to me that Tess could simply be *mistaken.* She is tired. She is worn out.

It is . . . possible . . . she saw another tall, blonde man in a blue blazer. With brown loafers. It's not an unusual uniform in a town thick with tourists. In fact, it could be called the mandatory tourist uniform.

Tess is quick to blame Jake now.

*Why oh why is this for me to bear?* Why, dear Lord, why have you given me Jake? I stifle a sob. Pa didn't want him. Ma didn't know what to do with him.

I don't want him. Nobody wants him.

Yet—Jake didn't ask for this. The sadness of my brother is too much for me to take in after one of the worst days of my life. That's it. I am dismissing this for the rest of our time here.

I turn over and go to sleep.

# Tess

## 2016

❀ ⋙∘◦◦∘⋘ ❀

### Laniakea Beach, Oahu
### August

❀ ⋙∘◦◦∘⋘ ❀

"John . . ." I whisper. An enormous humpback whale breaches the surface just offshore, Laniakea Beach. We watch as he continues to breach . . . *one, two, three . . . now six times.*

My husband is standing on the sand in his scuba suit, I look him up and down. Blonde. Tall. Fit. Handsome. Caring. *Perfect.*

Yesterday's madness disappears with the whale as she submerges. A horn, sounding from her blowhole is the signal.

I look around. *Hana is so different from Honolulu.* I see the touch of man, here. Large, brightly colored shiny houses dot the edges of Laniakea Beach, or Turtle Beach as it is known. It's a very small patch of fluffy white sand, with multiple tide pools and rock ledges.

John is eyeing a group of surfers, looking to catch waves

from the deep channel here. Lots of cameras. Sun umbrellas. Picnic baskets. Music from radios. The honk of a horn from the street. A siren. Yells from swimmers, laughter, splashing, noise.

I think of Hana. Of Marama.

It is good to compare, I realize. To be able to see the *before and the after.* Hana is Hawaii, before. Before man. Before industry. Wild, unspoiled Hawaii. The Polynesian islands as they once were. When Kauila ruled the seas and Hina ruled the skies.

I do not wish to make a judgment. I just sit back and observe. Being with the creatures of the earth teaches us. Guides us. Shapes us. Shapes our hearts. I observe, like a butterfly. I float in my space. I look. I see. But I am still a butterfly, these sights I see don't alter who I am inside.

Glancing up at the sky, I see Hina's sliver. She is there, waiting. Waiting to lead us. She leads Kauila to nest. She leads Kauila's hatchlings home. She leads the tides. There is a lesson in this. We all know to follow Hina. She is our moon. *Our moon to follow.* No matter what happens in life, we have her, to guide us.

It's what we all need, after all. A light to follow. Whether it is God, Hina or love. *We all need to follow the light in our hearts home.* Just like a turtle hatchling.

"Tess, would you come here, please," John is motioning to me, he is standing by an enormous crowd of people that have suddenly gathered at the water's edge.

I jump up, though it's not easy inside this rubber suit.

"Yes? What's up?" I say looking at the group.

"Tess, these nice folks want to swim with the turtles and to touch the turtles . . ."

"Aha," I say. I weave my way into the circle of the large crowd, I have done this before, I know just what to do. When I have their attention, I speak.

"Hello folks, my name is Tess McAdams. I'm a marine biologist . . . otherwise known as a turtle scientist," I say, raising my voice, and smiling.

"*I know you all love turtles*—I can see it in your eyes. Me too!" I say.

"But, turtles can get very, very sick when we touch them! Why, you ask? Because we humans have bacteria in our hands . . . yes right here," I raise hands, palms outward, to the group.

"I run a sea turtle hospital on Maui, and I promise you all— I have seen the results of this . . ."

The faces around me are stern.

"There is a horrible disease called, *fibropapilloma*. It's painful and attacks our dear sea turtles with tumors when people touch them."

I see eyes widen.

"The tumors can grow on the turtle's skin, internal organs, mouth and eyes," I add.

"I know you love turtles as I do, I see that," I say, walking around and looking at each person individually, "but you need to know that Hawaii loves the turtles too and in their best interests they have protected them . . . our sea turtles, our greens and hawksbills here in Hawaii, enjoy full protection under the federal Endangered Species Act and under Hawaii state law. It is illegal to chase, hunt, handle, injure or harass them in any way . . ."

I stop and pause.

"We didn't know Ms. McAdams," says a mother of three nearest to me.

"It is totally okay not to know, in fact most people don't! But we must *spread the turtle love,* folks . . . that is my job," I say.

They're all looking at me, and nodding.

"If you want to swim with the turtles—I suggest a few feet between you . . . but here's the good news: *sea turtles LOVE to visit!* They adore it. It's their favorite thing . . . in fact . . . don't be surprised if a turtle wants to hang out for . . . a few hours. . . this happens all the time."

"A few hours!" a little boy of about five cries out.

"Yep. They just love to be with people. they like to stare into your eyes . . ." I say.

"Wow! Cool!" the boy says, grinning.

I turn to John, who is waiting for me. He takes my hand and squeezes it.

# Peter

Well, this has been the strangest day of my life. *A bonzer, for sure!*

I mean, what are the odds of *yellow-dress-turtle-girl* appearing in the midst of my *National Geographic* shoot, here at Turtle Beach?

I'd just surfaced, off the west end of the channel. I shift my mask up, and boom—Tess McAdams—standing there, less than a dozen feet from me. In the sand, speaking to a crowd.

Course, I had to investigate. She didn't recognize me, with my diving get-up on, but I did her. In her diving suit as well, no less.

*Sigh.* I down the rum in my shot glass.

I open the digital viewer and start to flip through today's shots.

Magnificent. Mmhmm. Great close up of an angel fish. Moray eel in the coral, *National Geographic* will like that one.

Hawksbill. Woah. I stare.

*It's an opus shot.* Perfection. I hit the zoom button. More perfection. *The eyes.* God Almighty. The eyes have breathtaking clarity. *Iris. Pupil. Emotion. Depth. Age.*

Tears spring to my eyes. To have a reaction, like this? This is a photo capture of a world that needs to be known. Of a creature, that needs to be seen. Looking back in time, in her eyes. *I see it.*

Man, oh man. This is why I do what I do. You can never tell . . . when you're shooting . . . that it's—the shot. The one. Ten years.

7,700 hours. 920,000 photos. And now, the one. The Shot. Flawless. Thousands of images brought me to this one.

I click the log. Next photo pops up. My God. It's her. Tess.

It's an accidental snap, must have happened when I surfaced, finger on the trigger.

Blurry, but it's her—on the beach, people around her. Close up, though blurred. I must have left the lens on zoom—after I snapped *The Shot* of the turtle.

Jesus Christ. I click back to the previous photograph of the turtle. Then back to Tess. I'm an artist. I have a muse. She inspired my photo of my lifetime.

"Crikey, Peter Sloane," I say aloud to the bar, in my best Aussie accent. I order another rum.

It floods me with warmth. More warmth.

# Tess

What a difference a day makes.

The warmth of John's hand in mine as we walk along a Honolulu beach. A million lights dot the edges of this busy beach. It's not Hana. *It's the opposite of Hana!* I laugh aloud.

"Something funny, love?" John asks.

"Look . . ." I say, pointing at the millions of tiny dots of light.

"Yep. People." John whispers.

He turns, now.

His kiss is heavy. Warm. He presses harder. He opens my mouth with his tongue. I give him mine. We have healed from the wound.

"Later . . ." I say, giggling.

He smiles.

"And now . . . my darling adventurer . . . I have a surprise for you."

John abruptly changes direction. We walk toward the pier.

# John

Of course, I love *The Tess*. She is a beauty. She is my second love after my first, Tess, my wife.

But . . . Cats. C A T S. *Oh how I love catamarans.*

Thirty five hundred years ago the first Cat was built by the ingenious Polynesians. They looked like outrigger canoes, two bound together with a wooden frame, and a sail.

*Cats are fast.* They are graceful. They were made to move. They are pure speed. Ancient islanders loved them. The sight of a sleek Cat sets my pulse racing.

"Tess, come here," I say to my beloved wife, folding her small form into my arms. "Look . . ." I whisper in her ear.

She peers over my shoulder. A sleek catamaran is roped to the marina.

"No . . . ? For us?" she asks.

I take her hand and we step aboard.

# Tess

The Cat purrs.

There is a light wind on perfectly flat water . . . the sun is starting to sink.

"Just the sails tonight, doll," John says, as he centers the rudders, locks the wheel, disables the autopilot, and adjusts the traveller.

"Okay . . . yes, here we go . . . the sweet spot," he says, and I feel the Cat sigh. John's got the sail trim perfect. Direction stable.

I stand . . . and go to the helm. The motion of the boat has leveled out, the speed has picked up, and we're cruising along smoothly.

"I love you," I whisper.

"Me too," he whispers back.

We go below deck, and John takes me to bed.

# Sasha

## 2016

### Honu Hospital; Hana, Maui
### August

"Tess, John . . . *meet our new turtle savers,*" I announce to my bosses.

Four people gather around me. We join hands forming a line on the soft white sand. It's a beautiful blue-sky day here on Maui, in this quiet corner of the island.

"Tess, or *Turtle Mama,* as I sometimes call her, would love to hear your thoughts on who you are and why you love turtles," I say, nodding at the group. *"Please speak from the heart."*

Tess and John are seated opposite us. Tess has Hannah in her lap, a recovering turtle. Hannah has heavy bandages wrapped around her shell.

"Hi folks, please don't let Hannah distract you . . . she gets anxious when I leave her alone, she's recuperating from surgery last week," Tess says, holding Hannah's front flipper as she speaks.

"Hannah . . ." John whispers, stroking the damaged turtle's head softly. Hannah closes and opens her eyes as he does this, much like a puppy.

I smile, and turn to my group.

"Lani, Bane, Ema and Oke . . ." I say, introducing my group.

"Why don't each of you come forward say a few words . . ." I nod to Lani, to start.

"*Aloha*. I am Lani. I love the turtles. I more than love turtles. They are a part of my family. My grandparents have worshipped the honu all their lives. My earliest memory is swimming with the honu in the lagoon. My grandmother told me my aumakua is the honu."

"Welcome Lani. You are right. Honu are our aumakua. Our ancestral mother," Tess said, nodding at the girl.

"*Aloha*. My name is Bane. I just graduated from the university of Hawaii at Hilo. I majored in marine biology. I wanted a year in the field . . . I am honored to be with you folks. I come from Honolulu. We are descended from the Polynesians, so it is important for me to carry their flame, I love honu with all my heart. Thank you. Maholo."

"Welcome Bane. It is an honor to have you. I look forward to learning form you," John says, winking.

"Aloha! I am Ema. I work in the café in Hana, I also give tours all over the island, I am an expert in flora, fauna, marine animals though I have no professional education. My education comes from living here in nature. I bring my love of turtles to this job. I prefer them to people. Maholo, thank you."

"Maholo Ema. It is an honor to have you with us," Tess tells her.

"Aloha. I'm Oke. I am going to be honest, I heard about your technical work here with drones and nest sensors. I have ideas about possibly using transmitters on hatchlings . . . to track their voyage into the sea. I have spoken with Sasha about this . . . thank you."

I give a high five to Oke, and look at Tess.

"Oke, I cannot tell you how excited I am to hear this," Tess says, eyes shining. "Welcome to Honu Hospital, everyone!" she adds.

Tess and John are beaming at me. Beaming. Like two glowing moons.

*Life is good.*

# Tess

## 2016

❧

### Hana, Maui
### August

❧

"*Aha'aina . . .*" Marama's black eyes are glittering.

"*Aha'aina . . . really?*" I ask her.

"Yes. It is time," she says, squarely. "We must honor your triumphs, Tess, your gifts to Kauila's children."

Marama wants to celebrate with the traditional feast, the *aha'aina*. A luau.

"Come." Marama takes my hand, and walks me outside her hut. We sit down beneath a large drooping palm. It is so overgrown that its fronds touch the ground creating a private green space for us. I feel a secret is about to shared.

"I want to return to the old ways because I have had dreams . . . I have felt an unease. Something not right. Signs. The pueo, owl. Your troubles. Pele. There are signs. I have been reading them. There is . . . an imbalance, I fear . . ." she says to me, inside the ferns.

Her face is grave. "I . . . think . . . I fear . . . it is . . . *qaitu,*" she says.

"Ghosts!" I whisper, recognizing the Hawaiian word.

"Yes," she says quietly. "Evil spirits. The dead. Qaitu. I think . . . they have returned. I am not sure. I have yet to see them. I have been looking."

Marama shakes her head. She touches a fern and holds it to her cheek.

"Marama, I . . . agree. I have felt the shift too. Something . . . as you say, out of balance. With John and I, with the hospital . . . an evil, I feel. *An evil at war with good,*" I say, finally, at last. It feels good to get it out.

"Ah, child. Yes. You too, now. So, the thing to do is to start with honoring the good. The Gods will recognize this act. We will all come together at the *aha'aina.* The island must come together . . . like the strands of a lei," she declares.

I nod.

"I will then, dare the *qaitu* to show his face," she adds, in a fierce tone.

"You want to call out the ghosts! You want to show them we are not afraid of them. I see," I say. "Are you sure, Marama? Are you afraid?"

"I am not afraid," she says flatly. "It needs to be done."

I hold her hands tightly in my own. I look at them. Old, gnarled, brown. But, strong. So very strong. She is like the mother turtles . . . she is ancient but as solid as the earth itself.

Unshakable.

*"Ohe'o?"* I ask.

Not far from Marama's home, are seven sacred pools, created long ago by a rainforest stream. The pools are considered deeply spiritual. The natives call this place of healing, *Ohe'o.*

She squeezes my hand, *yes,* and we walk under a cathedral ceiling of drooping palms. I am much relieved to be back in my Hana paradise, where things have a rhyme, reason and method, and can be made to make sense.

Marama crooks her small finger at a cluster of moss-covered grey stones. It is the temple of *Kanekoela Heiau,* where she was trained long ago, a Kahuna of the secret arts.

As we walk, I realize that the old woman next to me seems to be *growing younger.* Her steps are quickening, leaping at times, doubling mine. She jumps to point at ferns and flowers. I watch her scurry up a palm tree trunk like a squirrel, to catch a Hawaiian blue butterfly. She places it on her shoulder and shimmies down the palm with the agility of a child.

*Is it the air we are breathing that has revived her?* I wonder. Dense, humid, full of white ginger perfume. It is, dizzying. I have to run to keep up with the tiny Hawaiian woman.

Marama points out her favorite things to me, bouncing from one side of the trail to the other. Giant banyan trees. Fresh picked strawberry guava. Footbridges across the raging waters.

A rushing sound has her skipping now. It gets louder and her skips are longer . . . three to four feet each. And then I see them up ahead. Strung like pearls, the seven sacred pools stretch before us.

As if the pools were hers, Marama dives into the first one easily. She disappears. I stand at the edge, peering into the sapphire blue. It is so clear that I can see the fish looking up at me from the depths. I can see their colors. I can see their gills moving.

But where is Marama? I scan the calm surface. Then, I see her little head pop up at the far side of the pool, her favorite place. Right beneath the waterfall.

*"Come, Tess . . ."* she calls to me.

I look down, and place a foot into the water. It is unlike any water I know. It has a *soft quality* to it, like honey, but not as thick. It is warm, heavy. I know it has volcanic minerals in it and this causes the unique viscosity. I also know that the natives believe this water has magic. It heals. It makes skin young. It seeps into the body, suffusing it with nutrients. It's like dipping into a pool of *happiness* and taking it with yourself when you leave.

I submerge. I am instantly *lulled.* My fingers move in the soft, swirly stuff. I rub my fingertips together under the water. So smooth. So silky.

I stand up and do it again—I rub my hands together. *I love this water.* It is just lovely, flowing stuff. I stretch my neck backwards, and breathe intense floral perfumes from hyacinth that grows above the pools. Yep. This is as close to bath-heaven, as a girl can get!

Submerging again, I swim out to Marama. The soft tickle of the outer waterfall threatens to lull me right to sleep . . . so I swim farther inside. It is more dangerous here, lovely pelting water is like a massage on my back. I decide to give in and close my eyes.

Marama and I rest in silence for a long time under the waterfall. The steady drumbeat of the falling water rattles my head, shaking all *unwanted thoughts free.* My muscles are relieved. I have no desire to do anything but this. So I stay, in pure bliss.

My thoughts splinter. They are unconnected and free. I don't try and group them together into meaning. Rather, I let them flow, like the waterfall itself, whichever way they wish.

The sea.

Hina.

Kauila.

My hatchlings.

A sleeping baby.

My eyes fly open! *A baby? Mine?* Or is it a turtle baby?

I close my eyes again to try and retrieve the vision. I look down at the sacred pool. I see a face there. It is a perfect oval shape. With large eyes. Enormous eyes. I stare harder . . . trying to see what else may be lurking.

"Tess . . ." Marama says just then, I look up to see her on the hot lava rocks, sunning herself. I decide not to disturb her with my vision. I swim over to the rocks and settle back, in the sun.

*"I ola o Mikololou i ka alelo,"* Marama whispers to me, *however much trouble one may have, there is always a way of escape.*

I see she has read my mind. She takes my hand.

"Watch *Hina,*" she says. "Follow her."

"Watch for signs, Tess," "Hina's light will let you see them clearly."

She is still holding my hand.

# John

## 2016

### Luau Beach; Hana, Maui
### August

The luau drums have started.

*Rat-a-tat-Rat-a-tat-Rat-a-tat-Rat-a-tat-Rat-a-tat.*

Rhythmic stimulation seeps into my brain, euphoria starts to build. The slower, steady beats, shift my soul into a state of deep relaxation and expanded awareness.

*Rat-a-tat-Rat-a-tat-Rat-a-tat-Rat-a-tat-Rat-a-tat.*

I feel the flow of our dynamic, interrelated universe. The beats connect me to it. Something profound happens with each *rat-a-tat*, I feel my body, mind and spirit integrating . . . and spinning backward in time. Three thousand five hundred years evaporate in an instant. My heart pumps. My blood rushes. Fire. Knives. Drums. *The sound of ancient Polynesia.*

I hear the call. The call of the warrior. I am the warrior. I have been for all of my life. I am *nature's warrior*, and she needs me to fight. She needs me to be strong in my battle for her. To stand up and take back her lands, her seas, her children. It is noble work.

The drums are getting louder. The *ailao* will begin soon. Each beat ricochets through my being, connecting me with the power of the universe. I externalize my human questions, and I internalize the universe's answers. I am enhanced. Racing through my veins is a heightened sense of empowerment and responsibility. I feel my core. I feel the power of nature.

The Samoan fire dance in my mind begins to ignite my hands and feet. They move, unconsciously, in the millennium-old custom as I prepare to perform the sacred rite. My fire soaked machete will twirl with prowess and skill and bravery.

All who watch me will be afraid. All who watch me will know my power. All who challenge nature's right to exist will have to challenge me.

**Ua mau ke ea o ka `aina i ka pono!** *The life of the land is preserved in righteousness!*

The drums are very loud now. My ears are ringing. I am in resonance with the natural rhythms of life. Rhythm and resonance order my world, the natural world. I understand! I see! *Dissonance and disharmony* arise only when we limit our capacity to resonate totally and completely with the *rhythms of life!*

"*Ua mau ke ea o ka `aina i ka pono!*" I cry aloud, above the din, "*the life of the land is preserved in righteousness!*"

My battle is before me—I am at war with the destroyers of

the earth. Images flash before my warrior eyes . . . the same label for each, *greed!* The ultimate enemy. I see him, and I name him. *I spin my flaming torches!* I whiz them around my warrior's body.

This is who I am! I'm a warrior. I hurl my flames at my enemy, those who seek to destroy my planet.

# Marama

I must defeat *qaitu. The ghosts. The dead.* I must show them our strength. I know they are angry. Our *aha'aina*, our luau will unite us, and the *qaitu* will see our power. Our power, together.

The *imu* is my first task, the sacred pit to roast our pig. Two by four feet wide. Unchanged for a thousand years.

"Fill it with small branches and twigs," I tell the helpers. "Then, cover that with wood."

I watch as Tess's people perform the ritual of the *imu*. Lani, Bane, Ema and Oke are serious with the task I have given them. My heart is glad. To see the young honoring our ancestral ways.

"Stones atop the wood," I instruct.

We will heat the stones later at the lighting ceremony. Just as my mother and grandmother and great grandmother once did.

"Maholo, maholo children . . . and now a layer of green . . ." I say, clapping my hands together, thanking them.

"To create steam, Marama?" asks Oke.

"Yes, child," I answer.

I look toward a rustling behind the trees. My mind spins backward, I am suddenly with my ancestors, in the time of the ancients. I see the men now, they are bringing the holy pig. I look at the face of the man I know to be my *great-great-great-*

*great-great grandfather* and I smile. He smiles back at me.

"The *puaa*, my Marama . . ." he says to me, using the Polynesian word for pig.

I watch as he carefully places the *puaa* in the *imu*. I walk to him, and cover it with dirt. Our hands touch. He stops and kisses my cheek. His face changes then, it becomes Oke's face. Oke is startled that I am holding his hand.

"It is okay, child . . . it is okay," I say. Then I stand, and recite the ancient prayer over the imu:

*"O ke aka kā 'oukou, 'o ka 'i'o kā mākou', yours the shadow; ours the flesh, dedicating a feast to the gods."*

# Jake

Drums.

*Rat-a-tat-Rat-a-tat-Rat-a-tat-Rat-a-tat-Rat-a-tat.*

Spider.

She's staring at me.

The black widow's eyes are red.

*Rat-a-tat-Rat-a-tat-Rat-a-tat-Rat-a-tat-Rat-a-tat.*

She stares harder at me.

Heart is pumping.

Blood is rushing.

She is angry—my black widow spider.

Her eyes smolder.

"What!" I scream at her.

She gathers her six arms close to her body.

She narrows her red eyes to slits.

"What do you want from me!" I am screaming now.

The spider starts to spin.

She spews grey stuff that is her webbing.

I am on my feet in my cabin, now.

Now I am angry, too.

"I hate you!" I scream at the creature in the ceiling.

The spider retreats to her web. She is hiding from me.

Then—a head pops out of her webbing. It hits my floor . . .

It is the head of a fly.

I look at it.

I understand.

She, the warrior, is having her feast.

I am the coward. I have nothing.

The drums are now so loud that my tiny hut is shaking.

*Rat-a-tat-Rat-a-tat-Rat-a-tat-Rat-a-tat-Rat-a-tat.*

I hear the call.

*The call of the warrior.*

I am the warrior.

I walk from my hut.

The drums guide my feet.

*Rat-a-tat-Rat-a-tat-Rat-a-tat-Rat-a-tat-Rat-a-tat.*

I see—flames ahead.

Fire!

Knives!

*Spinning, spinning, spinning,* circles of fire!

Like my spider, *spinning, spinning, spinning,* her web.

Both are preparing for battle.

Both take their prey.

I will spin. I will be the fire.

The spider will be afraid.

She will know my power.

I close my eyes. I am starting to transform.

*Rat-a-tat-Rat-a-tat-Rat-a-tat-Rat-a-tat-Rat-a-tat.*

Sound vibrations shake my body.

*Rat-a-tat-Rat-a-tat-Rat-a-tat-Rat-a-tat-Rat-a-tat.*

Thoughts shake loose, they are jagged edged.

*Rat-a-tat-Rat-a-tat-Rat-a-tat-Rat-a-tat-Rat-a-tat.*

They are fiery. They burn. Hot.

*Rat-a-tat-Rat-a-tat-Rat-a-tat-Rat-a-tat-Rat-a-tat.*

My battle is before me.
An image of the black widow spider explodes in my mind.
She is spinning a web made of fire.

*Rat-a-tat-Rat-a-tat-Rat-a-tat-Rat-a-tat-Rat-a-tat.*

I am ready for battle.

# Tess

The drums make me skittish. I press a shaky hand to my chest, thud-a-thud-a-thud. In time with the ancient rhythm.

*Rat-a-tat-Rat-a-tat-Rat-a-tat-Rat-a-tat-Rat-a-tat.*

The Tahitian drums sound the ancient call in universal island language. They align with our own hearts, pulling us in, one large pulsing people. We cannot fight it, our feet step, one after the other, in a trance-like state toward the sacred space. All of us. *Even, the qaitu.* Yet, Marama has no fear. As our Kahuna, it is her duty. Marama will tempt the ghosts. She must. She must challenge them.

As the drumbeats gets louder, I feel my own consciousness succumb. *Feelings, I've blocked, flash at me quickly, from behind shadows in my mind.* Flash of a face, my mother. Long ago scent of roses, in Mother's garden. A song now, an old Irish lullaby. My hands unconsciously twisting and threading and tying Marama's lei's. But unlike other luau's, I am not enchanted with the task.

*Rat-a-tat-Rat-a-tat-Rat-a-tat-Rat-a-tat-Rat-a-tat,* my heart hammers hard within me. The pink lokelani flowers in my hands weave into magnificent chains. Yet they are blurred.

*Rat-a-tat-Rat-a-tat-Rat-a-tat-Rat-a-tat-Rat-a-tat.*

I look toward the drumming, I see fire now. They are lighting the torches. The swords will be lit next. The warriors will come. They will show the evil spirits their power.

My hands continue to braid lokelani, leaves, mosses, blossoming grasses, and vines. The strands fall from my fingers in a beautiful heap at my feet.

But my eyes are fixed upon the spinning circles of fire.

# Marama

*The sacred ring of fire unites us.* Torches illuminate several hundred faces. So many! Everyone is here. I see the people. My people.

I look up at Hina. She shines brightly, an enormous orb above. Hina is with us.

I close my eyes. I feel the drum rhythm inside my body, a staccato surge of energy tying me to the past. *Rat-a-tat-Rat-a-tat-Rat-a-tat-Rat-a-tat-Rat-a-tat.* I'm inside a loop within myself and my people. It is silent, emotional. Like the bamboo wood's steady thuds, the *rat-a-tat* of the drums calls me home. Yes, it is time. *Let our luau begin.*

"*Aloha . . .*" I say, spreading my arms outward to the people. "*Aloha . . .*" they say back to me. Then, I raise my arms high to Hina, the moon, and I bow.

"*Kauila . . .*" I say, turning toward the sea. I bow again.

"*Kauila . . .*" the people repeat after me.

*Rat-a-tat-Rat-a-tat-Rat-a-tat-Rat-a-tat-Rat-a-tat.*

I raise my right hand sharply, my palm up. The drums stop.

I feel my face warmed by one hundred flaming torches around the luau stage. I can hear them flickering, crackling.

"*Kauila. Our aumakua. You know her story?*" I ask to the people. I walk closer to them. Their eyes glitter in the torch flames.

I see nodding heads. The torches burn brightly and show me their faces. As I read the faces in the rocks, I read these faces as well. These faces are real. The drums drew them here and opened their hearts. Now, they are ready to listen. *They are ready to hear.*

My voice is strong. Strong with eighty years of strength.

I use the English tongue, so the very youngest will understand:

*"Kauila was born on the black sandy shores of Punalu'u, on Big Island.*

*The daughter of two sea turtles . . . mother Honupo'okea and father Honu'ea.*

*Honupo'okea came out of the ocean to give birth to a very special egg!*

*Its color and shape similar to a piece of kauila wood. Honupo'okea buried her special egg in the sand . . . it was warmed by the Hawaiian sun until it was ready to hatch.*

*Before returning to the sea, Honupo'okea and Honu'ea used their flippers to dig deep into the earth forming a fresh water pond near their precious nest.*

*After a time, Honupo'okea returned to the black sandy beach to wait for her special egg to hatch.*

*Soon the egg cracked open!*

*A beautiful baby turtle emerged—dark and glossy, like kauila wood.*

*Mother and daughter made their way to the fresh water pond to live until Kauila was old enough to be on her own.*

*Kauila made Punalu'u her home and would often rest at the bottom of the fresh water pond.*

*Air bubbles from her breath would rise to the top of the pond delighting the children of Ka'u . . . Kauila loved all children and would sometime change herself into a little girl so that she could play with and watch over the children on the black sandy shores.*

*When it was time, Kauila followed her destiny and went home to the sea. It was a sacred journey . . . she followed the moon to find the ocean waves. And she follows the moon's light to come back to us to visit.*

*She is here—here with us today!*

*Under this incredible full moon . . . she knows we are here, let us all rise now . . . look toward the moon . . . and give thanks!*

My children have risen to their feet, they are slapping their palms together, now. They are standing up tall. Power surges through them. They are a strong tide, now. Coming in, cresting. I feel it. It is powerful. They are rejoicing Kauila. Good, loyal people of Maui. Our power is a strong one.

It is time to chant *oli*. The ancient Hawaiian chant is a rare gift, intoning it correctly, not easy. I close my eyes and lift my arms. My head and throat and body become sound chambers. Resonance echoes in my body.

I start with a single strong note, giving it a steady 'i'i vibrato. I don't change pitch or volume, but I move the sound around. I press it down into my *na'au*, diaphragm. I press it up into my throat . . . then higher up into my nasal sinuses.

*O ke au i kahuli wela ka honua*
*O ke au i kahuli lole ka lani*
*O ke au i kuka'iaka ka la*
*O ke au o Makali'i ka po*
*O ka malamalama ho'okumu honua*
*O ka walewale O ka walewale*
*E hoe'omalamalama i ka malama*

*At the time when the earth became hot*
*At the time when the heavens turned about*
*At the time when the sun was darkened*
*To cause the moon to shine*

*Hanau ka po ia honu kua nanuka*

*From the darkness of time came the sea turtle with its plated back*

*E hoe'omalamalama i ka malama!*
*E hoe'omalamalama i ka malama!*
*E hoe'omalamalama i ka malama!*

*To cause the moon to shine!*
*To cause the moon to shine!*
*To cause the moon to shine!*

I open my eyes. My people are dancing the hula. They are happy. They are strong. They are with me. Our power is united. *It is achieved.*

I raise both my hands, palms outward. *I bring them down together, victoriously.* The drums begin anew.

# John

*Rat-a-tat-Rat-a-tat-Rat-a-tat-Rat-a-tat-Rat-a-tat.*

My face is sweating under the black war paint. Red stripes like blood, trickle over my lips. Drumbeat rhythm pulses my heart. My Samoan fire knife spins in my hand. I snatch it back hard and flip it—to my other hand.

*Fire singes my wrist.*

I flip the knife again, in a circle. *I spin it.*

I imagine the enemy—*I spin it faster.* My feet move, instinctively, light, adept, nimble. A dance of skill. A dance of power.

I shift, I spin, the fire spins with me—searing the air and the night. Screams. Drums.

*Rat-a-tat-Rat-a-tat-Rat-a-tat-Rat-a-tat-Rat-a-tat.*

The drums are deafening. They are baiting me. The drums scream: more, *faster, now!*

I spin my knives faster. *The fire blurs to a solid red ring.*

Faster. Faster. Faster.

*Rat-a-tat-Rat-a-tat-Rat-a-tat-Rat-a-tat-Rat-a-tat.*

The night air is shaking. My soul is shaking. Spirits are shaking. Thoughts are shaking. Shaking free. *Breaking free.*

My *nifo oti,* my war knife, spins in an infinity loop of unbroken fire. The flames blow outward wildly—the crowd screams and backs away.

I twirl. I leap. I dance. I am the warrior. I am earth's warrior!

*"Alu ka pule i Hakalau! Pray to Hakalau . . . we are all in this together!"*

I have merged with the fire now. I am it—and it is me.

*Rat-a-tat-Rat-a-tat-Rat-a-tat-Rat-a-tat-Rat-a-tat.*

Then—all at once I am inside *a bright blue beam* from above. My entire body is ablaze in blue. The red fire is now blue fire. I look up to see Hina staring down at me. Her blue eyes bore into me. I'm blinded for a moment.

I throw a spinning knife *skyward*—it sails up, up, up, in Hina's blue beam. It dives back down, down, down, to my other hand.

The people cheer, they scream!

Then, they scream *again.* But now, their screams have changed. They are not joyous. They sound horrified.

I look at them, and then, at the stage I stand upon. *Another figure is on the stage with me.*

It's another fire-knife warrior.

His face is painted black with red stripes—like me. His hair is blonde.

Like mine.

Blue eyes that are a vacant blue, look at me, blindly.

Jake.

# Jake

*I am a warrior!* I am not a coward!

I see my enemy! *I spin my fire-knife!*

My flames spin a circle of red!

"*I AM A WARRIOR!*" I scream at the top of my warrior lungs.

*Then, I lunge at the enemy!* He is fast—he dodges my fire-tipped knife.

*I lunge again!* Again and again and again and again!

*There!* The fire-tip of my sword makes contact with the enemy! I have wounded him!

*Blood spurts from his leg!*

I lunge again! Another strike! *His arm spurts a torrent of blood!*

I am the spider! I have my prey!

I spin a fire-circle around him, *like the spider spinning her web!* I circle many times, faster, faster. I've got him! *I've trapped the enemy in my web!*

I lunge again! The enemy is down now, on the ground. I raise my fire-sword high.

"*QAITU!*" A scream stops me.

In horror, *I see the black widow spider standing before me!* How? How did she know where to find me?

I see her *red eyes!*

"*QAITU!* I see you. I do not fear you!" the black widow screams at me, her gnarled old hands in the air.

"*Look,* **QAITU**—*look around at us! All of us! None of us fear you!*" she screams at me.

"*We see you and we do not fear you,*" the black widow cries, circling me, now. She is moving in her crouched way, the way she moves when she is closing in on her kill. Soon . . . she will spin. Soon! I can feel it. *She will spin her web around me.*

"*Go back to where you come from qaitu!*" she screams. "*Go away!*"

"*Hele aku! Go away!*"

"***HELA AKU!***"

The black widow chants, the crowd repeats after her. Their voices combine. *They are now all spiders. They are all spinning. Spinning toward me.*

Red eyes everywhere.

"*GO AWAY!—**HELA AKU!**"* they scream.

"GO AWAY!"

"***HELA AKU!***"

"GO AWAY!"

"***HELA AKU!***"

"GO AWAY!"

"***HELA AKU!***"

"GO AWAY!"

They are coming at me now. *I take up my fire-knife—I wave it at them . . .*

The image of the fly's rolling head appears. In my mind, I watch it roll and then hit the wall.

The spoils! They want their spoils! *They want my head!*

No! I will not give them what they want. *No.* It is mine. *My spoils.* Not theirs. *I will have my spoils too.*

I take my knife—swing it high—and bring it down hard into my neck.

# She

My body floats.

On top.

Hina sparkles here.

Not white, but orange.

Also, red.

More orange.

More red.

Too much.

And, noise.

Unease.

I sigh.

Ripples.

Red, orange, red, orange, noise.

I submerge.

Deeper.

Peace.

# Tess

## 2016

### Hana, Maui
### September

Her large opalescent eyes are on me. I see a little *hope* there. Oil drips from my fingers. I quickly slip my net beneath the greasy water and scoop up the female hawksbill.

"Poor darling," I whisper to her.

"Has she ingested the oil?" John asks me.

"I think so . . ." I say, peering inside her mouth. I see black slick oil in her throat.

"Yes," I say.

I carry the hawksbill in my arms, through the net, and I gently place her in the triage room. Lani is waiting to clean her. I go back to my lookout and survey the black oily surface. I feel two things. Anger and resolve. We cannot wipe greed from the planet and this angers me. But we can raise awareness. We can do our part here on this little island in the middle of the great blue ocean.

"Anyone else, John . . . ?" I say.

John points at a large green sea turtle, five feet off our bow. She raises her head above the water's surface to breathe. But as she surfaces in the slick, I see her mouth open in the oil. She gulps and swallows.

I know it's in her digestive tract. I know her entire insides are becoming coated in oil, and mired. I watch her suffering, *trying and failing to swim.*

I wish I didn't know all of this, but we have had many oil spills in Hawaii. Large tankers travelling from the east to the west traverse our area. Pipelines, as well.

Flying across the deck, I throw my arm over the side and into the black sea, I scoop under her body with the net. Once aboard, I run with her to triage. She is moderately heavy, I try not to trip.

"Tess?" Lani asks, looking alarmed.

"I'm okay . . . please hand me the mayonnaise jar would you," I ask.

I open it, and put on surgical gloves. This wonderful non-toxic stuff is a miracle. I rub the turtle's face gently . . . her eyes, ears . . . mouth. I rinse . . . black oil trickles down the drain.

Her deep brown eyes still have a small sparkle. Her face is beautiful, variegated colors.

"Hi there . . ." I whisper to her.

She looks at me. I know she is scared. She is tired, perhaps even dying. Yet, I see a little love in her eyes.

I coat her shell thickly with mayonnaise . . . I rub it in, wide circles. I try to comfort her.

**"He nani lua 'ole**
**Ku'u wehi o nв lani**
**He kilohana 'oe**
**Na'u e pьlama mau**
**Hф'olu i ka poli e**
**Mehana i ke anu e."**

*I can smile when it's raining*
*And touch the warmth of the sun*
*I hear children laughing*
*In this place that I love.*

I always sing lullabies to my patients. It so helps to comfort them. I take a soft rag now, and rub very, very gently until the black oil covers the rag. I take a new rag and continue.

Her eyes haven't left mine.

*"He nani lua 'ole Ku'u wehi o nв lani,"* I sing softly.

The turtle's hawksbill shell comes alive like a piece of art. A shiny interplay of angular mosaics. Orange. Brown. Black.

"Oh Tess . . . my God . . . *she is beautiful,*" Lani says to me. I suck in my breath, sharply. She is.

I keep on task, polishing the hawksbill to a glow. Then I wrap her in a towel. We find the rocking chair that I reserve for such occasions. I sit and rock, with my patient. I see John watching me.

"Her name, my love?" he asks.

"Maya," I answer. I rock and hum and soon her eyes droop.

She is asleep.

When she awakes later, I will feed her. I will feed her mayonnaise, to clean out the oil from her insides.

But first . . . *a little Mama time.*

# John

The color of evil is iridescent black.

It's strange. As I look at this shiny black toxic stuff, I see a quixotic thing, I see rainbows swirling in it. Rainbows—stuck in it. They looked trapped. It's as if they fell and are now trying to escape the deadly stuff. The stuff that has no use but to cause destruction.

You can't get rid of this poisonous stuff. If it burns, it blackens the air. If it spills, it kills the ocean.

Evil liquid. *Oil.* Three of the most hated letters in Hawaii.

And just how did fifty-five hundred barrels of crude oil find its way into the bellies of our sea turtles?

Oh, a nasty thing called an oil pipeline carrying the stuff just underneath the homes of the turtles, ruptured. As they were sleeping—it broke open and flooded their lives.

Last night's memo from our local agency only had me fire up *The Tess* immediately:

> *"What we've learned from past oil spills is that trying to help the process can do more damage than letting nature take its course . . . it might make sense to not overdo the recovery process."*

We readied the boat and the supplies and set a course for the spill, straightaway.

"Ninety-four survivors, John," Lani calls up from triage. "All cleaned," she says.

"Terrific," I call down to the hull.

I turn the boat slowly to the west to search for more survivors. The wind is high, and the raw toxic smell of oil is overwhelming. It is an unnatural smell. Abrasive. It has no place here in the islands. It has no place on earth.

Black stains the edges of the beaches as I look up and down the shoreline. I see that the black oil hasn't traveled more than a foot or two up onto the beach. Yet. But for now, okay . . . Tess's nests should be all right.

I look over my shoulder and see my wife asleep with her new patient. Maya is sleeping soundly. I can see her shell rising and falling in Tess's arms.

My heart turns over. Like it did years ago, when I first saw my beloved on a beach in California. Standing in silhouette against a thousand leatherback mothers. I knew then, as I know now, I have found my soul mate.

My hands run over the edges of the wheel . . . the polished wood, the craftsmanship. My mind drifts backwards.

*Two little boys.*

*Holding hands.*

*Sitting on a pier, looking at a grey, blustery sea.*

*"Pa said we can out tomorrow to look for whales!" one boy says to the other.*

*"Really?" replies the other boy.*

*Their blue eyes lock.*

*The brisk air off the Pacific suddenly tears their blonde waves from their faces. It stings a little. They giggle.*

*But they don't drop hands.*

*The first boy knows not to expect any more conversation. His twin doesn't like to talk.*

*But it's okay. Brothers have other ways of talking.*

I let out a long, deep, sad sigh. Jake has been in the hospital now a few weeks. The psychiatric ward. No one will ever forget the luau.

Marama thinks my twin is possessed by qaitu. Ghosts. Angry ghosts of the dead.

I think it true that Jake is possessed by an anger, an anger that occupies him, perhaps beyond his understanding. But at some basic level, Jake is indeed angry.

I know he was deprived oxygen while in our mother's womb. I know, at some simple level of understanding, that my brother must be *angry at this fate* that has been decreed. He must be angry at what life has done to him. That he has to forever be *the lesser twin.* To crawl, *in my shadow.* A cruel twist of fate has done this to him. It is monstrous to live with, I know.

Somewhere inside his disability—there has to live a basic outrage as to—*why, why me?* And this *why, why me;* never gets answered. So the *why* turns into angst. Then sadness. Then, *anger.*

At its most simple, Jake has to know the exact replica of himself, me, is the perfect boy. *He, is the imperfect boy.* And there's no way to fix it.

Hence, anger. A bewildered, indignation.

Like touching a hot stove by accident at Christmas, burning your hand badly amidst the festivities. Why? Makes no sense. You are supposed to be happy now. Yet, you have serious burns to attend to. You don't want to, you don't have time. You want to be laughing. But you simply cannot. You have a burned hand. *You shouldn't, but you do.* Your anger is incredulous. *How the hell did this happen . . .* you say to yourself.

Jake must look at *his broken self, his burned hand,* and feel incredulous at the situation. *And, I, as the perfect twin need to understand. I need to save Jake,* save him from himself. *Like I save the earth from humans.*

Jake is self-destructing as the earth is self-destructing. Greed is killing the earth, anger is killing Jake.

But I must not lose faith—faith in the ultimate battle to win this war waged on our planet. *I can't lose faith in a brother that has to reckon with what is unreckonable.*

I look at Tess, and Maya. They are sleeping. Look at what love can do.

*Look at what love can do.*

*The Tess* glides gently on the rise and fall of the sea. Marama's words come back to me, from the night of the wretched luau. After Jake was taken away by ambulance.

*"I ka pule nō 'o Lohi'au a make"* . . . she'd said to me. *"It is when you are face to face with death, that you begin to pray."*

Yes, Marama. Prayer.

I pray for my brother, Jake.

# Lani

"Maya, please try . . . please get well," I whisper. "*Sacred honu, you can do it.*"

I am not as smart as the others. I know I don't have their schooling. The book learning. My school has been the island. The sea, the forest. The stars. The moon. *Tutu,* grandmother.

I look at the black toxic oil under my fingernails. I walk to the sink and turn on the hot water. I scrub with the soap.

They are incredible. These haoles. With their selfish, greedy ways. They look like Tess and John but they are as different as can be. They don't understand. They just don't understand.

I wash and wash and the oil refuses to budge. I see my nails remain black.

Yet the warm water is soothing. I let it run over my blackened fingers. I am reminded of the baths my grandmother would prepare for me. It was not as easy as this hot water tap that I have here. Years ago, at home, we would carry heated buckets of water from the fire pit into our hut. But we would sing as we worked, every chore had a song. It made work feel like fun, it made me feel happy. What made me even happier were grand-mother's stories. She taught me so much. I hear her voice and her wisdom, all the time.

*"Seventy years ago, Lani . . . an evil ship came into our waters . . . it came from a faraway shore. From a land of people who were asleep. They could not have been awake. If they had been awake they would know how wrong their actions were,"* she'd say to me.

*"The sleeping people?"* I'd asked.

*"Yes. The sleeping people. They did terrible things because they were asleep. They took from us, they stole land and even enslaved us. They made us stop worshipping our Gods. My mother had us pray for their awakening. Mother knew that forevermore their lives would be cursed for what they did to us, to the Polynesian people. Cursed forever! A terrible thing."*

I remember praying for the sleeping people. I prayed they would wake up. I still pray for them today.

I turn off the tap, and dry my hands.

Our patients . . . they need to be checked. Most are sedated. John injects them immediately with a painkiller and a sedative. Then, Tess washes them as they start to get sleepy from the meds.

I stroke one female's flipper. Suddenly memories shrink me down into a small, five year old Lani, stroking another turtle's flipper.

*"Lani, look . . . she is pregnant,"* Grandmother said, taking my hand and placing it on a stranded dying turtle we'd found. Her underside bulged.

*"Kauila demands we save her unborn children,"* she whispers fiercely.

*"Yes, Grandmother."* I knew of Kauila of course. The great sea turtle goddess who watches over us all.

We removed the mother turtle's eggs, and then carefully made a nest out of sand, leaves. Grandmother lit a fire nearby to warm it.

Later, when the babies finally hatched, we celebrated under Hina, when she was in her full fertile phase. The babies' mother had died, but we were able to save her children.

"*We are commanded to honor Kauila,*" Grandmother said. "*Yes, I promise,*" I replied.

"Your name means, heavens . . . sky, Lani," she instructed, "*look up and say a prayer to Hina, please.*"

I did as I was told. I always do.

*The Tess* surges and falls as I remember the past. I feel safe on the sea. The ocean is very lulling for our patients. It simulates their natural home. I love it too.

I walk to the triage unit and find Ipo. She was an early rescue. Very pregnant, this green sea turtle looks peaceful, wrapped in a pink towel.

Her heartbeat is strong, I hear, as I check her with my stethoscope. Good. I touch her skin; wet, cool, Good.

I feel anger rising as I watch her sleep. Oil is dangerous for sea turtle moms. They ingest the oil and pass oil compounds on to their developing young.

Worse than that—once laid, God forbid on an oil-slicked beach, the eggs absorb all oil components in the sand through the eggshell. Fetuses are destroyed this way.

I pat Ipo softly, on her flipper.

I move onto Kaimona. He has swallowed too much oil. John has him on a feeding tube and a breathing machine. Kaimona's eyes are half open and he looks at me.

"*Mai ka piko o ke po'o a ka poli o ka wāwae, a la'a ma nā kihi* 'ehā o ke kino" . . . I say to him, a traditional Hawaiian prayer, "*From the crown of the head to the soles of the feet, and the four corners of the body.*"

Kaimona's throat is clogged with oil, it sticks to the walls of his throat. To the 'papillae' that are there to help him breathe. We cleaned him the best we could. It is hard to undo the oil's damage, depending on how long the turtle was caught inside it. Kaimona is also showing signs of internal oil distress as well. When the toxic oil gets into his lungs and liver, it is deadly.

"I am sorry, Kauila . . ." I whisper, holding his flipper, "look what they have done to your children."

"Lani, honey . . . could you come up here please . . ."

It's Tess calling me from the deck. Her voice sounds heavy. I race up the stairs, two at a time. Tess and John are staring over the starboard side. They motion to me.

"Leatherback, far from home . . . she must have been driven into this shallow water by the oil . . . then it got to her," John says, flatly. I see an enormous turtle floating miserably, in the slick toxic stuff. The sun beating down on her shell is . . . *cooking her.* I can smell it.

"We've got to do something!" Tess cries. But even she knows that it would be impossible to hoist this two thousand pound creature aboard *The Tess.*

"I've radioed for help," John says.

"When will they arrive . . . ?" I ask, already knowing the answer. In a disaster of this magnitude, extra help is scarce, likely hours away.

"Tess . . . let's try ice . . . the ice from below . . ." John says, racing to the hull.

We chase after him and one by one, we haul bags of ice to the deck. Then, John dives into the water, and motions to Tess and I, to lower a bag down to him.

John swims with the bag to the dying leatherback turtle. He approaches slowly. He looks in her eyes for a minute. He touches her head, softly. Then he gently, gently moves the ice bag toward her.

By the time he has it positioned next to her back, she is working with him. It's incredible, the magic these people have with turtles. *John and Tess.*

The ice bag shifts easily atop the turtle's huge shell, as she dips one side of herself down to receive it. Tess and I dump three more bags into the sea, and John repeats his procedure.

Twenty minutes passes. The turtle's temperature starts to go down. In another twenty minutes, the turtle takes a turn for the better. John piles more ice on her back. Her eyes are brightening. She's moving her flippers.

"PETER?" cries Tess from the deck.

She is yelling at something she sees in the water. I look, there—a head. A diver's head. A camera. There is a diver, about twenty yards from the leatherback, with the biggest camera I have ever seen. He is bobbing in the water.

The diver pushes his mask up.

*"Ga'day Tess!"* What accent is that . . . Australian, I realize.

# Tess

"Peter . . . hello," I say, stunned.

"I'm working!" he says to me, bobbing in the water like a buoy. He lifts his enormous camera above the water. "I'm here on assignment. Filming for *National Geographic,* Tess . . . the spill. The oil spill."

"I see . . ." I manage a small smile, and gesture toward the boat. "We are covering the spill as well," I say.

John surfaces between us, then.

"John . . . this . . . is Peter Sloane . . ." I say as my husband pushes his mask up, off his face, wiping oil away from his cheeks as he does. He looks at me with a bewildered expression. I motion for him to turn around. The two men in the water look at each other. John turns to me then and speaks, "her underbelly is okay Tess, it's cooling down . . . *the ice is helping.*"

Then he looks at the diver in the water. "Hi . . . John McAdams."

"Peter Sloane. *National Geographic.* It's an honor to meet you John. You're doin' fine work here . . . mind if I film it?"

John narrows his eyes. Then he looks at me.

"*I met Peter in Waikiki, John . . . he's a photographer . . .*" I say, to the bobbing head in the water that is my husband. I glance at the other bobbing head, the photographer with whom I shared a drink.

This is the craziest situation I've ever been in.

"Aha." John is treading water. He swims to the boat and hoists himself up. He doesn't respond to Peter.

I hand him a towel. When he is dry, he hands me the towel. He turns to look at the photographer in the water again.

"Our business here means a lot to us Peter. Journalists often don't portray the truth as we would like them too, you ever encounter that?" he says.

"Mate, I'm with you on that one. Right there with you. I am a freelance photographer. Freelance only. I take assignments close to my heart. Your wife—Tess—whom I've been calling the turtle lady—impressed me more than any environmentalist I've ever met. She's the genuine article. I can only imagine you are the same. You're preachin' to the choir, mate . . ."

John smiles. He likes him, I see. I did too. What's not to like? An Aussie grassroots photographer with a pony tail who loves the earth as much as we do.

"Okay . . . Peter. Peter Sloane from Waikiki . . . but you're not really from Waikiki . . . I detect a down under accent, I believe . . ." John puts his hands on his hips and looks at Peter in the water.

"Australia," Peter calls out, grinning.

Then he swims to the leatherback. He puts the enormous camera on his back. He takes the turtle's face in his hands. She softens to him. It is clear that he has spent a long time in the sea. A long time. He doesn't rush. He stays with the turtle.

John watches. "Mmhmm," he says. "I need a sweater Tess," he says to me, going below deck.

I watch Peter with the leatherback. "Peter . . . do you want to come aboard?" Amazingly, both he and the turtle turn to look at me.

"Not just yet Tess, I'm good . . . I think this turtle here would like to visit with you . . . ?" Peter calls up to me.

I look at Lani, she nods. "Peter this is Lani, our right-hand gal," I say. Peter salutes Lani from the water.

I don't hesitate. I zip up my wetsuit and grab a mask. I slip into the water feet first, careful not to splash. Then, I swim gently over to them.

I take the leatherback's flipper. I know what to do.

Peter is watching me. But I go on autopilot and he is no longer there, I am alone with the turtle in my mind.

"Sweet darling . . . here I am . . ." I croon to the sick turtle. Her enormous heavy eyelids rise. She is looking at me. I take her other flipper. She is now looking at me with full concentration. I see nothing but her.

"You will be fine . . . Kauila is with you now . . ." I whisper.

She looks at me for long moments. I see confusion, distress, pain, in her eyes. *She doesn't understand why this is happening to her.*

As the oils dribbles over her head I can see that she feels helpless. And that this is a new feeling for her. She and her kind have survived millions of years because of an acute sense of survival, adaption. But this—oil—is unexpected. Unprecedented. Two hundred million years of changing seas, of reading the signs, of evolving with the earth and now this. *Inescapable toxic poison.*

She looks away from me and lowers her head, down into the water. Then she raises it up again. She does this a few more times and stops to look at me. I realize—she needs to submerge. She has been here, above the water, baking in the sun.

I know this. She knows this. I nod to her, as if to say, it's okay. I will submerge with her. She will not be alone.

I push my mask onto my face. I hold her flippers. I let her guide us. We drop beneath the surface.

She comes to life here immediately. She moves. She lets me hold one of her flippers, and joyfully moves the other three. Then I realize she is submerging slowly, she is doing this for me. She doesn't want to make me submerge too fast to hurt me. In reply, I let go—I look at her—my eyes say *go*, it is okay, I will wait.

But she stays . . . she thrusts her flippers back against my human hands. She stays here, a few feet beneath the surface.

I let go again and back away. She seems to acknowledge this and dives—quickly. Fast downward, away from the oil. I watch her to make sure she isn't nose-diving, as would be the case in most exhausted, oil-ill sea turtles.

Maybe John's ice did revive her? I stay put, for a while. My tank sustains me. She appears then, from below, she is returning to me.

I feel a pull on my arm. It is John . . . and Peter. I am alarmed at seeing both of them—in masks—staring at me like I am crazy.

John motions forcefully—thumbs up—time to ascend. Peter is filming. He is there with his enormous camera. He hasn't stopped filming.

I look at the leatherback mother. I shift my head to the right. I am asking her. She pauses. A creature two hundred million years old doesn't make hasty decisions.

The men—however, are anxious. John taps my tank and then

points upward. He is afraid I will run out of air.

The leatherback seems to sense this, and swims beneath me, in one great push, she and I ascend.

I fly through the air. I break the surface . . . then settle back down. Emergency sheriff boats are finally here, I see. I climb aboard *The Tess*.

The leatherback is fitted with a large sling, then very slowly and very carefully, she is hoisted up, and aboard the sheriff's boat.

I see John hop aboard and administer oxygen to the large turtle. A SWAT team of marine biologists finish what I started, and set to cleaning her shell fully, with mayonnaise.

I grip the railing, then let go. I breathe deeply, yes . . . she will be okay. She will survive. I can see her looking at me from the other boat. Her eyes look bright and her chest is moving, she is breathing normally.

Another person is next to me, I realize. I look up. All I see is a large glass lens. A camera.

Peter is behind it. Still filming.

# Jake

White.

White walls.

White floor.

White sheets.

White gown.

White doctors.

White nurses.

I smile.

I like white.
It feels clean.

# Peter

## 2016

### New York, New York
### · October

"Pete."

Chris is in khaki pants and a white shirt. I glance at his feet. Shiny loafers. They look Italian. How he has changed. But it's okay. I like to visit him here in Manhattan. Well, for a few days, anyway.

"She's beautiful Peter."

"Yes, a magnificent leatherback, largest I've ever seen in fact . . ." I say.

"I wasn't talking about the turtle, buddy," Pete says, looking up at me over his Italian-looking glasses.

"Ah," I say, smiling.

His voice is matter-of-fact.

"Her too, of course," Chris remarks, his trained eye narrowing at the splayed photographs across the large conference room table.

"Mmhmm," he mutters, going from one photo to another.

I look over his tall, lanky build, outside to the looming skyscrapers. I remember him in art school. Long hair and black tee shirts.

"This is good. Incredible. Astonishing."

Chris is looking at the zoom shot of Tess and the leatherback descending, *hand-in-flipper*.

"Yeah," I say.

"She's a biologist? Stanford? What's she doin' in Hana, Hawaii?" he asks, putting a magnifying loop to his eye.

"She moved there with her husband," I say. "Another biologist . . . I think he's also a surgeon, veterinarian."

"I see. Love brought her to Hawaii, then?"

"Turtles brought her to Hawaii," I say, a little too quickly. Chris looks at me, smiles, then back at Tess.

"They run a turtle hospital. And a rescue, release program."

"Yeah, but a million people do that. Sorry, Pete. But it's not new. This, however, *is new . . .*"

He hands me a photo of Tess underwater, holding the ailing leatherback's flippers, human and turtle gazing at each other.

"Yeah I know Chris. I know. It's what I've been trying to tell you."

Chris drops the lens. He turns to me.

"This is a cover story, Pete. It's extraordinary. Turtle hospitals and rescues are not uncommon, and other than the philanthropy aspect—they aren't really that extraordinary. *This woman, however, is.*"

"That's why I called you mate," I say. I put my hands on my hips. "It's . . . pretty much, the most extraordinary thing I've ever photographed, the two species together. It adds another dimension, Chris. It electrifies what would, already be a terrific photo alone. Adding this—mermaid—to the photo takes the sea creature and elevates it to a universal level."

"I totally, one hundred percent, agree, Peter."

Aha, my full name. Chris loves the work.

"That's the angle then, for the magazine, heck, we can spin this into a television show as well. I'll call a board meeting."

Chris takes his Italian glasses off and rubs his eyes. "Tell me about them . . . both biologists . . . married . . . what's the husband like?" He puts his glasses back on. In that one fluid motion he goes from hippie artist I knew for years to stylin' city dude. I laugh aloud.

"Yes?" he says.

"Well, what I know is . . . they're both Stanford grads . . . marine biologists. They are rescuin' turtles in a different way. They—Tess—always communicates with the turtles, Chris. As if they are her children. I've been in the field a long, long time. *I've never seen this.* I mean—I, can get close to the turtles. I have had this happen to me. I am in the water, oh, three hundred days a year. Crikey, maybe three hundred twenty-five. So I have a comfort zone with the turtles. *But . . . Tess is different.* I don't know what it is but these . . . my . . . pictures capture it. You see it too."

"The evidence," I say, pointing to the photographs all over the table. I fold my hands into my lap.

"Agreed," he says, looking at me directly in my eyes. "This woman and turtles, extraordinary. Cover story."

I recognize his look. I've seen it a few times before. It's Chris being absolutely sure about a major decision.

"Can you get me more?"

I smile.

Oh yeah. Yeah. I can do that.

# Tess

## 2016
❦

### Hana, Maui
### October
❦

"John . . ." I whisper.

My husband opens one eye. It fixes upon my face. I've just been to the hospital, and I'm very excited. I lower my voice even more.

"I know it's early babe, but . . . I think I'd like to sleep at the beach tonight . . . Sasha's sensors have picked up some motion in the beach nests . . ." I say, softly.

"Mmhmm," John says, and closes his eye.

I stand and tiptoe out.

My hands are shaking, I have *new mom jitters.* I jump onto my bicycle and peddle back to my babies. Well, the monitor of their nests.

The sun is just coming up . . . the sky yawns in deep pink and purple. I smile and glance upwards at Hina, who is readying her retreat.

"Tonight, Hina . . ." I whisper aloud, "They will need you tonight, my babies will want to follow your light home . . ." I say.

I see Honu Hospital up ahead and I make a sharp detour to the back, to my hatchery. I hope off my bike and race for the door. Lullaby music trickles through.

I step inside and check the *hatchery babies*. I peer inside their incubator nests . . . did one shake? A teeny, tiny bit? My eyes are glued to the sand surface . . . and the sleeping shells beneath. Then, I turn to check on my *beach babies*.

I walk into the adjoining room. Sasha's computer screen monitor has two feeds, drones and sensors. I click onto the sensors page. Ah! Five of the six are registering activity. Pre-hatch activity!

# Peter

"Hello?" the voice says.

"Tess, it's Peter. Peter Sloane here . . . how are ya lass?" My hearts skips a beat—she picked up my call.

"Peter . . . how are you?"

"Oh, I'm dandy Tess, just dandy . . . I was in New York a bit, but thankfully I'm back out 'ere in Hawaii. Where I belong. Camera in hand."

"Wonderful, I understand. I prefer the sea to cement, myself," she says, laughing.

"Righto, me too, me too. How've ya been Tess?"

There is a pause, now, it worries me.

"Fine . . . fine Peter . . . sorry, I'm just now at the hospital . . . we're expecting a frenzy out at the beach nests . . . so I'm tidying up here so I can leave for the beach soon."

"*Really!*" I try to reign in my excitement. Crikey, these are the photographs I need to complete the story . . . *a hatch . . . a freakin' release?* With Mama Turtle in my lens? It's almost too good to be true.

"Just a sec, Peter," she tells me and I hear the phone receiver click on a counter.

Lullaby music creeps into my ear. God Almighty. The woman

plays lullaby music for the unborn hatchlings. I eye my camera in the corner of the hotel room. Which lens will I need to shoot all this, I ponder . . .

"Peter, I'm back . . . I need to fly now, check the nests . . ."

"Absolutely, *Mama Turtle*," I say . . . trying out my new name for her, imagining the headline in the magazine; *Mama Turtle on Maui.*

"Tess, are you, ah, are you, ah . . . free? Maybe later . . . I mean, you and John?" I stammer.

A pause.

"Of course, Peter."

Yes! A smile explodes on my face.

"It's not just fer pleasure Tess. I've got an idea . . . just now actually. Originally, I was wanting to do some hatchling shots here on Maui. Hatchings, and that *amazing dash to the sea.* You know the one, I'm sure Tess," I pause and try to catch my breath. My new idea is simmering and getting ready to boil over. I take a deep breath to calm myself.

"But maybe . . . maybe there is something better? Maybe we can do some *images of your work?* You by the nests, tendin' em. Watchin' over 'em as they dash . . . *home?"*

She is silent on the phone. I wait. Maybe I have said too much? We Aussies have a tendency to be pushy I know. But this . . . this is a story like no other. It's perfect. "I know you are busy and all . . ." I start to say. She cuts me off.

"I'd love to, Peter. It's a fine idea. You want to publish these photos, yes? In a magazine? Was it *National Geographic* . . . you mentioned to me in Honolulu?"

"Ah . . . yeah . . . yeah . . . that's right Tess . . . indeed it was . . ." My hands are shaking.

Then, a few moments of silence go by and I think, perhaps I need to call her back, give her time to think about it further. But then she starts speaking . . . *so quickly* I have to sit down. I hold my cellular with both hands.

"*Passionate publicity—that is what we need.* What the turtles need. They need people to see, understand, and care. *And love them.* They need *awareness* for their cause. They need *love* for our work. The turtles need people to desire to help, to care. About *them,* the turtles."

I'm too astonished to respond. I hold onto my cellular, eyes popping out of my head.

"You know what—*remarkable timing*, Peter. *Let's do it.* I'm sure John will agree. We can shoot a whole story for you. My hatchlings' journey. *Their amazingly brave, courageous journey.* How hard they *struggle* for this thing called life. We can show them as *little miracles.* And we can describe the evil of *poaching*—the snuffing out the lives of these brave little *one-inch miracle babies.* These little creatures whose struggle is beyond the bravery of many people I know. Yes . . . I see it in my head, now. My hatchling's magical journey . . . *sand to sea.* The sixty-day incubation. The actual hatch. The dig upward through the sand from the subterranean nest . . . that first gulp of fresh air under the moon . . . and the brave, courageous crawl home to the sea. *How's that sound?*"

As I haven't breathed in five minutes I find I cannot speak.

"Peter, are you there?"

I cough, sputter. This woman just laid out the entire cover story spread for me.

"Tess . . . ah . . . yes . . . ah . . . yes . . ."

"Good!" she says.

"Thank . . . you . . ." comes tumbling out of my mouth.

"Come around four this afternoon, Peter . . . or whenever you are free," she says.

"Tonight?"

"Yes. Hana beach."

# Tess

❦

"He's Australian?" Sasha asks me.

"Yep," I answer, folding up a large green tent.

"Hmmm. A photographer?"

"A terrific one," I say. "He's a bit of a rogue . . . he's an adventurer," I laugh. "He showed up at the spill, popped his head right out of the oily water."

"Lani mentioned that much," Sasha said. "She said he was covered in oil, camera covered in oil, and he just started snapping off photos."

"He was on assignment, he was covering the spill for *National Geographic*."

"I see . . . a journalist?," she asked.

"He's a freelancer . . . he shoots what he wants to, what touches him."

"I see," she says. "As long as he's cool . . . *you know*."

"He cares about his work. He's an artist. He loves his work . . . he's very cool," I smile.

"Let me take the tent to the truck for you. Blankets too? Sleeping bags?"

"Sure Sasha . . . thanks," I tell her, I pat her back as I leave.

Peter is a dedicated artist. He loves, what he does, he loves his subjects. He cares. I was drawn to him. He is also a professional, I think to myself. This story could put the turtles on the map. It'll let everyone know about their hospital, their mission. It's an amazing stroke of luck.

Marama would say this is good, here we have a weapon against evil . . . awareness . . . opening people's eyes to evil so it can be conquered. United people, against evil.

*Peter is a godsend,* I think to myself.

Kauila wants this, I am sure.

# Peter

"*Chris, it's a go,*" I say into my cellular, "more photographs, a night shoot. Hatchlings under a full moon. Race to the sea."

"My God, Pete. Awesome. This is gonna be big. Huge. I ran it by several sea turtle foundations. Even, my contact at the EPA. I mean, they saw Tess's pictures. She's a mermaid, Pete. A real living mermaid."

"Yep . . . yep I'm excited," I say.

"Pete . . ." Chris is laughing, "my contact at Vogue asked for Tess's contact . . . it's that face of hers . . . eyes like . . . Twiggy, buddy . . ."

"Christopher, stop," I say sharply. "She's not into that scene at all."

"Okay, okay . . . back to this story, I've got a writer here who will do a searing editorial for us. Passionate activist. Also a scientist from Columbia who's been following all five species for decades. I'll tell ya Pete—these are some amazing creatures. *Two hundred million years old,* my research tells me. Here, when the dinosaurs were here. And you tell me this gal, Tess—*communicates with them?* So . . . we could do . . . like a Dr. Doolittle spin to the piece?"

I know this is the biggest thing in Christopher's career thus far, maybe mine too . . . it's hard to remain calm. But I think of Tess, her *fragility*. I remember her crying into her yellow dress. She's fragile.

"Chris, mate . . . it all sounds good, but the lass . . . she's fragile mate, sensitive . . . *I think that's how she can talk to the turtles,* to be honest, Chris. She has something about her. Sixth sense maybe? She seems to pick up on vibes in a way I've never seen. I met her in tears y'know . . . at a café in Waikiki."

"No! My God man, that's the *opener* to the story! Crying about the turtles!"

"No, Chris! That's for your ears only. What I'm trying to tell you is that this lass is soft, open . . . big heart. Maybe too big, I don't know. We gotta be gentle."

"Alright, alright . . . but you shoot me your best shots Pete, okay? You owe me buddy . . . I want to see this *big heart* of hers, through your lens. Show me her face, the turtles' faces . . . show me the magic. The *magic,* mate."

He calls me *mate* in my Australian slang. Wow. He really wants this, bad.

"You like what you saw in the oil spill images?" I ask.

*"Loved what I saw.* That's how I got the cover, Pete."

"Okay then. More of the same. Much more."

*"Hot damn!* Peter, this is gonna put us on the map," he tells me.

"Yep," I reply.

"Go to it," he says, hanging up.

I get up and walk to the white desk in the corner of my hotel room. Tess looks up at me from a dozen photos.

In one she is looking at the sick turtle, covered in oil. It's a side view shot. The turtle's face is front view. I sit and look at this one, this image.

The turtle's eyes are large, shaped like almonds tilted to the side with heavy double lids. Her nose is beaked, two small holes are her nostrils. The oil shines on her face. *It's the ancient face of a dinosaur.*

I flip to the next image. The leatherback's eyes are softer, looking at Tess.

I flip to the next photo, and the next. Then I flip backwards. Then, forwards.

*I see it.* I see it now. It is hard to see immediately, because the leatherback's face is so heavily formed, an ancient face from epochs ago. But as I flip through a dozen shots, back and forth, I see it.

*A smile.*

The turtle's beaked mouth deepens in the corners as Tess attends to her. With every touch of Tess's hand, stroking the face, gently wiping mayonnaise over its head to remove the oil . . . the corners of the turtle's mouth curve a little more upward.

The leatherback is *smiling* at Tess. Tess, her rescuer.

"Cold-blooded reptile? My foot!" I cry aloud to the empty room.

I sit down and take out my pen. I need to make notes.

# Tess

My face is an inch from the sand.

I look at the tiny, yellow grains. I place the flat of my hand on the sand surface. I close my eyes. *Are you ready, my loves . . . ?* I ask in my mind.

What was *that?* A twitch? I open my eyes. I see a crab crawl over my hand.

"Aha!" I say to the crab.

"Anything yet?" John asks me from the tent.

"No . . . not yet," I say to him. I sit up and look out to the sea.

"Soon, though, dearest . . ." I say to him. Yes, soon.

*Soon my babies will hatch.* They will flex their legs inside their shells. The shell will stretch . . . rubbery shells that don't crack easily. Then my babies will flex even more. And then . . . the *first cracking sounds.* The other babies will hear this! It is an exciting thing to hear this for the very first time. They will then, start to *frenzy* . . . all babies pushing outward, inside their eggs. *Crack, crack, crack.* Shells, breaking open . . . into the cool, dry sand. Then it's time to really start to *work.* My babies are strong. They use their little legs, and beaks to dig, dig, dig. Upward. Together they are strong, *creating tunnels* upward, for others to follow behind.

I squeal, I laugh, I clasp my hands together as these *new mother thoughts* fill my mind.

"Tess?" John calls from the tent.

I don't answer him. My mind is still with my children. I see them frenzying like good, little *healthy* children. *They help each other,* as they know I would wish them to.

I see all the eggs cracking open inside subterranean nests, babies digging out, and then up. And then, at last, the first of them pops her little hatchling head above the surface of the sand.

*Tears spring to my eyes,* as I think of the little darling, opening her eyes to see the world for the *very first time.* She will be surprised. She will be scared. But, she is a courageous adventurer. She will breathe, real air. *Her first breath,* fresh salty air from the sea.

And, of course, Hina will be there to greet her, to let her know all is well. My hatchling will open her eyes and see Hina's moonlight. She will feel *safe, calm, loved.* She will push up with her tiny limbs, and pop herself fully, onto the soft white sand.

Hina will bathe her in moonlight. Hina will fill her eyes with moonlight. And then, the *real magic begins.*

My babies know what to do. They are smart, born with this wisdom. *They know to follow Hina.* And as they all emerge from their subterranean nests, they instantly look for Hina above, to guide them. *Home.*

They follow Hina's pointing fingers, to the sea, where they *sparkle and sparkle and sparkle.* My babies love sparkle, they are riveted. *They are mesmerized by Hina's pretty, sparkly fingers!* Off they go. They race towards the glittery sparkly diamond-fingers of light upon the watery waves of the sea.

The beacons of flickering light speak to my babies. They whisper, *come . . . come here.* And they follow, all of them. My darling babies are *wise,* they know to *follow the moon home.*

I look up to see John staring down at me. He says nothing.

He bends down and takes me in his arms for a long squeeze. Then he goes back to the tent.

I place my hand back upon the sand surface.

I wait.

# John

"Hello there, Peter."

"Hello mate! Awful nice of you to let me barge in. Good onya, I do appreciate it, mate."

That's *two mates in one sentence.* Awful enthusiastic of him, I think to myself.

"Anything for our turtles," I say to him.

*"Righto. Righto. Righto."*

Okay, three righto's, now.

I watch him set up a tent next to ours. He's got two large, square trunks . . . must be his camera equipment.

"John—help Peter, dear," Tess calls to me, coming out of the sea.

We both look at her. She's a mermaid. And—she's my mermaid. I look at Peter, he is looking at my wife.

"Let me help you Pete," I say grabbing one of his cases roughly.

"Woah—*mate*—gentle, gentle," he says, taking an end of the case in his hands.

Three mates, now.

"How long have you been taking pictures?" I ask him. Tess walks into our tent.

"Oh . . . well . . . forever, forever and a day. Since I was a kid, really. Queensland."

"Queensland . . . where in Queensland?" I ask.

"Cairns," he answers, looking me in the eye.

"Ah . . . Cairns . . . *Great Barrier Reef*," I breathe. Now he has my full attention.

"Yep . . . 'tis a marvel, mate," he says.

I don't mind this *fourth mate* . . . not at all.

"My God . . . you grew up diving the Reef?" I ask, my head spinning at the prospect of this, the world's largest coral reef. Peter sits down and faces me.

"It's amazing John. Amazing. For a man like me . . . I mean, just mind-boggling. I never, ever tire of shooting it. Ever. Endless possibility down there . . . *endless*," he says looking me in the eye. "You've been, yourself?"

"Oh . . . I've wanted to . . . many times Peter . . . I have been . . . busy . . . here . . . with Tess and Honu Hospital . . . tell me more . . . *mate*." I smile widely and he laughs a deep-bellied Australian laugh.

His accent is addicting. A congenial touch added to this place I have dreamed of all my life, the Great Barrier Reef of Australia.

"Beer, boys?" Tess is here handing us each a beer. We don't look up, we just take the bottles. "Thanks Tess," I say my eyes on Peter.

"Well, of course you know that the reef itself contains an abundance of marine life *not seen anywhere else in the world*," Peter says, taking a long swallow of his beer.

"Y'have to be a good swimmer, ya do. It comprises over three thousand individual reef systems and coral cays . . ."

"Yesss . . ." I say, downing the beer, trying to imagine *three thousand reefs*.

"And that's just the magic, below. Above? Literally hundreds of unspoiled, untouched islands with perfect beaches, no human has stood upon."

*"Jesus . . ."* I sigh. *"One of the seven wonders of the world."*

"Yep. You can see it from space," Peter says.

"Tess . . . darling . . . another round, love?" I call.

"Diving at *night* . . . that's my pick . . ." Peter mused.

"Night dives . . ." I muse, "it must just . . . burgeon . . . at night. Come alive."

"Bloody spectacular, mate. Pure adrenaline. Pure thrill."

I stare at him, jealous now, for the *second time.*

"I mean, John, you just don't know what's gonna happen at night. A *shark* could swim within a couple of meters of you, and you might not know it. Floating in a dark ocean, shifting and swaying with the current. I had a flashlight all right, but that was it, mate, a spot of light in the blackness. Ah . . . but the images . . . my God in heaven, the images to be gotten . . ."

We downed another beer. I don't think I've blinked in ten minutes.

"The coral looks different under the shine of a light, John. And the sleeping fish! Amazing. Floating, still. I saw, and shot—the biggest parrotfish I've ever seen . . . melted rainbow colors glistening under my lens. About twenty meters down, under a huge piece of coral."

"I'm there. I have to see it," I say to my new mate, Peter Sloane. "I'll make time."

"The huge drop-off on the outer reef edge is where I like best . . . it's an endless wall of coral extending downward into dense blue openness. On the other side sleeps an impenetrable wall of blue ocean."

"When you next go, you take me with you," I say, imagining the endless blue.

*"Full body stinger suit, mate* . . . the jellies there can kill you," he warns.

*"Right!"* I say, loudly. "Poison tentacles that can stop the heart with a touch, I studied them."

"So, you have to know my next question . . ." I say smiling slyly at him.

*"Turtles?"* he asks.

"Turtles," I say.

"Well, that's my specialty, mate. One of the best encounters . . . a spread I did for *National Geographic* in fact—was with a large hawksbill . . . she suddenly dove deep, she was hungry, wanted food. So I followed her. She had a magnificent sharp beak, I got amazing close ups . . . terrific zoom lens . . . she found and feasted on crabs and shrimp for a half hour, knew I was there—didn't care, amazing . . . she let me film her entire meal . . . *crikey,* made me hungry just to watch her!" Peter let out an enormous Aussie laugh then.

"Soon after her, I spied a large green, she was nosing around in the sponges, her jagged edged beak nibbling on plants and algae . . . she cruised too, had me chasin' her . . . I dove a bit beyond what would be considered safety zone, but I was in *my zone,* y'know mate? I couldn't let the shot go . . . gotta be careful of that . . ."

He stops, then, looking up at the stars and the darkness around us. "When did it get dark?" he says.

"Heck, you're right, sun's gone down," I say, looking up at the sky, stars sparkling brightly above us.

"I'll be darned! John, I got to talkin' too much. Apologies."

"No! Man, it was great . . . I dive here of course but I dream of the Reef. It's next on the list. Lotta dangers facing it . . . aren't there? Same, as we have here. Globally warmed waters, oil spills, pollution, fishing . . ."

"And *poaching*," Peter finishes my sentence.

"Boys . . . I'm turning in, now . . ." Tess calls from the tent.

"Darlin' I'm sorry," I say, standing up.

I stick my hand out to shake Peter's.

"Damn glad to meet ya Peter."

"Same here mate, same here."

# Tess

John comes inside the tent with a wide smile on his face. A satisfied smile.

"What a great guy, Tess . . ."

"Mmhmm," I reply, looking at him closely.

"I mean . . . he's like me . . . he's an adventurer. He grew up diving the Great Barrier Reef . . ."

"Mmhmm . . ." I say.

"We need to go, Tess, my love . . . we need to go . . . will you? I want to see the Reef . . ."

"Of course, John, sure."

I know my husband's taste for adrenaline. But honestly, the thought of the greatest coral reef in the world? Home, to my turtles? *Oh yes.*

"We can set up another hospital, Tess. Maybe Sasha can run it? We can do great good my darling . . . Honu Hospital II."

He looks at me with the look that melts me. I go to him.

# Peter

Well I'll be god darned. He's a *mate!* I'll be god darned. As terrific as she was, he is just as terrific.

I turn my lens over in my hands.

He really thought my work was terrific. I mean, he really, was diggin' my life, my work, I think to myself. I let this feeling sink in. It's mighty fine it is.

I take a tripod out of my bag and walk to the first marked nesting site. I see Tess has orange meshing on poles around the site. I place my tripod inside the mesh wall. Then I take my Canon, the newer one, on the side of it painted, *Canon EOS-1Ds Mark III SLR,* and I gently place it on the tripod.

An hour later, my equipment is ready. I almost want to wake my sleeping new mate to show him. It's then I realize something.

I'm channeling Charles.

I look up at the sky, noting the bright full moon. The stars around it, sparkling. One part of my mind is excited about the perfect lighting for the shoot, the moon so illustriously full will record the hatch perfectly.

Another part of my mind is still on Charles. I see his face in my mind, he is ten, I am five. He is showing me how to use his camera. I don't have much interest.

"Pete, listen, you can play ball later, mate. Look here, this is a lens, can you say that? L-E-N-S. It's where the picture get captured, in here . . . see?"

"Charlie, gimmee my ball back. I don't want to look at the lins."

"*LENS*, Peter, *Lens*. With an *e*, mate."

"LENS. I see. Okay. The glass part. Where the picture gets stuck. Now can I have my ball, Charlie . . . ?"

"You can have yer bloody ball in a second Pete. Take this camera, now, hold it—don't drop it. Okay. Find something to snap. It's fun. You want to snap . . . that kangaroo? See her over by the trees?" Charles shifts my body to face a faraway cluster of trees and shrubs and a mother kanga there.

"Wow! Charles . . . she's . . . she's . . . up close in the lens!" I cry, as my older brother twists the metal piece around the lens piece for me.

I pull my head back—yep—the kanga is still very far this way, then I put my eye in front of this . . . this magic lens . . . and she is right in front of me.

"WOW!!!!" I yell, too loudly. And the kangaroo promptly hops away in fright.

"Peter, you never ever yell when shooting, okay buddy?" Charles says to me, using Mama's voice.

For the next two hours we walk through the dusty outback looking for kangaroos. When I finally find one, I am ready. I have searched, I have waited.

Charles helps me twist the kangaroo into my view, he puts his hand on top of mine and shows me how to do it.

I twist forward, backward, until I have her. I can see her face. Her ears. Her mouth. *When I have her eyes, I pause.* Charles places his pointer finger on top of mine, and whispers . . . "Petey, good boy . . . now press down and take the photo . . .

*when you can see her eyes . . ."*

I look . . . I watch. Then a crazy thing happens.

The kangaroo sees ME.

Me.

She is looking right at me. Her black eyes are the shape of almonds. They are soft and kind. I am so stunned I forget to snap the photo. But—then I do.

CLICK. *My first photo.*

My heart is pounding, I can't stop smiling.

"Charles! I did it! I did it Charles!"

"You did it my Petey boy!" My brother's face said it all, he was so *proud* of me.

"You always want the one, the photograph that is, *the one . . .* you will know it when you see it Peter . . . I cannot describe it beyond that. You will know you have magic when you see magic."

Magic. I've been chasing after it all my life. Since that day, really.

Since, Charle's death a few years ago. In my heart I knew he was chasing, *the one,* the perfect shot. He must have had it in his sights, in his lens. Maybe it was a stingray, maybe a shark. Maybe a turtle. He stayed with his shot, he waited. Waited for the eyes.

He waited too long.

His camera, his film survived the dive, even if he did not. He would have liked that. It made the cover of *Life Magazine.* It was their cover story. It won awards. It made me proud.

"Miss you Charlie," I whisper to the moon. I let a tear sneak down my cheek, before wiping it away.

I lay back on the sand. I try to sleep a little.

# Tess

John is asleep. He is sleeping with a smile on his face. How . . . curious. I watch him. He is hugging his pillow too. I am glad he likes Peter so much.

We both adore Peter. It makes sense of course . . . that John would adore an activist . . . a crusader for our cause . . . an adventurer, an artist.

But there is something more. Then, I realize what it is. A brother. John has a *brother* he can talk to, share with.

My husband was robbed of a brother. Jake is a kind of . . . half brother, though not in the vernacular sense of course as they share the same parents. *No, Jake is half of what he should have been,* he should have been a whole counterpart of John. Two wholes, connected. Instead, *he is a half, John a whole.* The missing half of Jake was lost at birth.

It has not been easy for John.

I suddenly feel a great depth of sadness for my husband. And for his tragic twin. Though I don't like Jake, I don't like the half missing from Jake . . . *the half of his heart that is supposed to love, care and feel compassion* . . . I do understand the tragedy. For both of them.

And Peter . . . reminded John of that today. Now I understand.

I stand up and walk outside the tent . . . into a blaze of blue light.

"Hina . . ." I whisper, stepping into her light. I know she is listening.

I look down then—at the moon sparkle on the sand, illuminating it into a bed of *shining glass beads.* I dig my toes into it . . . I watch the sparkle beads sift over my feet like loose *gemstones.* Smiling, my eyes trace the sparkle to the waves where they explode in *shimmer.* Diamonds dot the foamy peaks. It is impossible for me not to follow this glittery path. Mesmerized, I saunter along it, to the water. Everything is awash in moonglow. The night is warm and sweet.

"Hina . . . you are so easy to follow. Thank you. My babies are almost ready for you . . ."

"Tess?"

I spin around, to see Peter standing behind me.

His face is blue, in Hina's glow. He has a camera in his left hand.

"Sorry to disturb lassie . . ." he says, grinning. He looks like a boy all of a sudden. A boy about to ask for a treat before dinner.

"Can I photograph you Tess? As part of the storyline . . . where it all begins . . . here, under the moon . . . ?

*The story. My story. My babies. I like it. I like it a lot.*

"Sure, Peter . . . tell me what to do," I say to him. We are both blue-skinned in the surreal moonlight.

"Pretend I'm not here . . . as you were . . . kneeling in the surf . . . the lighting is breathtaking . . . *just do your thing . . .*" he says, putting the lens to his eye.

I can do that. I can do that easily, I think to myself. I turn and face the sea. I put my hands on my hips. Then I let them loose at my sides.

Oh, let's have some *fun* with this Tess, I say to myself.

I lift my arms to Hina. I hold them like this for a few moments. Then I let them drop in ballerina grace. I walk to the waves and step in. I lean forward and stir the waves with my hands . . . letting the seawater drip through my fingers.

I splash my face gently with water . . . and smooth it over my hair. It is warm. It is so inviting that I let myself slip into it like one would a blanket. I swim slow laps back and forth under Hina's luminous light. It is brighter than I can ever recall.

I dive down beneath the wet shimmer, and resurface in more *silvery, slippery glow.* I imagine my babies arriving here soon . . . their first taste of the sea, this lovely warm silvery stuff, so easy to find, *so swimmably soft.*

I propel through the water, my feet becoming flippers, my body weight centering, the shell that is my back holds me static above the reef drop-off. I decide to go over it, for a look, my babies will soon be here and it's important I find food for them . . . there should be *algae* down there. I move slowly, and then dive down hard. The strong moonlight penetrates many feet, *extraordinary,* I can see everything clearly. Lobsters, crabs, coral, and yes, mountains and mountains of algae. Good. I dive a little deeper, *good*—even more algae.

I resurface with the stuff between my teeth, and crawl to the sand. It is quite good, very fresh, and the smaller variety, good for little mouths that will be quite hungry.

*Click-click-click-click.*

I turn to the strange sound and I see Peter snapping his camera at me. I decide to ignore him. It isn't hard, I have so much to do. I walk to the nesting sites and place my hands on top of the sand.

Nothing yet.

I don't need to check the sensors activity on the laptop computer in my tent, this way is easier for me. I lay down in the middle of the sites and look up at Hina. I decide it's time to sing. I choose the lullaby I play in my hospital hatchery . . . the one Marama suggested.

*He nani lua 'ole*
*Ku'u wehi o nɐ lani*
*He kilohana 'oe*
*Na'u e pʉlama mau*
*Hɸ'olu i ka poli e*
*Mehana i ke anu e.*

*I can smile when it's raining*
*And touch the warmth of the sun*
*I hear children laughing*
*In this place that I love.*

*Mau loa ke aloha*
*i kɸ pu'uwai hɐmama*
*He u'i lani 'oe*
*Na'u e mɐlama mau*
*Aia i ka la'i e*
*Hemolele i ka mɐlie.*

*I can smile when it's raining*
*And touch the warmth of the sun*
*I hear children laughing*
*In this place that I love.*

I pause. I sit up. I place a hand atop the closest nest. I feel it!
A stirring. Faint, but there. I stay seated and start singing again
. . . a little louder.

*He nani lua 'ole*
*Ku'u wehi o nɐ lani*
*He kilohana 'oe*
*Na'u e pɯlama mau*
*Hɸ'olu i ka poli e*
*Mehana i ke anu e.*

*I can smile when it's raining*
*And touch the warmth of the sun*
*I hear children laughing*
*In this place that I love.*

*Mau loa ke aloha*
*i kɸ pu'uwai hɐmama*
*He u'i lani 'oe*
*Na'u e mɐlama mau*
*Aia i ka la'i e*
*Hemolele i ka mɐlie.*

*I can smile when it's raining*
*And touch the warmth of the sun*
*I hear children laughing*
*In this place that I love.*

Moving grains of sand start to tumble inside the first site.
Then the second . . . then the third. Soon the six sites are tumbly

sparkling mounds of activity.

*It is clear—the frenzy has begun!*

I glance around me, gauging the quickest path to the sea but Hina has already mapped it. She extends *a long shining finger* from the nests, around the higher dunes to the lower ones and on out to the sea.

It is only then that I notice the tripods have come to life, their lights on and their lens swiveling. As the sand moves faster and faster, the lens' drop down low.

I try to ignore this and keep my mind on my work.

I start to sing again . . . as I know their subterranean digging has likely brought them up near the surface now, three feet of sand beneath them, little scared babies . . . waiting for me.

> *He nani lua 'ole*
> *Ku'u wehi o nɐ lani*
> *He kilohana 'oe*
> *Na'u e pɯlama mau*
> *Hɸ'olu i ka poli e*
> *Mehana i ke anu e.*

> *I can smile when it's raining*
> *And touch the warmth of the sun*
> *I hear children laughing*
> *In this place that I love.*

Hina hears me and does a magnificent thing then . . . she throws down *six separate hands,* with *outstretched palms* above all six nests.

*"He nani lua 'ole . . ."* I start to sing, when a teeny tiny little head pops up, out of nest two.

I know better than to move. I continue singing, very softly.

*"Ku'u wehi o na lani . . ."* The tiny head turns to me. Another head pops up. Then another, and another. Tiny sets of glittery eyes fix on my face.

*"He kilohana 'oe . . ."* Nest four erupts with a dozen baby heads. They all look at me.

*"Na'u e pьilama mau . . ."* Nest five and nest six now have heads popping up. More stares.

*"Hφ'olu i ka poli e . . ."* All my nests now have dozens of babies teeming in Hina's cupped hands. I sing and I watch them stretch their tiny one-inch bodies. They are flexing their unused flippers. Some attempt to take a step. Some fall over.

I continue singing for a few more minutes.

Then Hina shrinks *upward*—the babies take notice. She pauses in the night sky, as if drawing a breath.

Then she blasts an enormous shining beam of light across the sand to the sea. *It is a very clear path to follow.*

"Follow the moon my babies . . . look, you see Hina? *She is your moon to follow!*" I use my softest voice and start to crawl in the moonlight to demonstrate to the hatchlings.

Instinct takes over and they catapult themselves crazily, I hear them giggling as they trip and spill and tumble over one another and the little sand hills.

"Hahaha," I laugh aloud with them. Oh, my babies like to play!

They right themselves onto Hina's path and within seconds, I watch with pride as my children become runners. Real runners. Grace and stealth take over. I am flabbergasted. They race pell-mell faster, faster.

I know what I need to do now, I stand and give a last look at the nests, now emptying.

Then, I run to the waves.

My heart heaves as I know this briefest of visits is all I will have. I fall to the wet mud, and feel the surf under my knees.

I look. *The first are arriving.*

I lay down on the mud, my cheek suctions to the sticky stuff. At this low vantage point, I can see their tiny bodies better.

The first one arrives. Her flippers are so tiny, they hardly make a sound on the mud. She is a glowing little hatchling, her eyes sparkling happily in the moonshine.

She flippers up to my face, and then past and into the waves.

*A two hundred million year old instinct drives her onward.* I am honored to witness this . . . though, as always, my heart hurts a little as I see her unbroken stride.

Plop, plop, plop. One by one, into the sea. Tears of joy stream down my cheeks.

"Goodbye my lovelies . . . *I will miss you,*" I whisper.

The last hatchling crawls next to my nose and flings herself upon some foam. She moves out with the tide and disappears.

*"Kauila . . . they are yours now,"* I say.

And then, for an unknown reason, I feel my chest cramp. I know it is wrong. But I can't help it. Sobs bubble up.

I cry for my babies.

I cry for my mother.

It passes. Afterward, I lay on the sand in Hina's glow. "You are always here for me, aren't you Hina . . ." I say, drying my face.

I stand and turn around. Peter is a few feet from me. He has recorded the entire night. I look at him and then walk back to my tent.

My work, tonight, is done.

# Peter

Dawn is breaking.

I look at my equipment, now neatly packed into boxes and trunks. I look at the sky, at the stars.

"I've done my best work tonight, Charlie," I whisper.

And then, I have no more profound thoughts. My mind needs time to absorb what I've witnessed. Hands shaking, I climb into my rental car.

I leave the beach as the first light of dawn licks the sky.

# She

Darlings!

Here you are.

I will watch over you,

As you grow.

As you thrive.

As you prosper.

I will watch over you.

Always.

# Tess

## 2016

### Hana, Maui
### November

I take the new lullaby discs out of the shed, carefully. I stick them under my jacket so the light rain doesn't get them wet. Marama suggested Keali'i Reichel. *Beautiful soothing chords so soft they'd comfort a butterfly,* she'd said. Well, I need something. I try not to panic. I tiptoe back to the hatchery.

My watch reads six a.m. I've been up all night. I couldn't leave the hospital. They are late—my hatchery babies are *late.* This could be a problem. A serious problem. Three months . . . that's all they need, more than three is a risk.

Yet the incubating eggs have been still.

My stethoscope reads heartbeats—all are well. Just . . . not wanting to hatch. I know there are risks with trying to duplicate nature. But these eggs are rescue's. Nests that had been destroyed, mothers that had perished . . . these orphans needed help, my help. Without my interference, they would surely die. But interfering with nature, I know, is a risk.

Marama loves my work here, and I know, my heart is in the right place. Yet . . . the non-hatching troubles me deeply. I remember a particular hatch . . . a year ago, with John, and the hatchling that flipped over. She tripped, then tumbled over a dune and landed on her back. She tried and tried and tried to right herself, to flip herself over. John had to forcefully hold me back. *"We cannot interfere, my love . . ."* he said, very sad.

"Just this once . . ." I had whispered, knowing his answer before he spoke.

"If we do it once, we do it always," he'd said. Yet when the hatchling managed to heave herself over, and stand at last, John was the one jumping up and down, cheering her on.

I walk to the incubators. I look round the room. I have the light turned down, low, the temperature is perfect. I glance at the disc I have playing. Ocean sounds. I switch it for Keali'i Reichel's lullabies.

*What could be the problem here?* I sit down and put my head in my arms.

I look inside myself. I ask the question. Mothers and children have a unique attachment. They can sense things. They know things. Could these hatchlings be reading my heart vibrations? Perhaps, they have deduced what I subconsciously feel, that I do not want them to hatch . . . *and leave me?*

I know what I need to do.

*"Hatch my lovelies . . . hatch . . ."* I whisper, walking

around the hospital room, with new resolve. I imagine the brave burst to the sea, that sand-to-sea run that sets the pace for all of their little lives. It is inside that *self-empowering moment,* that first *accomplishment,* the *declaration to survive . . .* that will see my hatchlings through all their lives. They must, *must* feel that I want this for them.

The clock on the wall taps out seconds. I watch. I close my eyes.

*Visualization.* That's what it's called to see a thing happening in the mind. Maybe it will help if I visualize things?

I imagine an *egg.* A baby inside it. It is a *cozy warm egg.* The baby likes it, she is wrapped up tightly. But . . . she is starting to feel just a wee bit cramped. She is growing after all, and the egg is shrinking around her. In fact . . . her flipper wants to extend. Yes. It wants to press *outward.* Now another flipper wants to flex . . . be free. In fact, the baby's head wants to shake itself out too. As much as she loves her egg, her home, and all she has ever known, maybe . . . it is time to *explore?*

I keep this thought in my head. I add to it, *many more eggs,* and babies inside. Some girls, some boys. Everyone starts to feel the urge—*to play.* They sense each other, for sure. They know there are lots of them in eggs all around, they can hear the heartbeats like a soft reassuring *tap-tap-tap.* My goodness, what fun would it might be, to break free from the egg and *meet* each other? This idea starts to get stronger and more flippers and heads press outward against the shells.

*I see it all in my mind.* I start to smile widely as I do. It is only natural for children to want to play! I check the clock on the wall, and I close my eyes to listen to the lullaby. When I open them, I spy a small *twitch* in the incubator, a piece of straw moves slightly. It's small, but I see it. Then a small *wobble* from the incubator across the room. And, another. Ever so slightly.

I walk to the glass cases. Four eggs are rocking now, ever so slowly. Some are smooth in their motion, others jerk back and forth quickly, and then stop. Ah, many different *personalities* I see!

I smile.

I wait.

Wobbling. Jerking. Shaking.

I go to the music and turn it up a bit. I know it will comfort my babies now, at this hatching moment in their lives.

*Where is my cellular?* There, by my clipboard. I grab it and dial Sasha. No answer. I dial Lani.

"Lani—it's me, I'm at the hatchery, eggs are shaking, hatchlings are getting ready to frenzy . . . can you assemble the troops? Bane, Ema, Oke. Great. Thanks."

I go to my laptop and I refresh the *Honu Hatchery* page . . . I type my favorite words there:

*Hospital Hatchery Shake-up: Release imminent!*

I grab my cellular again. "Ema? You heard from Lani? Good—please call Bane and Oke—oh you did already? Great. Let's all meet here in a half hour. I expect the babies to spend about an hour hatching. We will need to load them into the truck, inside their sand crates . . . sundown is five fifteen . . ."

I walk outside to check the temperature. It is a perfect, warm, Hawaiian day. Light breeze off the Pacific. I look up.

"Hello Mahina, I think they will be ready soon . . ." I whisper, using the Hawaiian word for moon. Her daytime outline is translucent against the blue sky.

I walk back into the hatchery—the eggs are all moving now!

I turn the music dial up higher. Ukulele combines with Hawaiian voices . . .

*He nani lua 'ole*
*Ku'u wehi o nʙ lani*
*He kilohana 'oe*
*Na'u e pʙlama mau*
*Hɸ'olu i ka poli e*
*Mehana i ke anu e.*

*I can smile when it's raining*
*And touch the warmth of the sun*
*I hear children laughing*
*In this place that I love.*

*Mau loa ke aloha*
*i kɸ pu'uwai hʙmama*
*He u'i lani 'oe*
*Na'u e mʙlama mau*
*Aia i ka la'i e*
*Hemolele i ka mʙlie.*

*I can smile when it's raining*
*And touch the warmth of the sun*
*I hear children laughing*
*In this place that I love.*

Come, children. Come, I whisper.

# Sasha

*Beep-beep-beep-beep . . .*
My computer awakens me, abruptly.
I stumble out of bed and over to the inbox . . .

*To: Sasha*
*From: Tess*
*Subject: Hatchery news—babies—about to frenzy!*

I fly into my clothes. I can't stop smiling.
Outside, however, I stop—cold in my tracks.
My tires are all flat. They have been . . . cut open. Slashed.
With a knife. I stare, dizzy.
Then I race for the old rusty bicycle in the yard.

# Oke

"Yes ma'am . . . okay Tess, I am on my way."

The frenzy has begun! My heart thumps as I catapult myself across my bedroom. But, in a moment—I am on the floor. I have tripped over my ukulele. Laughing, I right myself.

Keys in hand, I run for my Jeep, I know Tess will need the extra nest boxes I have stored there.

Then, I stop. I almost trip again. The tires of my truck have been slashed. All four. My eyes don't blink for five consecutive seconds.

I dial John at home on my cellular with shaking fingers.

"John—my tires are—*what?*" John's tires are slashed as well. He tells me that Lani, Bane, Ema and Oke—all have slashed tires.

Tess is alone at Honu Hospital.

# Tess

I look at my cellular—its message light is blinking madly. I smile. Releases are always so *exciting*. I decide to listen later. My babies need me first.

They are all shaking in unison now. Several eggs have small cracks, it's easy to imagine little flippers pressing outward inside their shells.

Then—*a cough.* Behind me.

I turn.

He is standing there, a *large knife* in hand. A black rag covers his face beneath his eyes.

Blue eyes.

*Blue eyes I recognize.*

# Sasha

I peddle on the old bicycle like a robot. I fly over pot holes and puddles. Mud splatters me. I peddle faster. My mind is spinning. *Oke's words* burn in my brain.

"All? Everyone? Oke, you are sure?" I'd screamed into my cell.

"Yes," he'd said. "All."

This isn't a *lone wolf situation.*

No.

This is an operation.

*Planned.*

Tess is alone at the hospital. My mind replays the events. How would someone know the nests would frenzy today?

Only someone, *at Honu Hospital,* would have that information. Someone close to Tess and John. *An inside job.* A horrible thought started in the base of my stomach.

But—Jake is in the sanitarium? Under lock and key?

Isn't he?

I stop pedaling and dial 911.

# Oke

My legs are pumping as fast as they can down Hana highway's old dirt road. I draw on strength I have built from many years of running on this island.

Carry me now, I tell my legs silently.

*Hewa,* I think in Hawaiian. Evil.

*Diabolo.* The devil.

# Tess

I can't breathe.

The blue-eyed, blonde man is dirty, his clothes are stained. I am afraid to utter his name.

"Please . . . don't hurt me. I will do as you wish." I stammer in a broken whisper.

The man walks to the disc player. Lullaby music drifts from it. In a fraction of a second—he raises his arm up high, and then forming a fist, he brings it down—*smashing* the player to a million shards of broken plastic.

He shatters both the player and his arm simultaneously. Blood and bits of plastic spray everywhere. He seems unaffected.

As if he cannot feel pain.

*I scream.*

I look at the eggs in boxes around me. They have all stopped vibrating.

*They know. My babies know.*

He reads my mind.

In another second, he is tying my hands together with rope from his waist. He pulls too tightly, cutting my wrists. I don't cry out.

"Marama . . . *help me* . . ." I pray inside my head.

He turns to the silent incubators. He eyes the eggs. He walks to the first one and roughly lifts it, yanking hard on the electrical plug in the wall that warms it. He gets irritated quickly when it doesn't pull out of the wall socket right away. He yanks harder, smashing the eggs against each other, inside. Then, horrifically, he turns the incubator over and dumps the eggs onto the floor. Shells smash open as they hit the cold tile hospital floor. Amniotic fluid spills everywhere.

I see frightened *hatchling eyes* looking up at me, from a dozen cracked open shells.

I cry silently.

*"Marama . . ."*

He is now yanking, and dumping all the incubators' contents onto the floor in a murderous pile of shells, fluid and bodies. *It is murder.* I watch my babies die. Their eyes look up at me, one after another, after another, after another.

**"KAUILA!"** I scream aloud through my gag.

He stops.

Turns.

Then he walks to me in one hard step, raises his bloodied arm again, and brings it down upon my face.

# John

I am peddling on my bike as fast as my athletic legs will allow. Then I peddle faster. Left leg, right leg, left leg, right leg, faster, faster, faster. Obstacle thoughts like flaming knives pummel my mind, as I try to focus on one thing only; *speed*. I must get there, I must get to *Honu Hospital,* now.

But the fiery thoughts plague me. *Bubble cave. Waikiki. The luau.* With a great heave—I push them off and power to the finish line.

# Sasha

My lungs are about to explode. As I near Honu Hospital, I hear sirens. Police. My dilapidated bike careens crazily into the driveway.

"Tesssssss . . . ?" I yell, as I fly off the bike.

"Who are you?" A police officer is blocking the hospital front door.

"I called you! I am Sasha Jones! I work here!"

His face looks grave.

"These are my friends! Is Tess McAdams okay?" I cry.

I look behind the officer. Tess is sitting on the floor of the hospital. Paramedics hover above her.

Oke arrives just then, out of breath.

"What the—?" he yells.

"Folks. Everyone take it easy. We've contained the situation. Tess McAdams has suffered an attack but is recuperating. We can't let you in—this is a crime scene."

The police officer crosses his arms, and stares us down hard. "Do you, either of you, have any idea of who would want to hurt Mrs. McAdams? Hurt her hospital here? Motives?"

I look at Oke.

"Yes, I know someone. You're damn right, I do," I say to the officer.

His eyes open wide and he grabs a pad from his pocket. He flips it open and clicks his pen.

"Name?" he asks me.

"Jake," I say.

"J-A-K-E, M-C-A-D-A-M-S," I say again, spelling both names out, slowly.

"Brother of John McAdams," I say, John is the husband of Tess McAdams.

Just then, John arrives. He is panting haphazardly. He steps off his bicycle and collapses.

"John McAdams?" The police officer speaks sharply to him.

John nods from the ground.

"Your wife has been attacked," the officer says flatly.

"Her condition is stable. She took a blow to the head, paramedics say it's a surface wound only. The perpetrator escaped. Before he did, though, he assaulted the hatchery. Smashed the incubating eggs. Presumably, took a few as hostages, but the rest of the victims, those left behind on the floor, unfortunately did not survive, Mr. McAdams. The other hospital patients, appear to be intact, however. The perp—seemed interested in eggs only. Perpetrator, I mean. We are looking at several charges here: breaking and entering, aggravated assault, and poaching."

John is staring blindly at the officer.

"Mr. McAdams, these employees of yours. They gave me a name. A suspect. Can you confirm this person? The officer's face is grave.

John tries to stand.

"Jake McAdams. Your brother. Can you confirm this name for me?"

The officer glares at John.

John closes his eyes.

# Marama

## Hana, Maui
## October

*Great Ku!* I look up at the Tiki God. His wide, toothy grimace is a warning. Ku's enormous legs are bowed for battle.

"Almighty Ku," I begin, "I have seen *Qaitu*, I have seen ghosts." *"Ku! I have seen the dead!"*

He glares at me.

"They came up from Po-Milu. They came from their dark spirit world and have inhabited a *haole* . . ."

I bow deeper in humility before the God. With my head down, I continue to speak, "he has the *ghost sickness* . . ." I say. "Great and mighty Ku, the haole has a *very bad* ghost sickness . . ."

I look up. Will the Tiki God speak to me?

Ku looks angry. His teeth are savage. Surely this great warrior will know what to do.

"God of War . . . how do I drive out this evil?" I whisper, "I tried to reason with the haole, but his sickness is deep, great Ku."

I take a deep breath. The quiet here inside this wooden *heiau*, surrounds me.

Mother taught me that qaitu must be driven out, and back to the underworld. Otherwise, they cause imbalance. It can be deadly.

Ku continues to stare at me, his gaze unbroken.

I stand and approach the altar. I place my offering in front of Ku. I've wrapped it in leaves. It is a piece of broken shell. Broken hatchling shell. From the attack on Honu Hospital. A little piece of life left behind. A sacrifice for Ku.

"Great and fierce Ku, husband of the moon goddess Hina, you who have caused light to shine in upon the world . . . hear my prayer . . ."

*He nui a me ka inaina Ku . . . husband o ka mahina Akua Wahine Hina . . . oukou ka poe i i malamalama mai ka mahina, ma luna o ke ao . . . hear i ka'u pule . . .*

I intone my prayer in the old way.

And then—a reply!

Hina reaches down through the ceiling, through the opening at the top of this chapel. She slips through and down and circles me in a moonbeam hug. I wrap my arms around hers.

In my mind, I hear her words.

*E hahai mai oe ia'u. E hahai i ka mahina. Oe i ka hope-mahina e hana ia mea. Malu hoomakaukauia'i ia oe ilaila,* Follow me. Follow the moon. You have a moon to follow—do it. Follow my wisdom, truth awaits you.

Yes. I understand. I look up at Ku.

"Thank you, great Ku!"

*I have my answer.*

# John

## 2016

### Hana, Maui
### November

"He must go, John. He must." My wife won't look at me. Her voice is low. I cover my face with my hands.

"But . . ." I whisper hoarsely.

"No *buts!* No more buts John!" Tess cries. My scientific mind replies. "Proof. Facts. Data. Tess, there is *no data* to support your accusation . . ."

"*WHAT?*" My wife is standing now.

"He has been at the *sanitarium.*" I say. I stand and go to her. My surfboard is against the bedroom wall behind her. I look at it. I soften my voice.

"Jake has been under security watch. Tess, look at me, Jake has been under security camera watch, twenty-four hours a day, seven days a week . . ." I say, holding her face in my hands.

"No. Something happened. He must have broken out. He likes to sneak around. It's a *game* to him, John, A game. Jake is not who you think he is, John. He is a pretender. *He is always pretending.* He was In Waikiki. In a proper blue blazer. And shiny Italian loafers. He was there to *stalk* us. "*He is pretending to be you!* It's a game to him. He's playing it, that's all. He's a *leprechaun.*"

I feel my Irish pride rising. I push it back down. Not now.

"Whomever it was, that attacked you and the hatchlings at Honu Hospital, Tess, it couldn't have been my brother."

My wife's perfect oval face is red. Her enormous eyes are bigger than I have ever seen.

"I called the hospital, Tess. They *confirmed this,*" I add.

"Impossible," she says, flatly.

"It's true," I say.

"*He killed my babies John! He killed my babies!*" Tess's words fall like broken hatchling shells onto the floor between us.

"John, either he goes or I go," she says.

"He has gone, Tess. He has gone to live at the sanitarium. He is there now. Under lock and key."

I walk to Tess and attempt to embrace her. She steps away from me.

"John. It was *him.* I looked into his eyes. They were your eyes. Your hair. Your build. Your height. Your walk. It was you. The *other-you.* Your *evil* twin. It was *him* in Bubble Cave. It was *him* in Waikiki."

I listen to her. My mind throws an image at me, then. The four men at Spitting Cave. Three Hawaiians . . . and a haole.

A blonde haole. Tess doesn't know about this.

I push the image back. "We can't know any of that. All we can know, is what has been confirmed. Jake was at the Maui sanitarium the day of the break in at the hospital."

Tess turns and faces the wall.

"It had to be someone else, Tess. Another poacher. A haole from the mainland. Blue eyes are common. Blonde hair is common. Turtles fetch *thirty-five hundred dollars each* on the black market. Eggs . . . can be *fifty dollars apiece.* It could be any soulless, Godless, evil bastard out there."

She turns to face me. "John. I have been married to you for nine years. I know you. I know Jake. It was him." Then she stomps out of the room. The door slams behind her.

I am shaking so badly I have to sit down. I look at my hands. I turn them over. I look at the knuckles, the lines, the nails.

As boys Jake and I used to compare hands. And feet. No difference. Same.

Is my wife right? Or is she losing it? Her babies being *murdered* in front of her could easily fracture her large heart, I know. She could have been so traumatized that she saw, whom she has always distrusted. My brother.

Yet—I called the hospital. They told me Jake had been there. All day, all night. I drove to the hospital. I looked at records. I interviewed nurses. They all tell me he was there. A nurse showed me his vitals taken at five a.m. Signed by her. His meeting with his doctor at seven a.m. Signed by the doctor. His therapy appointment at eight a.m. Signed by the therapist.

Yet.

Yet . . . ?

Yet.

My mind races.

It is . . . perfect. A perfect revenge. Revenge for the curse. Revenge for his *cursed birth*.

An *imperfect* second son born, after a perfect first brother born.

A *simple* son. Dull blue eyes. Oxygen deprived.

He must dream of a different scenario?

Jake's uncomplicated, simple dream of the scenario where he becomes normal. A dream, where he *takes back* what should have been rightfully his. The dream, where he as a warrior returns to claim his birthright. With *fiery knives* in his hands.

I understand it all. Of course I do. Would I do any differently? Would I?

What other destiny does any warrior have, but to right wrongs? I rake my hair with my fingers.

*"Nooo . . ."* I cry aloud.

I look down at my fingers. I see two palms pressed together. My palms and Jake's palms. As boys we would measure our hands to see whose was bigger. It was always *the same.*

I breathe in very, very deeply. I hold the breath inside my chest for five seconds. I let it out slowly.

The hospital *swears* he was there. There are *witnesses*. There are *signatures*.

I rub my eyes. Then I get up and walk out of the house and into the night. The moon overwhelms me with a tsunami of light.

"Hina. Help me," I say quietly. Soft blue light seeps into my skin. I hold up my hands in the blue blaze. My five pointed fingers create a shadow monster on the sand behind them. I flutter my fingers and the monster comes to life.

Marama says things are *not always as they appear to be.*

# She

I lift my head.

I breathe.

Sweet night air.

Hina, atop water.

Her path.

I see.

Hina moves.

Across heaven.

I follow her.

I always have.

I always will.

I remember.

I never forget.

Anything.

Ever.

# Peter

As much as I hate New York City, I was glad to make this trip. I was glad to shuffle through JFK airport. I was happy to wait forty-five minutes in the taxi line. Crikey, I was thrilled to drag heavy photographic equipment six blocks to *National Geographic Headquarters* on Fifth Avenue.

Chris has been in his glass-walled conference room an hour. Shades, drawn.

I wanted to leave the photos with him, alone. I felt they needed to be viewed privately. It's an emotional experience, best shared with no one.

It was for me, when I laid all my shots, out after the shoot. Took me several hours and *three vodka tonics* to take it all in.

Sometimes there are no words to express what photographs express.

I believe this is one of those cases.

It is more than a human connecting to an animal species. Something happens with Tess McAdams and the turtles. Something *inexplicable.* As I told Chris in a voicemail, you just have to see this to believe it.

There is something that happened in my lens, between this human woman and the ancient reptile babies, that is a statement on all of us being connected at some level.

It is bigger than activism, as I told Chris.

It's the joining of two species. Somehow, someway, these two species were able to meaningfully connect.

*"What do you mean she becomes a turtle?"* Chris had asked me, calling from some noisy midtown bar. I heard music and yelling in the background.

"Hard to explain mate . . . can you . . . Chris, can you walk outside a minute . . . I can hardly hear you . . ."

"I just ordered fried zucchini buddy . . . so . . . she pretends to have a *shell?*"

"Nah . . . not like that . . . hard to explain . . . but I've been shootin' turtles for years Chris . . . she . . . she sorta floats arms and legs hanging down, her back above . . . then she dives . . . she seems to stay under an inordinate amount of time . . . I don't know . . . it's . . . just . . . ya gotta see the photos . . ."

"Pete—didn't hear a word you said mate . . . call me when you land in New York."

I look at the closed conference room door. I decide to go downstairs and get some coffee.

The elevator is jammed with people who all wear the same face; disgruntled panic. I look around. Then I glance at the elevator buttons, "'scuse me mate, might ya press ground floor me?" I say to the guy in a suit that looks like he is about to implode. His exasperated face cracks me up, and I laugh. I don't mean to be rude of course. Pressing a button is after all, a mighty large request.

Soon, I find myself standing in line for coffee, listening to the screeches, horns, and yells of the street. The smell of exhaust mixes with a sickly sweet donut aroma.

Looking up, I see steel. Structures as tall as the great pyramids of Giza. My eyes enjoy traveling the straight lines that pierce the sky.

And then—I see her! Hina. *Tess's moon.*

A small sliver of pale white above a skyscraper, she is here with me. Watching.

I laugh aloud! She is watching over Tess's photos upstairs. She wants to see Christopher's reaction.

*I'll be darned.* Well, so do I.

I decide to walk to the park. A bit of green, yes. Central Park is a magnificent attempt to bring nature into this steel metropolis of noise. My feet pick up their pace as I see trees. A stone bridge...a pond, now. The noise abates . . . ducks, squirrels scatter on the walkway. My heart is lightening. There, a meadow! I walk off the paved path and onto the grass.

Damn, why didn't I bring a small camera, I say to myself realizing my shoulder is empty. I left everything in Chris's office.

Gone is the noise, the cement. Photographer's eye candy spills before me. I pass several natural-looking lakes and ponds, glassy calm surfaces, I see frogs and ducks. The walking path takes me under a stone bridge and I hear the whinny of a horse! A bridle path is next to a large area of natural woods.

I look up. Imposing skyscrapers have been silenced, and replaced with this lovely sound of galloping hooves. A whinny. Then, a splash in the pond, as a family of ducks plays.

I whistle as I walk. An ice-skating rink is around the next bend in the path, and then, I hear sounds that don't seem possible.

The distinct *roar of a lion*. A *chimpanzee cry*. The low *grumble of a seal*. The *screech* of . . . what sounds like a *macaw*.

A zoo? A zoo.

I see a sign for *Central Park Zoo* . . . and before I can stop myself, I've bought a ticket and I'm inside.

Instantly, my wildlife photographer brain clicks to, *on*.

"*Hello, Polar's* . . ." I say to the two enormous bears behind glass. My mind, mentally clicks the shot. I feel a buzz in my pocket. Must be Chris on my cellular. I can't stop now . . . snow leopards, sea lions greet me next. Then, tamarins, lemurs and snow monkeys! A large anteater, a red panda, a mouse deer, a sloth, rock cavies, harbor seals, fruit bats, a banded mongoose . . . spill into mental view finder, one after another. My heart is happy. Mental clicks going off at rapid shutter-speed.

Another buzz in pocket—but here is a swan goose, bufflehead ducks, and my God! An African pygmy goose. Rainforest birds screech at—damn—I must never forget a camera again—a golden weaver, a Victoria crowned pigeon, a scarlet ibis and a white-rumped shama. As well as a Bali mynah, keel-billed toucans, blue-grey tanager, an emerald starling and fairy bluebirds.

Buzzz . . . says my back pocket once again.

Parrots! A blue-headed macaw, blue-throated conures, Derbyan parakeets, and Fischer's lovebirds.

Buzz, buzz, buzz.

What was it Tess said? *Look hard and remember!* Now I see my photographic favorites, the colors that sing on film, frogs! Tiny colorful poison dart frogs, waxy monkey frogs, Panamanian golden frogs and smokey jungle frogs. A Puerto Rican crested toad. A Surinam toad.

Oh my God—an emerald tree boa! And there—several blood pythons and Dumeril's ground boas, too.

TURTLES! A pig-nosed turtle, a red-footed tortoise and a Burmese mountain tortoise. Next to them are lizards, a giant Madagascar day gecko, an Orient knight anole and a prehensile-tailed skink.

Buzzzzzzzzzzzz.

I shove my hand into my back pocket and grab the phone, *"Yeah?"* I yell into it.

"GET BACK HERE NOW, PETER!"

I laugh out loud. Yep. Christopher's been bitten by the Tess McAdams bug. Now we can both be sick with this incredible creature of nature.

I run through the zoo and out to the park, and up to Fifth Avenue. Taxis scream their horns at me as I fly across the street. I sprint down Fifth Avenue smiling. I reach *National Geographic* and bound into the elevator. Within a few minutes I'm rapping on Chris's conference room door.

"Come in, mate," he says, opening the door. Six people are inside. Tess's photos are all over the large table.

"I'm Margaret Jones, Peter, Director of publicity," a woman with a severe black haired bun and black glasses says to me. Her lips are the color of blood.

"Pleased to meet ya," I say in my best Australian drawl.

She doesn't smile. She looks me in my eyes and then takes her glasses off.

"Peter, I speak for the group. These are the most profound

photographs of the miracle of *chelonioidea* that we've ever seen," she says.

*Chelonioidea.* This lassie doesn't fool around, using sea turtles' scientific name.

I walk around the room. The photographs are laid out in a storyboard. I start at the beginning. Tess walking into the sea. Swimming. In the dunes. The nests. The hatch. The crawl. The sea. The moon. Tess. The entire night is captured there, the story I have told. In, my photographs.

Suddenly, I'm not in New York City. I am on a Maui beach at midnight. The moonlight is all the lighting I need, playing in the shadows of Tess and her hatchlings.

*Faces. Eyes.* I grip the table.

I look—their faces! Of the *turtles.* Of *Tess.* I feel dizzy.

It all comes rushing back to me. The night. It is all written in their faces.

Here a tiny turtle hatchling struggles to dig its hind flippers out of the sand, I see exhaustion on its tiny face. *The struggle for life.*

There, Tess's face, awash in moonglow, diamond-tears on her cheeks, as she watches her babies battle it out.

And again, in the waves, her blonde mermaid head, moonglow-white, watching the babies swim away.

I hear the whisper of night, a sound of breeze and palms rustling. I smell the salty sea in my nostrils. My vision is black and white now, it is calming, soothing.

Then, the last photo.

My chest heaves, I can't stifle the sob.

It is a zoom shot of Tess's face, sideways, laying on the mud in the surf. A tiny hatchling is silhouetted in front of her enormous eyes. The turtle's back is to my camera, she is looking directly at Tess. And, Tess is looking directly at the turtle. Tears spill from Tess's eyes, silvery rivulets. She is saying goodbye. Forever. To the hatchling.

"Pete . . . Peter . . . it is okay mate . . ." I feel a hand on my back.

I put my face in my hands. The room is silent. Then, I turn around. Six adults are staring at me.

I turn to Chris. "Chris . . . it's just that . . ."

Chris finishes my sentence, "It's *the one*. You took the one, the shot of your lifetime. The one perfect shot that summarizes all your work. The one shot," he says.

I nod. Then I sit down. Margaret gives me a bottle of water. She opens the cap for me. She waits a minute, as I drink it down.

"Peter, what we'd like to do, is this," Margaret says in a business voice. "We'd like to have this photo essay of Mrs. McAdams and the chelonioidea hatchlings as the cover for our Christmas edition, we will have to rush but it is possible. We are pulling all other cover ideas and we are going with this story. I have also been on the phone with the Museum of Natural History as well as the Metropolitan Museum of Art—we are going to do a live exhibit, a walk through for Christmas . . . your photographs will be blown up on forty-foot boards. The world will see your work Mr. Sloane. The world wants to see this, they need to see this story, Mr. Sloane. Er—Peter."

I look at the woman with the severe hairstyle. She removes her glasses, again.

"This is bigger than Tess McAdams, Peter. It is bigger than the hatchlings. This is a statement on life. This says to the world . . ." Margaret pauses and picks up a piece of paper, and reading aloud, continues, "Look. Look what we can do if we love the planet, love one another, love all of God's creatures."

I am nodding. My life's work. On the world stage.

"Crrrrrikey," I stammer.

"You are an artist Peter," Chris says to me, "this is your heart and soul, we understand that." He sits down next to me. "You're gonna change the world, Peter . . . how the world sees turtles."

"Mr. Sloane, we will do a finalé statement on *poaching*, as we know Tess's mission is saving sea turtles from human greed, be it pollution in our oceans, plastics, oil spills, or greed from poachers who harvest the turtles for their shells. We will expose the black market aspects of the greed. We want people to be," Margaret stops again and reads from the paper, "awed, moved to tears, and then moved to action-via-awareness," she finishes.

"Yes . . . yes . . . yes . . ." I stutter.

"Pete, here have some more water . . ." Chris hands me another water bottle.

"This will bring endless publicity to the cause Mr. Sloane. The sea turtles will have a spotlight that otherwise could never be had. We expect this to shake the world. Your clients can expect federal grants, private donations. Honu Hospital on Maui will benefit hugely Mr. Sloane . . ."

I hear the words that I know Tess and John long for. "I will fly back to Hawaii. I will speak to them. My friends."

# John

"Tess . . . I'm just off the phone with Peter . . ."

I look at my wife, she is cleaning out the hatchling crates. She's on her knees scrubbing the crates with bleach, she wants to rid them of any scent, new hatchlings can detect scent . . . and we can't afford new crates for every new hatch.

"Mmmm . . ." she says.

I see her wince as she shifts her weight, she is still healing from the attack at the hospital.

"Doll, Peter . . . called . . . he is in New York City."

"Mmmm . . ." she says, scrubbing at a corner hard.

"Tess . . ."

"Damn it! John, this crate just cracked. We'll have to discard it. I'm sorry . . ."

"Tess . . ."

"Yes?" My wife finally turns around.

"Peter is in New York City. He showed your photos to *National Geographic*. I guess . . . he took photos of you before the hatch . . . in the sea . . . and after the hatch as well . . . ? He said he was shooting for hours."

My wife looks at me silently. Her enormous blue eyes fix on my face.

"I don't really remember him, John. I was in my head . . . I was doing what I do . . . for the children . . . my babies."

I nod. "I know, love," I say softly.

"I remember he wanted a few shots of the hatchlings . . ." she says.

"He got a lot more than a few shots, Tess. He got some very . . . intimate . . . photographs of you . . . with your babies. *National Geographic* went crazy. They . . . apparently went totally crazy . . . they love the shots and they are doing a cover story . . . as well as a live photo essay exhibit . . . to walk through . . . at . . . the Museum of Natural History . . . in Manhattan . . . New York City, Tess."

Tess is staring at me. She has never been to New York.

"The Metropolitan Museum of art is going to host the exhibit as well . . ."

Tess tucks her knees under her arms. She is curled up in a ball.

"So . . . Tess . . . two things, honey, one—it's extremely personal photography . . . you will want to see these shots . . . you need to know that the world, the entire world will see them . . . you . . . and the hatchlings . . . and, two, Tess; the world, will then know of our work here. It will be worldwide exposure. The turtles . . . they will benefit Tess. Our hospital will benefit."

"I know . . . I . . . told Peter it was a great idea . . ." she says in a whisper.

I go to her. I sit on the floor and put my arms around her. "I know you are, maybe scared, now, of the photos and what they show . . . it was . . . a great idea before, but now it has become real. I know it's private for you darling. I know they are Kauila's babies. It will help a lot for you to see the photos. Approve some, disapprove others. All your call."

Tess puts her head on my shoulder and nods.

"This will expose the world to the turtles and to their needs . . . and to poaching," I say.

"Mmmm," she says.

"Yes. We will receive attention from the EPA, from corporations . . . everyone will know the evil that happens on the black market . . . the poachers will be dissuaded . . . police will crack down . . . corporations will make policies to be aware . . . green . . . it will be a domino effect . . ."

"Yes," Tess says, shaking her head. "I want to see my photos, John," she adds.

"Peter is sending them. He wanted to prepare them for you, not loose shots . . . he wanted to have *National Geographic* do a preliminary layout. Is that okay?"

"Of course. Of course, John, I want to help. Peter is an artist. I am sure . . . he . . . captured what he considers . . . art . . ." she tells me, "it's just so private . . . as you say."

"Yes, he seems a good man, Tess . . . he does," I say.

"I just don't want our lives to change John . . . we can let the world in . . . but I want to be able to keep them out as well . . . you know?"

I nod at her. I agree, utterly.

We all have things we would not want made public. Skeletons in the closet.

# PART 3

# Joe

## 1975

❦

### Kinsale; Cork, Ireland
### October

❦

*"'Aye . . . Joe."*

I watch my father pace the small, airless room that stinks of the guts of millions of fish that have traversed here.

It's three o'clock in the morning.

Yet, Pa wants to talk. We are expected at the pier. In Castletownbere. Three forty-five, they leave. The fish do not wait.

His steely blue eyes sear into mine.

*"Joe, Joe. Joe McAdams. I had higher hopes for ye, Joe. I did, I did, God in his heaven, knows I did."*

I look at my shoes. My toe waves at me from a hole.

"Tis America that'll be yer future, boy. Not Ireland. We Irish have done well, we have, in America. John Kennedy, m'boy."

Pa's eyes glitter softly. He falls, heavily, into a chair. The seat explodes billows of peat dust.

His hands, rough, calloused, old before their time from the sea, rest on his knees. They've not known much rest in their fifty years of fishing.

He takes a long swig of his beer. I look at his deeply lined face. A map of his life.

"'Aye. *'Tis a thing,* isn't it. 'Tis a thing. 'Tis a thing."

My toe escapes the hole in my shoe. It tries to breathe in this tiny room. It can't and retreats back into my shoe.

"So. How far 'long is the lass?" Pa asks, flatly.

"A month." My voice shakes.

"A month. Well. 'Aye, I reckon her kin'll look after 'er."

"They be good kin too. Aye. They'll keep it quiet."

Pa shifts in his seat. His reputation means everything to him.

"Her father's a sailor in Tinsdale. A good church man. Aye, I know they'll be doin' the right thing. They've a side business in town, too. A rooming house, I hear," Pa says, starting to slur his words.

*"Cha d'dhùin doras nach d'fhosgail doras . . ."* he adds.

I look at my father. Gaelic always resonates louder for me. *No door ever closed, but another opened . . .* Pa's words echo in my head. So I am to look at this as an opportunity? This tragedy? My secret?

*"Cha sgeul-rùin e 's fios aig triùir air,"* I say back to him. *It's no secret if three know it.* The Irish do not keep secrets well.

*"NONSENSE!"* he explodes, jumping to his feet, "no one need know!"

The fish blood splatters on his clothes are deep stains.

No amount of washing will make them go away.

*"Cha mhisd' a' ghealach na coin a bhith comhartaich rithe,"*
I say softly . . . *the moon is none the worse for the dogs' barking at her.*

Our family name will survive, I think . . . regardless of whether our secret stays hidden or not. Fiona's pregnancy is a fact.

Pa rounds on me. Hands on his hips. He is angry now. I have pushed too far.

*"Am fear nach dèan cur sa Mhàrt, cha bhuain e san Fhoghar."*
*He who will not sow in March will not reap in autumn.*

The sagging peat walls around us seemed to laugh at his threats.

The smell of fish is everywhere. In the house, on our clothes, in our noses, in our souls.

"You will reap as I *demand,* boy."

I stand now, too. If he wants it to be this way, then let it be this way. I am a man now. I am eighteen years old.

"Ye will be off to America, boy. Ye will plant yer seeds. Ye will tend 'em. Ye will reap our family's *honor.* Then, 'aye, ye will bring it home to yer ole Pa."

"McAdams is a fine name *now,* Pa," I say.

Pa stares wildly.

"I like my life here. Fiona likes our lives here. We live with the sea. We like it here," I whisper.

"Let's go, boy," he says, angrily. He turns to a peg on the wall and throws a jacket at me. Then he motions to the door. He doesn't bother to lock the cottage. There's nothing to steal.

At three a.m. in Kinsale, not another soul is stirring.

"We're late," he says.

Pa's old truck crunches to a halt on the roadside, the headlights reveal a lone heron wading in the tide below.

The gangway opens before us. Pa's forty-foot inshore trawler is waiting. He has skippered it for six years. *The Graine*. Named for my mother. Dead, now ten years.

He flicks a light switch in the wheelhouse and fires up the diesel engine. I busy myself with the moorings. Our passage out of Kinsale this morning is streaked with the light of an Irish dawn, bold and brazen reds, oranges and purples.

"Hurry up, boy," yells the skipper, Pa, deadpan. The passion of our chat earlier now gone. He turns his attention to the sea.

"Prawns, Pa?" I ask, already knowing the answer.

"Aye," he replies.

"The prawn-fishing grounds we're heading for are more than an hour away.

"Put the kettle on, boy. Make use of yerself."

*The Graine* is small, unassuming. Which is funny, as Graine McAdams was none of those things. She was a loud, brash, sailor's wife. Full of fun, and drink and merrymaking.

*The Graine* has two of everything still.

Two bunks, two cups, two chairs and two spoons. I think of Fiona. Her long black hair, her eyes of blue. And our son . . . if he is to be, coming soon. Three, spoons it will be. Three cups. Three chairs. Three bunks.

"Joe—lookee 'ere!" It's Pa calling me.

I go to him and see fourteen fishing trawlers leaving port out of Kinsale. Dingle has more, but still, fourteen is a large number for us.

"No lobster pots today Pa? I ask. Lobster potting has come to replace shrimping, though its more labor intensive.

As the lights of Kinsale Harbor fade into the distance, Pa grabs a tin whistle from the shelf and plays a familiar tune.

*Me and my cousin, one Arthur McBride,*
*As we went a-walking down by the seaside,*
*Now mark you what followed, and what did betide,*
*For it being on Christmas morning . . .*

I listen, I close my eyes. Fatigue doesn't exist in this life. This life of the sea. Fatigue is simply a *part* of things. It is like breathing.

Pa unfurls the hauling system and guides it into the ocean. One hundred fifty meters of steel cable follows the net down into the surf.

Massive stocks of white fish are below in these waters, A box sells for one hundred pounds back at the harbor, so a couple of boxes would cover our diesel costs for the day, with a little change to spare.

I look at the sky. Purple staining red now. We are late, Pa is right. Prawns are most numerous at dawn, hence an extremely early start.

"Pour the tea, Joe," Pa barks after the nets are set.

I do as I'm told.

My thoughts drift to Fiona. He shape. The curve of her hip. Her full lips.

She is the daughter of another fisherman here in Tinsdale. Pa respects her Pa. They have known each other for years. Yet, he drives me to leave here. To leave her. Leave for America. It's the *Rising* of course. Always the *Easter Rising*. And failure of the Irish to sustain it. This anger drives Pa and so he drives me. To be more. Always more.

"Ten, Joe."

Pa points to his watch.

We put on oilskins and begin hauling in the nets. It's not easy—but we manage with effort, to drag them on board.

"Pa!" I cry.

He smiles . . . "Aye, boy . . . have a look . . ."

We may have been trawling for prawns, but these nets don't discriminate.

Pa pulls at a piece of cord and, suddenly, every sea creature imaginable is flapping or wriggling about on the deck: prawns, monkfish, brill, megrim, dogfish, starfish and something I don't recognize.

My heart races—I am glad for Pa, and us.

"That's a proper McAdams catch it is, it is . . ." Pa declares.

It's an awesome sight. A ling slithers at my feet, its mouth an expression of anguish.

Pa shovels some of the catch, both dead and alive, back into the sea, sparking frenzy among the gulls that have been trailing us for miles.

He reaches for his knife, and I am mesmerized, just as I was as a boy, at his skill. Pa guts and sorts hundreds of fish in a matter of minutes.

"Not enough," Pa says.

Two boxes of prawns. Scarcely enough, in other words, to cover the cost of the day's diesel.

"Don't worry, Pa . . . let's press on . . . the day is young," I say, patting my old Pa on the back.

He looks me in the eye.

"The sea's a friend. A brother, Joe. Never forget this. What she gives us—we must give back. We must *honor her.* Always."

"Aye, Pa," I say, my eyes filling. I understand. He wants better for me. Better than this. Yet, he is proud of his toils. He loves the sea.

An hour later, I pull in the nets, myself. Pa is having a smoke below. At first all I see is miles of seaweed. Then empty cans of soda. Then—cod. Endless bodies, flopping.

*"Go sabhailte Dia sinn!"* I shout. Yes, it seems God has saved us.

Piled high in a crate, they look like enormous elephant ears with mouths. Pa and I start to sort through the haul, and I am glad to be here, with my Pa, doing honest Irish work. I am proud.

"I want to bring honor to the McAdams name, Pa," I say, as my knife guts a cod open. Its eyes bug out.

"I know ye do, boy, I know," he says. He guts faster than I do. He doesn't look into the fish's eyes as they explode.

"Just, make somethin' of yerself. At university. Do that. Do that first, 'aye. Then ye come on home. First ye do me proud—then ye can come home. Come home educated. Do that and I'll be proud, boy. You'll do yer old Pa proud that way, y'will."

We gut another hundred cod bodies.

He speaks again.

"'Tis a bloodthirsty battle we have 'ere in Ireland, Joe. Must be fought not from below, but from above. Not in the streets. In government. Ye go learn in America. Then ye come back home. And ye fight fer Ireland here."

I nod.

Then, suddenly I think of Fiona.

Her black curls that spill to her waist. Her blue eyes that shine with hope. Trust. Love. For me.

Fiona.

I look at the fish I am about to gut. It still breathes. It is looking at me. I thrust my knife in its belly. It dies, its eyes fixed on mine. So this is what it feels like to betray.

*Is í ding di féin a scoileann an dair.* I say the Gaelic words to myself as I don't dare say them aloud. *Beware of the enemy within.*

Pa stops. He pats my back. We look at the sky. A sliver crescent moon is there, Pa points to it.

I look at him. His old, lined face. I think of his life. Sacrificed for me. I take his hand in mine. I look back at the crescent moon. Curving downward, like an ear waiting to hear something. And then—strangely, my heaviness lightens.

"Yes," I say to the moon, and to Pa. "Yes?" Pa is looking at me. "Yes, *America.*"

A new feeling, now. Hope. It is hope. Hope is the color of that white moon above our boat. It dilutes everything else.

I leave Ireland a week later. And I never look back.

# Fiona

## 1976

❧ ⁓⊕∘⊙⁓ ❧

### Kinsale Cork, Ireland
### October

❧ ⁓⊕∘⊙⁓ ❧

"Yer a big boy, ye are little Flanagan . . ."

"'Aye, that's it darlin'," I say. My boy walks well already! Aye, he's a strong one, he is. He looks right fine in a proper woolen sweater and trousers, my own knitted pattern too, he wears it proud.

'Tis the same pattern for all the menfolk fishing from our village. Mine own hands created it. To keep our men safe at sea. And to identify 'em if they are taken by the Lord's own hand.

"Careful my boy, easy there Flanagan," I say, as I watch him inspect some thatch on the floor that's fallen from our roof. A mouse darts out of it as he pokes away.

"*Fall down Ma!*" he cries at me, raising the soddy thatch.

"Right ye are li'l Flanagan! A smart boy ye are! Like yer Pa." I nod to him to go and put the thatch in the fire. He obeys immediately, keeping back from the flames as I've taught him.

"Aye!" he cries, victory hands in the air, when the task is done.

*"Ha ha ha . . ."* My mum and I explode in laughter.

"A *fine* boy, Fiona . . . a right fine lad here, ye have . . ." she says.

I look at my child. With eyes as blue as any Irish sky. A son o'Ireland, he is, 'tis a true *son of the sea.*

**"Gráím thú . . ."** I love you my son, I say to him.

**"Gwáím thuuuú . . ."** he says back to me in his own Gaelic.

'Aye, I've one good thing in d'world . . . one good thing, my own son. Love him so much I do. My own, wee boy.

I stand up and walk to him, my dress stained with fish innards, scales and oil doesn't keep little Flanagan from hugging me tight. He places his wee hand into mine own. I close my fingers around his.

Then—I wince. My fingernails are torn, 'aye, my hands look like an old maids.'

'Tis true though, I'm also a child of the sea. I am, Pa and Ma's hands when theirs are busy on the boat. But I must make my livin'. I must help to put food on the table. I must.

"'Aye, you're a son of the sea, my Flanagan . . . like yer Pa."

My words make the wee boy smile.

*"Wike me Pa!"* he cries.

Again, me own Ma laughs from the corner, pausing at her wool spinning. I wish I could spend the day with him, I do.

"Best be gettin' to the dock Fiona," she says, then.

"Ma . . . a moment, Ma."

"'Aye, ye can't be late girl. Ye cant be late, them fish need' cleanin' before sellin', they do," Ma says, her voice a sharp blade to my ears.

I hug my boy to me. He's a stocky fine boy, he is. Good eater.

Good fighter, too. When half the village had **eitinn,** the cough, the dreaded tuberculosis, my boy fought it off, he did. Fought it right off. Not everyone, did.

As small as Kinsale is, it became smaller still when **eitinn** arrived. It came from a dark and evil place. From a foreign land of wickedness. A dark and damp place of trolls and demons. Aye, I was sure o'it, I was. It crept into our homes, our pubs, our churches. 'Twas a rank and devilish pest, it was.

But we Irish—Irish o'the sea, we are strong, we are. The strongest Irish that ever there was, we are. Like mine own son here, strong like his Pa and mine own Pa too. Good Irish stock, dear boy. *Fine, Irish stock.*

'Aye, we speak Irish here in Kinsale, just the old tongue, we answer to only ourselves and the sea. We are proud, we are. We are strong. Our four hundred sixty-five cottages have five hundred families livin' in 'em. We're eight hundred fifty men, with eighty God-fearin' boats.

I remember the night Pa pledged to defeat **eitinn,** he spoke under a full **gealach,** a full magnificent moon. He pounded his fists, and his voice scared us all.

"Let us together drive this vermin from our own shores! Back to the sea with it! Be gone, **eitinn!**"

And the very next morning, nary a man, nor woman, nor child was sick with the pestilence. Not a cough was heard in all o'Kinsale. Pa is God fearin' man, but sometimes times call fer the old ways.

"A good omen, **gealach** is. A good omen," I say aloud. Ma nods at me but motions to the door.

"Isn't that right my Flanagan," I say to my own dear son. He looks at me.

"Aye, Ma, *gealachhhhh.*"

I laugh long and hard. I love me own fine son.

"Fiona . . . go," Ma stands now. She is a haggard old woman, worked every day of her life. My heart breaks when I look at her sometimes, but then I also know the strength she has in her heart. A strength I've needed me own self, as I wait for my man to come home. Come home to me in Kinsale. Come back from across the sea. To his family. To me, And Flanagan.

But Joe McAdams will come back, McAdams are tied to the sea. They cannot leave it. They will die if they do. That's how I know me own Joe will come back to me.

I stand and take my coat.

Yesterday was a fourteen-hour day, today will be the same. Aye, a good catch yesterday though, 'tis a grand thing really, I have to clean many a fish today . . . herring, mackerel, skad, turbot, haddock, sole, hake, cod, ling, bream, gurnet and pilchards.

Off with me. I bend to kiss my boy goodbye.

"Little Flanagan . . . my dearest boy . . . be happy my lad, yer Pa's away in a fine, grand land . . . but he's comin' back, sure as day, he is . . . he's comin' back fer us," I whisper.

Flanagan's eyes are the color of the sea, a *brave, courageous blue.*

"Go to your Nanna now, dear boy, time fer a nap," I say, as he goes to his cot. Ma tends to him there.

"Sleep now so as fairies don't steal ye away . . ." I call, as I leave.

Ma closes her eyes and sings . . .

*Seoithín, seo hó, mo stór é, mo leanbh*
*Mo sheoid gan cealg, mo chuid gan tsaoil mhór*
*Seothín seo ho, nach mór é an taitneamh*
*Mo stóirín na leaba, na chodladh gan brón.*

*Curfá:*
*A leanbh mo chléibh go n-eirí do chodhladh leat*
*Séan is sonas gach oíche do chóir*
*Tá mise le do thaobh ag guídhe ort na mbeannacht*
*Seothín a leanbh is codail go foill.*

*Ar mhullach an tí tá síodha geala*
*Faol chaoin re an Earra ag imirt is spoirt*
*Seo iad aniar iad le glaoch ar mo leanbh*
*Le mian é tharraingt isteach san lios mór.*

*Curfá*

*Hush-a-bye, baby, my darling, my child*
*My flawless jewel, my piece of the world*
*Hush-a-bye, baby, isn't it a great joy*
*My little one in bed without any sorrows.*

*Child of my heart, sleep calmly*
*And well all night and be happy*
*I'm by your side praying for blessings on you,*
*Hush-a-bye, baby and sleep for now.*

*On top of the house there are white fairies*
*Playing and frolicking under the gentle moonlight*
*Here they come calling my baby*
*To draw him into their great fairy mound.*

# Joe

"Two sons, Mr. McAdams. Twins."

The doctor's face looks stern. Eyes blank.

Strange.

"Aye, thanks be to ya, " I say. These Americans are hard to read. Not like the Irish, whose eyes are open windows.

"May I see m'boys?" I ask him.

"Right this way," the doctor leads me down a long white hallway. He stops at the end, in front of a glass panel.

"There," he points.

Two wee babes are inside. Wrapped in blue blankets they are, in two wee baskets with the proud name o'McAdams there for all to read. They are sleeping as peacefully as two lambs in spring.

Me own sons.

"Mr. McAdams," the doctor starts to say, taking my arm.

Again, the American and his face like a dead fish.

"'Aye—?"

"Joooooooe!" My own dear wife interrupts us—calling from down d'hallway. In a wheelchair, she is, poor thing, exhausted from the birth. A nurse in white pushes her to me.

"Fine boys, Joe," she cries.

"Mine own darling, my love, aye, they are fine lads! God be praised Mary o'mine," I say, hugging my American wife as tightly as I can.

"Yes, it wasn't so bad . . . not nearly what I thought it might be," she whispers into my ear. I look at her, and take her face in my hands.

"You've made an Irishman happy my Mary lass, you have," I say through tears.

*I am happy, I am. Aye, a beautiful lass for a wife. Two fine lads. And entrance to a university too, a fine place o'learnin' for me to make d'most o'myself.*

The old Irish blessing plays in my head . . .

*O Thou, to whom to love and be are one, hear my faith cry for them who are more thine than mine. Give each of them what is best for each. I cannot tell what it is. But Thou knowest. I only ask Thou love them and keep them With the loving and keeping Thou didst . . . Show to Mary's Son and Thine.*

I glance away, then.

That American doctor and his nurse are huddled like two codfish in a net.

I don't like this, I don't.

Their expressions are dark. Aye, the nurse's face is as white as bone. She's nodding, she is, at the doctor.

They look at me.

A wind blows hard off the sea then, in my mind. I hear Pa yellin' to me to draw the sails in fast. Storm a-comin.

I look hard at the two o'them. Aye, I know this look. I know it well, in fact.

Betrayal.

# Fiona

## 1977
❧ ～✴◦◦◦◦～ ❧

### Kinsale Cork, Ireland
### November
❧ ～✴◦◦◦◦～ ❧

*"Filleann an feall ar an bhfeallaire."* The bad deed returns on
the bad-deed doer.

I hold my boy close. He's gotten tall, he has.

*"Filleann an feall ar an bhfeallaire?"* Flanagan asks me, in
perfectly accented Gaelic.

"'Aye," I reply. My eyes are full. My son looks at me. Then he
jumps up, runs to the center of the room, all decorated for his
birthday today and throws his little arms out to the sides.

> *"Filleann an feall ar an bhfeallaire!"*
>
> *"Filleann an feall ar an bhfeallaire!"*
>
> *"Filleann an feall ar an bhfeallaire!"*

He is dancing now, a small child playing at a new game, with a new song. I jump up and interrupt my wee lad.

"Happy birthday darling boy," I say to Flanagan, in the bravest voice I can muster.

He takes my hands and we spin and dance and laugh,

*"Lá breithe shona duit!!!!"* I sing at the top of my lungs, wishing my child a proud birthday in our Gaelic tongue.

I glance at the un-ringing phone. The phone that hasnt rung in almost a year. Okay, Joe. Do as you will. But dont you forget that I will do as I will, as well.

"We Irish are clever . . . a thing's not done until it is *DONE*," I say, aloud, to myself.

Then I add, in Gaelic . . .

*Brìgh gach cluiche gu dheireadh.*
*The essence of a game is at its end.*

# PART 4

# Tess

## 2016

### New York, New York
### December

I look into the woman's enormous eyes.

They are full of many things.

Her eyes are bigger than usual, on the exhibit wall in the museum, each eye is about . . . four by six feet, to be exact.

I step back from the thirty foot black and white photograph that covers the wall.

Yes, the eyes say it all. No words necessary.

I glance up at the lettering above the first photo . . .

**_Sand-to-Sea, A Mother's Love_**

_Photography by Peter Sloane_

I look back at the eyes. Everyone is looking at her eyes. I look around the room, The museum is packed. New York is very different from anywhere else I've ever been. Millions and millions of people clog every corner. On the sidewalks, streets, inside the buildings, like this one.

I am back to her enormous eyes.

I see sadness. I see gladness. I see a mother's love. Sadness at her children leaving, gladness because they leave for their new lives.

The lighting is surreal. Expert. Her face is an oval, white with moonlight.

And then there is the hatchling. Tiny. In, silhouette. A tiny eclipsed body in front of an enormous moon-mother face. The perspective is genius. A magnificent shining orb that is a face, is watching over the baby. It is Hina, her eyes on Kauila's child. I am drawn to the face. Her eyes pull me in. I step up onto the platform and over the red rope.

There is something more in those eyes.

Wistfulness. There is courage there . . . yes. But also a wistful longing. Like the eyes of a *hatchling*.

Suddenly I am hurtling back in time . . . to a day long ago.

"Mama . . ." I put my hands in the air to be picked up.

Mama reaches down and scoops me in one motion. Weeeeeee . . . it's fun to sail through the air.

"Mama," I say, putting my arms around her neck and snuggling her cheek.

"Tessie . . ." she purrs in my ear.

She walks with me to the stove and stirs a big pot of soup. "Mama . . ."

"Yesssss . . ."

"Am I too big to pick up?

"Nooooo"

"I am, I'm too big . . ."

"Not at all Tess O'Conner. You are not too big to pick up."

"Okay," I giggle.

But I do feel too big. After all I'm almost four years old. I touch Mama's hair.

"Pretty . . ." I say to her.

"Thank ye darling,'" Mama says, in her special way of talking. She sounds different from the other mothers. Her words bounce up and down like a song. The other mothers sound like talking. Talking's okay. But it's not like singing!

"Thank ye darlin' . . ." I say, imitating Mama.

"That's me Irish lass . . . ye sound like a true lassie of the isle . . ."

"A true lassie of the isle . . ." I repeat . . .

Mama laughs. She laughs too hard, she starts to cough. She has to put me down.

"Mama . . . too much laughing!" I cry, clapping my hands together. Mama stops and puts her hands on her hips.

She clears her voice. Then she takes my hands in hers and swings me around in a circle . . . she starts to really sing!

*How many miles to Dub-l-in?*
*Three score\* and ten,*
*Will we be there by candle-light?*
*Yes and back again;*
*Hupp, hupp my little horse,*
*Hupp, hupp, again.*

I laugh as I spin, and I sing with her.

*Hupp, hupp my little horse,*
*Hupp, hupp, again.*

I let go of Mama's hands and I spin as fast as I can . . . I hear her laughing and clapping.

"Go, Tessie, go!"

I spin faster!

Then . . . I feel myself tip . . . but I keep spinning because it is so much fun . . . I collide with a table and I hear a loud *womp* noise. I realize the *womp* noise is me. I have landed on the ground. The room is still spinning.

"Tess!"

Mama comes tearing over to me.

"My goodness Tessie girl! You were a-spinnin like the wind, you were . . ."

She takes me in her arms. I look over her shoulder at the items strewn across the floor from the table falling over. A book is open, and a photograph is there. The eyes in the photograph stare up at me.

They are enormous eyes! *Big!*

A pretty lady's eyes. Perfectly round, longer on the top and bottom. She looks like a fairy princess. She just needs a crown and she would be one!

"Mama . . ." I say, "a fairy princess . . . look . . . she has big eyes!"

I feel Mama freeze without turning around. She makes a noise. She puts me down and turns around. She slowly gathers up the books and magazines on the floor. She takes the photo and looks at it.

"Here Tessie, say hello to Claire . . ."

"Hello Claire . . ." I say to the princess in the picture.

"Is she a princess, Mama?" I ask.

"I always think of her as a princess Tessie . . . she can be your princess too, would you like that?"

"Yes, Mama!"

"I'll tell you what Tess, if you promise to be real, real careful . . . I mean real careful—for that there's the only princess photo I've got—you can put her in your own room . . ."

"I can!" I shout.

"Yes—but only if you are careful with her," Mama says to me. Her face is very serious.

"I promise, Mama!"

That night, after my bath, I got into bed with my dollies. The princess doll is my favorite. She has a gold crown, it stays on her head, even when she sleeps.

I realize I forgot something! I pop out of my bed and get the princess photograph.

"Goodnight Princess Claire," I whisper to it.

I decide to put the photograph on the pillow next to my head. I don't want Princess Claire to be lonely during the night.

Every morning, I carefully put Princess Claire back on my dresser so Mama could see her there.

Princess Claire has eyes so big they can see me wherever I stand in my room. I try to stand in all four corners . . . to test the princess. Yep—she sees me. Her eyes travel up and over the furniture and past my toys and around my clothes and find me wherever I am. I hide in my closet . . . poke my head out—there she is! Big eyes seeing me! I feel safe with her near me.

*"Isn't that Tess McAdams—the woman in the photos?"* a voice in the museum yells loudly, behind me. I turn. I realize I am in the museum, back in the present moment. I see a thousand faces turn to me. A *gasp* erupts.

I turn back again and look at the enormous thirty-foot photograph behind me. The woman there. The enormous eyes. *Princess Claire's eyes.*

My mother. My mother, Claire O'Conner looks at me from the looming wall. *My real mother,* even though I called Grandmother, *Mother.* Grandmother didn't want to tell a young child that her own mother had died.

The photograph is unmistakable. Claire's eyes. My eyes. And, suddenly, everything makes sense to me as I look at the moonglow photo that Peter took of my face, which is suddenly, very clearly now—my own mother's face. Wistfulness, courage and longing are there, my mother's, and mine, in the blue light of the magnificent photograph.

"Yes—I am Tess O'Conner," I say loudly.

"O'Conner?" calls a woman from the crowd.

"Well, Tess McAdams now. These photographs document my work in Hawaii. On the island of Maui. I save sea turtles there. It is my life's work. I have a hospital, a rescue boat, a hatchery. We are in the business of saving sea turtles from the world's greed."

The crowd is silent.

"I *understand* sea turtles. I *understand* their plight," I continue.

"I know what it is, to feel small and alone. To feel *helpless.*

I know the joy in seeing a shining face to trust. Courage comes when we follow the light, we trust it guide us home."

I turn and motion to the photographs.

"These hatchlings grow beneath the sand and hatch, they dig upwards and break the surface of the sand. They see the moon," I motion to the shining face, the big eyes. My face, my mother's eyes.

*"They see mother . . . in the form of a shining moon above, and they follow her light home to the sea,"* I say to the people, "or so says Hawaiian legend."

"Are you Hawaiian?" someone calls from the crowd.

"No. But I live in Hawaii now."

"But she's Hawaiian in 'er heart!" an Aussie voice calls from the back of the crowd. Everyone turns to see Peter Sloane standing there.

"I can vouch for this . . . Tessie McAdams is the spirit of Hawaii . . . in fact she is the spirit of each and every baby turtle. She's pure courage, folks."

Peter makes his way through the throngs of people and reaches me at the front.

"Mr. Sloane . . . hello, Mitch Johnson, New York Times . . . you shot this series, yes?"

"Sure did," Peter says in his best Australian drawl.

"Did Ms. McAdams pose for you . . . or was it . . . spontaneous . . . ?" the reporter asked.

"Ms. McAdams didn't know I was there. I believe . . . she thought I was asleep in my tent. Or . . . on a night dive with her husband."

"Ms. McAdams . . . do you have anything to say about the series . . . this photo essay?" A woman calls from behind the

New York Times journalist.

I look at her. Then, at the crowd.

"Look hard at these photos . . . look hard and remember. Your heart knows what the right thing to do is. Those without voices, need our help the most. The turtles. We must speak for the turtles."

I smile at Peter and glance back at the photograph covering the wall. *"I love you, Princess Claire,"* I whisper.

Then I leave the museum. I don't want to be late for my flight back to Hawaii.

# Marama

Hana, Maui
December 24

He wants a meeting. John. *Haoles* make me nervous. Before the haoles, we were free. Our way of life was ours. Not theirs.

Then, the haoles. Now, we suffer with imbalance. The sun rises and the sun sets. The tides come and the tides recede. The moon rises and falls. Yet our people are not in sync. We have lost our place in all of this. We are not in rhythm with nature. We have lost our footing.

It is because of the *qaitu* presence. There is a grievance. The ghosts of ancestors have risen up from the underworld. They are here. They have disrupted our balance. We must regain balance!

Ku gave his wisdom. As Kahuna—I must follow his words. Hina—his wife will show the way. She knows the way, we have only to follow her.

*Hina's light will lead us away from darkness.* Hina is our moon to follow. I shall tell this to the haole, as Kahuna, as commanded by Ku.

I place my face in my hands. When I rise from my chair, I feel calmed. Yes. I know what to do. I close the door to my hut carefully.

Then I stop, and drop three bamboo stalks in front of it. I arrange them into the shape of an arrow.

I walk a few steps away from the door, and lay another stalk. I walk a few more steps, and drop another. A few more steps then, and another.

I drop bamboo stalks behind me as I walk to the southeast corner of the bamboo forest. The side that skirts the cliff, above the sea.

Beautiful soft purple light surrounds me.

Twilight.

I smile. Hina will be here soon to keep me company.

Walking through the deepening inkiness, I listen to the forest speak. The hum of birds' wings overhead in the trees, tells me to trust. Scampering little feet under bushes reminds me to laugh.

Chirps of crickets. Belly burps of frogs. It's a song of *togetherness.* My feet fall silently.

I have walked this path since I was old enough to walk. I have trusted these feet to carry me since I was old enough to realize they would carry me. *They will always carry me.* Yes, I say to the forest. I have heard you.

Just then Hina sends down a kiss. A long blue beam curls around my face and touches my cheeks. I raise my arms to her. Hina! A moon to follow. I am safe. At peace. It is Hina, she has balanced me.

I decide to sing her a song . . .

*Kamali'i 'ike 'ole I ka helu po, Little children who cannot count the nights*
*Muku Nei, muku, ka malama, Muku is here, Muku the dark moon*
*Hilo nei, kau ka Hoaka, Hilo, followed by Hoaka*
*'Eha ku, 'Eha 'ole, eae, Four ku, four 'ole*
*Huna, Mohalu, Hua, Akua,*
*Huna, Mohalu, Hua, Akua*

My voice echoes inside my chest and spreads outward to my limbs. The vibrations fill me with joy. Inside this joy I see the forest around me with love. I look at the bend of a palm. The flash of eyes, under a rock. The opening, of a flower. I bend my body to greet the flower. I fall to the ground and smile at who is under the rock. I touch the petals of the flower delicately, their scent fills my nose.

I walk in Hina's wake, jumping from puddles of blue light. One after another, after another. Hina is a fine leader! She leads me to explosions of roots—erupting from the floor, colored lavender in her light. And to cries from the canopy of the forest, a tail here, a claw there. Darting, pausing.

I breathe very deeply, a life giving scent . . . vegetation, moisture, soil, and plants and wood.

Oh . . . now, tickles on my feet! I look down to see leaf-cutter ants, carrying harvest leaves crossing over my feet . . . they are funny in their march, observing my feet to be no more than a bump in the road. I watch them parade to their giant underground nests where I know they will store the bits of plants to make the fungus they eat.

Hina throws down a huge plume of light and I glimpse a rare sight; a spectacular blue butterfly, her wings a translucent blend of sapphires and purples, made ever more exquisite in this magnificent early evening light.

Then, Hina flexes her beaming fingers, uncovering a brightly colored green and black poison dart frog, who is a friend to all that honor his space.

I stop now. I look at the frog. I look up at Hina. She has paused here for me. *Is this a message?*

I crouch to my knees, in front of the frog. I bring my face very close to his. He looks at me and darts his tongue at me quickly. His eyes are cloudy.

*Caution.* That is what he says.

Then, breaking my gaze with the frog is the cry of a toucan, from high in the canopy.

*Hmmm,* I think to myself.

I continue on my way. I sing again . . .

**Kamali'i 'ike 'ole I ka helu po**
*Little children who cannot count the nights*
**Muku Nei, muku, ka malama**
*Muku is here, Muku the dark moon*
**Hilo nei, kau ka Hoaka**
*Hilo, followed by Hoaka*
**'Eha ku, 'Eha 'ole, eae**
*Four ku, four 'ole*
**Huna, Mohalu, Hua, Akua**
**Huna, Mohalu, Hua, Akua**

And then, suddenly, beneath my singing, a low, steady rhythm grows louder . . .

*Click.*
*Click.*
*Click.*
*Clack.*
*Clack.*
*Clack.*
*Wacketty.*
*Woocketty.*
*Wicketty.*
*Thud.*
*Thud.*
*Thud.*

Trunks and stalks hit together in rhyme, in rhythm. As many times as I have traversed this path, as many times from a child to an old woman of eighty, it is always the same. A rush of excitement. A serenaded joy. A show. A symphony.

The bamboo greets me, in soft staccato, and grows louder. With every footfall I am closer.

Here at this entrance, the clicks and the clacks and the thuds are paired with a rush, rush, rush sound of the sea. Waves lap and crash upon the shore and combine to create a special rendition that only adds to the percussion of the sound.

I drop my last bamboo stalk. I've finished my trail for the haole.

A very strong sea breeze wafts up from below suddenly, it is a conductor's wand.

*And—the bamboo trunks begin to really play for me.*

Low notes of the widest stalks are pleasant alto thuds. Atop those are the lighter clickety, clackety beats of the short thin stems. Mid sized stalks carry a bouncy full melody that echoes the others' harmony.

My feet rise instinctively, I am on my toes. I kick softly to the right, then softly to the left.

I spin.

My feet find their alighted steps as they have done since I was a child.

I dance.

*Clicketty-clacketty-thud-thud-thud-wop-wop-wop . . . clicketty-thud-wop . . .*

My toes are strong and propel me like a grasshopper . . . I bounce. I jump. I spring.

My arms fly out to the sides in time with my feet, which are in time with the bamboo music.

*Hina joins me.* We spin and sway in layers of shine. Her dancing glows the bamboo forest in an incredible white-green hue. We spin, and spin, and spin.

*"MARAMA!"*

A foreign noise ends the dance. It cuts through the forest. Imbalance. Bamboo stops. The butterflies freeze. Slithers halt. Canopy is silent. We are interrupted, Hina and I. Abruptly, I stop dancing. He is here. The haole has found my trail.

I turn.

*But—what is this?*

I rub my eyes. I look again.

*Two?*

I back up and take a deep breath.

I see—*two haoles?*

Then—another!

*Three haoles!*

I cry out—I turn, I look around to the forest. I see the poison dart frog, still staring at me from the floor.

I turn back once again. My eyes deceive me. I must be going mad. A spell has taken me—because I now see *FOUR*.

*Four haoles.*

*No!*

*I rub my eyes with my fists.*

I open my eyes. Something is wrong. My old eyes are seeing four yellow-haired haoles.

One is behind a tall trunk.

Across from him, a second is next to a rotten stalk.

To the left of him is a third between young stalks.

Behind the three—a fourth. A fourth haole.

I am frozen.

Not one—but four *qaitu* confront me! All at once.

Ku . . . Ku said to follow the moon. Hina.

*"Hina?"* . . . I breathe, looking upwards. And—she sends down a spotlight of blue.

It floods the area. I see, now. Four blonde haoles.

**Qaitu! Four Qaitu!**

I am starting to shake.

"Hina . . . help me . . ." I cry aloud.

Then—*as if by the same evil*—an angry, fierce wind—rips the bamboo trunks and stalks wildly. I hear the cracking of some of them breaking. Others bend into painful ninety-degree angles, and hold this horrific position.

When they snap back—it as if a thousand sling-shots go off. The sound they make is like none I've ever heard before. It is a  scream. A sound of necks that are trunks, breaking.

I look at the haoles.

*I hold up both my hands to them!* None of them move.

**"Qaitu!** *Speak!"* I cry aloud, shaking the forest with my wail.

**"What is your grievance?"**

Silence.

**"A Kahuna orders you! I will hear you now!"**

Hina moves in closer and illuminates their faces for me. I see why they haven't answered!

They are all staring open-mouthed at—*eachother!* It is as if I am not here at all. All four haoles, all yellow-haired haoles are staring at one another. Mouths hanging open. Then Hina intervenes.

*Ku's wife rises in the sky . . .*

She extends a long winding finger of light out through the trees and over the cliff to the sea.

A white flash of light explodes as the tip of her finger hits the water. A million little bombs go off as the water comes alive.

The four haoles turn toward the sea.

I suddenly realize what Hina is doing. She is summoning someone. Her.

"Kauila," I whisper.

Hina's finger withdraws slightly, and the blinding sparkle of light dims a bit.

A shell, surfaces. It pauses.

Then, it moves slowly following Hina's finger. The shell is heading our way.

The four haoles swing their heads from the sea—to me.

They look at me. They start walking. They form a circle around me. Their blonde heads glow in the moonlight like four beacons.

"Marama! Here I am—it is me—John!" one haole yells at me.

"No I am John," yells the haole to his right. He looks just like him.

"Jake—why are you here!" yells the one who calls himself John to the one who is his mirror image.

"Maybe I am John!" yells a third haole, in a voice that is coy. He looks like the other two.

"Flanagan!" yells the fourth blonde haole, his voice is gravelly, and old. Yes, Hina's light shows he is much older than the others.

"Aye, boy, I've been looking for ye, I have," the old haole says.

**"Brìgh gach cluiche gu dheireadh,"** the haole called Flanagan says in a language I don't recognize, though it has the same music that our Hawaiian language has.

"*The essence of a game is at its end,*" Flanagan adds, looking at all of us.

"'Tis not ye brothers' fault, Flanagan. Tis mine," the older haole says.

"How are YOU here, Pa? What is going on?" cries the one that called himself John, first.

The older haole looks at John, then at the ground.

"I've been following him, I have." He points to Flanagan. "Me own son."

"You are my brother?" yells the first to call himself John.

"Aye." The one called Flanagan answered, with the foreign tongue that sounds like Hawaiian music. His words have a flattened sound, different from the other haoles.

The old haole puts his face in his hands. "Tis true," he says, "I meant to send for her. I did, I did, Flanagan. Tis me own fault."

"Yer a liar, ye are, Joe McAdams," Flanagan replies.

"Another brother." It was the second haole who called himself John, who is really *Jake*, that is speaking now.

"ANOTHER BROTHER." Jake's words ricochet like bullets across the dark forest. The sharp-pitched wail freezes my blood.

"JAKE—JAKE . . . TAKE IT EASY," John says to his twin. He moves to take his arm. Jake snaps it away.

"Are you, *simple*, too?" Jake asks Flanagan. "ARE YOU?" he screams.

"No, not I," Flanagan says. "Aye, I was born clever. Smart. Too smart. *'Aye, too smart for me' own good.'*"

Then, the haole called Flanagan speaks again, but in a different way. He sounds like the haole, John. His speech, sounds like John's speech. He has changed the way he speaks, to sound exactly like John.

*"Yes, I was born too smart for my own good,"* Flanagan says.

Joe McAdams is staring at his three sons. His face haunts me. I have seen this face before. When I was a girl, the honu that died leaving her eggs in my care, had this face.

*"An American accent. And an Irish accent,"* John says to Flanagan.

Then he raises his voice at him. "Tell me, just how long have you been here, Flanagan?"

"Aye, brother o'mine, I've always been here. Left Kinsale, I did, after me' own Ma died. After he—killed her down dead."

Flanagan smiles at John, and repeats himself, in the American accent, *"Yes, brother of mine, I've always been here. Left Kinsale, after my mother died. After, he—killed her."*

John's mouth drops open.

"I wanted to come back, Flanagan," Joe interrupts. "I wanted to, son."

"Aye. But didya? Didya Pa?" Flanagan yells. "I found her. I did, I found her. Drowned in the sea. Stones in her pockets. She waited, Pa."

Joe is looking at his shoes. They are old, I see. Holes, in the toes.

"Ma waited, and waited, and waited. Like, a good Irish lass. She waited for you like she waits for d'tide. D'tide, it comes in every morn, Pa, as ye know. And she always told me ye were like d'tide. That, the Irish were like d'tide. Reliable. Honest. Good. Decent. Loyal."

Flanagan smiles then. He takes a cigarette from his shirt pocket and lights it. He takes a long deep drag, then, blows it out slowly. Jake coughs next to him.

John's face is red, and his eyes are bulging. He continues to look at Flanagan. He sees that he is blonde, like himself. Blue eyed, like himself. *Like himself . . . and Jake.* He remembers the smell of cigarettes in Oahu.

Jake doesn't smoke.

*"It was you,"* John spits, his words drop like stones.

*"You.* Bubble Cave. Waikiki. Oahu. Honu Hospital."

*"It has been you, all the time."*

Flanagan looks at John. ***"Brìgh gach cluiche gu dheireadh,"*** he says, cursing.

John spits at his Gaelic curse. He rounds on him, face red with rage.

"Yes—this game is at its *end,* Flanagan, in Gaelic and in English!

It was you—you, Flanagan . . . who has been killing our turtles! Your operation, isn't it! *You are the killer.* You are the *poacher. It was YOU—not Jake, all along!* It was you who attacked my wife."

John looks at Flanagan with the face of Ku.

"You had me—all of us—believing it was *Jake,*" John cries.

***"Brigh gach cluiche gu dheireadh,"*** Flanagan says again.

***"Tá tú diabhal!"*** John spits back at him. *"Devil,"* he adds.

Flanagan looks at Jake, then. Hina shines brightly on their faces. There is such a resemblance between all the boys.

"'Twas easy. 'Aye twas. You, with all yer learnin'. Me with none o'dat. You all high n'mighty. "Aye . . . like Pa. High n'mighty. But *I fooled ya,* didn't I. Right under yer noses. Made a tidy bundle of money, too." Flanagan slapped his thigh hard, and hollers an eerie laugh. It echoes off the bamboo trunks.

*"Tttt-iii-dddd-yyy bundle of money, I did,"* he repeats, singing, sounding out each letter like a five year old might do. A rank, cigarette smell emanates from him. It is a heavy, sickly smell.

"Naw, I ain't stupid. Not I," Flanagan looks at his father, who looks a great deal older than he did moments ago.

Then Flanagan turns to face Jake. "Tis such a, *shame,*" he said to him, in a sarcastic voice. "A shame, 'tis, 'tis . . ." He looks Jake up and down. He sees the way Jake holds his hands in a clasping, nervous way. His legs bowed a little, confused, scared.

Flanagan mimics him. He copies his stance, clasps his own hands and bends his legs.

"'Aye . . . the easiest to fool of all, right here, 'tis slow and stupid right here, in plain sight," Flanagan says, mocking his brother.

Jake tries to straighten up. Balls up his fists at his side. Straightens his legs.

Flanagan laughs and spins around to Joe.

"So. This is what ye prefer, ya do, Pa? Slow n'stupid. Better that, than Flanagan. Joe prefers slow n'stupid to his own kin home in Kinsale." Flanagan's face is as white as a corpse in the blazing moonlight. He moves closer to Joe. He holds up a fist.

*"Cha tèid nì sam bith san dòrn dùinte!"* he yells at his father. *"Nothing can get into a closed fist, Pa."*

Joe looks at his son and says nothing.

Then—*a screeching sound* explodes. It is coming from Flanagan. *A scream.* A wail. It lifts my skin from my bones. It is a foreign sound, not from these Polynesian shores. I look at Flanagan, and I see his face is suddenly *twisted into another face.* This face, *a woman's face,* is screaming, a wailing, piercing cry.

Joe falls to his knees—he appears to recognize this new screaming face.

*Three ear-shattering screams explode from Flanagan's throat.*

He has thrust his arms wide open and his eyes are turned up inside his head.

"Banshee!" screams Joe, his face, acute horror. *"Banshee! Ye come from Ireland ye have! Ye come for me, ye do . . . !"*

Flanagan opens his mouth as wide as he can—and screams the banshee scream again. Joe doubles backward. Stumbles. Holds his hands to his ears.

*"'Tis Fiona! 'Tis dead Fiona—come back fer her old Joe as a banshee!"* Joe cries. Then he collapses to the forest floor.

*Banshee* . . . I know this word. I know this word . . . a haole from long ago . . . yes. A haole told grandmother of a *qaitu* spirit called *banshee* . . . yes. The banshee spirit was a *qaitu* that rose to tell of a death. *The banshee foretells death!*

The banshee wailing stops abruptly. Flanagan's head drops to the side. His face returns to normal.

Then, Hina jumps from Flanagan's face—to the simple haole's face. The haole, Jake. Something is happening now, to Jake. I watch, in horror.

It is like . . . the pieces of Jake's face . . . are falling apart. The glue that was holding them together melt. Pieces fall away from each other.

All of a sudden—Jake throws his arms out. He grabs at something under his coat. A long object. It flashes in the moonlight. A knife. But, not any *ordinary knife*. This one is tipped in gasoline. I can smell it. Jake draws out a match, lights the knife and begins to dance with it. *Spin* with it. Around and around and around.

I hear something, then from far away.

*A scraping sound.*

Low.

Heavy.

Grinding.

Dragging.

I turn.

*Something large is coming from the darkness.*

Its outline takes shape in the shadows. It is . . . as large as a house. The scraping sound gets louder.

*The quarreling haoles don't notice.*

Yet, the thing is moving quicker now. Scraping gives way to loud booms.

Feet.

**Boom—boom—boom—boom.**

My body jumps with every boom. I hold onto a bamboo trunk.

**BOOM—BOOM—BOOM—BOOM.**

As I bounce up and down with the moving earth, I look at the haoles, they are trying to fight off Jake and his flaming-knife. They are screaming, yelling, kicking, tearing. A bloody, fiery battle.

*"Arrrgghhh"* screams the haole called Jake, as he pounces onto Flanagan with the fire sword.

*"Be gone ye simple fool!"* cries Flanagan, kicking him hard in the stomach, the tip of the fire sword lancing his chest.

*"Stop!!!!"* screams John, as he throws himself between the two, the fire from the sword suddenly ignites Flanagan's shirt.

The haole father throws himself at all of them . . . *"STOP! STOOOOOOOOP me boys!"* he screams.

The fire jumps from one brother to the next brother to the next brother to the father.

Then—all is muted in a huge *WHOOOOOOOOOOOOOOSH,* as an ocean wind explodes upward, out of the sea—it rattles the bamboo trunks wildly with its force! The forest becomes a screaming thudding thunder! Two-foot wide trunks bend all the way to the ground—then—SNAP—in the opposite direction. The deafening percussion drowns out all sound. I feel my eardrums snapping.

**THUD-THUD-THUD-THUD-THUD-THUD.**

**THUD-THUD-THUD-THUD-THUD-THUD.**

**THUD-THUD-THUD-THUD-THUD-THUD.**

The four fighting, flaming haoles have now become a silent movie, as the bamboo crashes deafeningly. Then, something nudges me from behind.

I turn.

*And, everything stops for me.*

*Everything.*

*Stops.*

Eighty years. I have waited eighty years. Eighty years melt into this moment.

Her eyes.

I am lost in her eyes.

Sparkling as brightly as black diamonds.

*Sparkling with love.*

*The love of a million mothers.*

Tears stream down my old, withered cheeks. She looks at me and pauses, opening and closing her huge eyes slowly. Then, she nods for me to step aside.

*I do as Kauila commands.*

She begins her long, slow, crunching, grinding crawl toward the fire. Limbs are flying out of its flames. Her dark silhouette as big as a boulder, approaches.

Then—Hina throws down both her hands in an outward gesture, illuminating Kauila's form.

Seven feet high. Ten feet long. Eight feet wide.

My vantage point uniquely frames her enormous turtle body with flames around it, as she stands, looking at the screaming haoles.

Then—she charges.

Into the flames.

Then—a loud chomping sound.

Then—screams.

I race from my hiding space to see better. She has Flanagan in her jaw! And then with one powerful swinging motion of her enormous head—she knifes him from the right—to the left, flinging him, hard, a hundred feet.

He hits a tree. The intense cracking sound tells me his bones are shattered, crushed, instantly—in this one mighty crash.

Kauila turns, facing the other burning haoles. She rears up—takes a deep breath, lowers her head—and charges, smashing into them, with the blinding full force of her armored shell.

In an instant—the three haoles are sent hurtling—flying through the dark night like fiery catapults, in all directions. *It's a death throw.*

Joe hits a wide bamboo trunk, his head splits open immediately.

John and Jake—fly together as one flaming mass—shooting through the trees, and out over the cliff. They hit the water together. And, submerge.

Hina shines down upon Kauila.

I look at her.

She is part of a long ago earth landscape. A time, before the ancients. *The time, before time.* She looks like the first sea turtle ever to be born. The very *first* one. That is what she looks like, to me.

I can't help myself, I sit down and gaze upon her. Her front and back legs are trees. Her shell is the helmet shape of a *leatherback*, but far more elaborate, sharp nobs running front to back, like armor.

As I watch her, I realize her chest is moving up and down. Her skin expands and contracts.

*Kauila is sighing.*

Then, she turns around and looks to the sea. Her enormous

head has a grace to it. It waves softly to the right and softly to the left as she takes in the view. She doesn't rush. She takes her time.

Then Kauila looks up at Hina.

Slowly, Hina sends a finger of light down through the bamboo. It snakes down through the upper canopy, through the branches. It spills across the white bark of the trees.

It finally reaches the great turtle.

The blue beam finger touches one side of Kauila's face, then the other.

Then, the fingers spread outward, sliding over her shell like a sister's hand. Hina is stroking Kauila's shell as one would rub the back of a distressed child.

The prehistoric turtle folds her legs beneath her and settles onto the forest floor. Then, she closes her eyes.

All is quiet.

I get up.

I don't look back—it's time to go home.

# John

*Clarity.* As I drown, it comes. *The clarity of blindness.*

Images flutter before my dying eyes. Pa. Me. Flanagan. Jake. Pa was blinded by ambition. I was blinded by pride. Flanagan was blinded by revenge. And, Jake, permanently blinded by fate.

We, four McAdams men, could not see the truth. We were blind, in the *darkness.* Out of the *light* . . . so we couldn't find our way home.

*Is í ding di féin a scoileann an dair,* Beware of the enemy within, the qaitu within . . . as my lungs heave and ache for air, I feel the enemy within my chest. It is a strong enemy. *It hurts.*

*Is í ding di féin a scoileann an dair,* Beware of the enemy within, the qaitu, within . . . as greed destroys the earth, humanity feels the enemy within its soul. It is a strong enemy. *It hurts.*

The turtles knew. They knew to escape the darkness by following the light home. Hina's light, home.

My closing eyes catch sight of Jake's lifeless body spiraling downward past me into the watery abyss, finally at peace.

*Tess.* How I will miss you. I am suddenly, incomprehensibly sad.

*Clarity.* As I die, it comes.

# Tess

Three hard knocks.

John!

I fling open the door. Christmas bells jingle.

On my steps is a stranger dressed in blue. A sharp Maui wind sails over his shoulder, into my house from the sea.

"Mrs. McAdams . . . there's been . . . an accident . . ."

His mouth is moving, but suddenly I can't hear him.

My mind transports me to Marama, I am with her in the bamboo forest. The steady ocean wind is with us there as well, its strength thuds millions of bamboo trunks together. Click-click-click-thud-thud-thud.

I can hear nothing else.

The man in blue still appears to be speaking.

Bamboo percussion is thunderous now . . . low thuds from wide bamboo trunks, staccato, higher notes from thinner stalks.

Then, Hina, the moon goddess interrupts the man in blue. She looks down, drenching him in light.

She extends a finger, pointing at the sea. How it sparkles in her sheen. The waves wink at me.

"Mrs. McAdams . . . ?"

I can hear him now.

"Ma'am . . . ?"

I look at him.

His head is fair, it catches the moonlight. I am reminded of my husband. John.

"Please ma'am . . ." the man on my steps says to me.

But Hina's glowing arms are around me, tight. I look to the sea, a silent flicker of diamonds.

> ***Nana ka maka;***
> ***ho`olohe ka pepeiao;***
> ***pa`a ka waha . . .***
>
> *Observe with the eyes;*
> *listen with the ears;*
> *shut the mouth.*
> *Thus one learns.*

Polynesian words echo in my mind. I do as Hina commands.

# Marama

On the floor of my hut, I rest awhile. I breathe easily. My heart is light as I sleep.

Later, I open my eyes to see Hina, once again, her index finger pointing at me to come, come with her. I rise, and smooth my clothes. I open the door and follow her finger as it lights the path down through the forest.

Her light is very strong tonight, it is easy to follow her. I walk in the blue beam through the forest heading west, and then out . . . as it leads me to Hana's most secluded beach. The sand, the water shimmer, like diamonds. I don't think I've ever seen such sparkle.

I look hard now at what Hina is illuminating so brightly for me. The water, the waves, the surf, blindingly bright with moonlight.

Tess!

I go to her in silence. We take hands. We say nothing. We wait. We keep our eyes on the moon.

# She

He is light.

I rise slowly.

Up, up, up.

The surface, now.

I swim.

Soon, the shore.

The path.

I hurry.

Sand. Forest.

I arrive.

I shift, he slides, the floor.

I look up.

I nod at Ku.

I leave him.

Then, I go.

# Marama

We don't have to wait long.

A dark object on the sea, suddenly comes into view under Hina's gaze.

*"Kauila,"* I whisper as her form becomes larger. She comes ashore and looks at me. Then, at Tess.

I take Tess's hand and crawl atop Kauila's back, pulling the slight girl up high onto the enormous shell with me.

Kauila turns and soon we are in the water. Hina's blazing moonbeams draw a line across the waves to our destination.

We start to glide toward it.

Tess's face is awash in blue moonglow.

# She

I swim.
Soon, the shore.
The path.
I hurry.
Sand. Forest.
I arrive, again.
I shift, they slide, the floor.
I look up.
I nod at Ku.
Three, now.
Two, embrace.
The third, stares.
Eyes, like mine.
Wise.
My head moves.
Her head moves.
Then, I go.
I always, remember.
I never forget.
Her eyes are with me.
Forever.

# Tess

I take my husband in my arms.
He is wet, he smells like the sea.
Hina hugs us as we hug each other.
Awash in moonglow, all is made right.
Love wins.

# THE END

# Epilogue

# Sean

## 2024

### Hana, Maui
### December 24

"Liam . . . can you pass me my mask, please?

"Sure. Here."

I put my mask on, I pull the straps real tight like Papa says to. I see that Liam has done his properly."

"Ready?" I say to my twin. I have my flippers tucked under my right arm. Liam has his, tucked under his left arm. We are then able to grasp hands.

"Let's go!" I yell.

We run down the beach in front of our house . . . and across the sand . . . we hold hands, as we have always done. Papa says its best for brothers to do things together. Especially special brothers like us. *Twins.*

Splash! We are in the water. We plop down and fumble for our fins. Liam giggles, which gets me giggling. We get the fish-feet on and pop our breathing tubes into our mouths. We hold hands again and wade out, backwards. Soon we are underneath the sea.

We've done this *a thousand times*. But it's just like Mama says, every time is new. A new adventure, meeting new friends, as well as old. And we are to be on our best behavior, every time. Respect the homes we are visiting. *Look, don't touch.*

Humphrey! I see my friend Humphrey, then! Oh, I am so glad to see my dear friend. I swim nearer to the large green sea turtle with the awesome fake flipper that Papa made for him. Prosthet-ic, I mean. It's a hard word to say.

I wave to Liam, I mouth the word through my mask, *HUMPHREY,* and point to the great green sea turtle. The fake flipper is sooo cool. Liam sees Humphrey and swims over quickly. We know to stay back, several feet. We know how to respect Humphrey's space.

*He sees us!*

Liam copies Humphrey's posture and lets his arms and legs hang down, centering his back. I do the same.

Mama trained us to swim with turtles this way. We both look at each other and start by hanging our heads forward heavily. Then, we raise our heads slowly, in a lobbing sort of way, looking back and forth. Humphrey does the same. After a few moments, he turns with his right flippers and waits a moment, we turn, then Humphrey swims off and we follow. As he knows we will.

We follow Humphrey along the coastal reef of Hana. He picks up his pace and our flippers match his speed. He stops suddenly, and we do as well, he sees algae growing from a cluster of brain coral. With a soft jettison of his hind flippers, he is able to grab the algae with his beak, yank it once, and swallow. Liam looks at me in awe. That—we cannot do. Yet.

I watch Papa's fake flipper working perfectly with Humphrey's three real ones. It is as if Humphrey's accident never happened. Papa was able to reverse time. He was able to return Humphrey to the life he had before the speedboat hit him.

Mama says that helping the turtles is helping the planet. And helping the planet is what we are supposed to do. We know Mama is right. A lot of people do. She doesn't like it when people call her, *the turtle lady,* but she is glad for our new hospital. The one dedicated to *"The Turtle Lady of Hawaii."* It's where Humphrey's robot flipper was created.

Liam and I laugh when we see the photos of the old hospital. It looks a lot like the snack shack in Hana! The new hospital looks a real *people-hospital.* Except, there are only sea turtles in the rooms. But lots of people with cameras are there, not in the beds of course, they are talking to Papa about the patients. The robot flippers, especially.

Humphrey is leading us deeper into the big blue. I see Liam following along, his bright purple flippers moving just as Mama taught us, low, on-purpose kicks, using our backs as gravity centers. I watch the reef disappear behind us, and follow.

Soon, though, I realize I am losing sense of shore and sea. Papa has warned us about this. I wonder why Liam is flippering along as if he has forgotten this? I forget my on-purpose kicking and speed up, using energy I should be conserving. I yank on the purple flipper in front of me. Liam stops, turns, then points to

Humphrey. The great green sea turtle is so large I can see him clearly here, just a few feet beneath the surface, Maui sunshine is strong and lights up the sea at this shallow depth.

I see what Liam sees, Humphrey is powering along . . . he is on task. He has a goal. He . . . wants to show us something. *Ah, I understand.* Liam thinks Humphrey needs us to help him with something. It is not a fun swim for Humphrey. Nor a food swim. No. This is a mission. As if to confirm my thinking, Humphrey stops, suddenly. He turns and looks at us. His fake flipper catches sunbeams that have filtered down from above. It flashes wildly, like a siren. Liam looks at me. *Humphrey needs our help.* When he turns to swim, we both follow.

# Liam

Papa would be proud. That's all I can think as I power behind Humphrey. I remember when we found him. I was the one who saw the blood first. It was a huge red pond in the ocean. Papa sped toward it in our rescue boat. I had the binoculars and I saw Humphrey's white underbelly, streaked with the red as he floated. I was sure he was dead. I saw the bleeding stump of what used to be his flipper. The wake of the speedboat that hit him, still rocked his dying body. I felt tears form in my eyes but fought them back. Papa taught me to be strong for those who have lost their strength. Humphrey needs me, I thought as Papa dropped anchor. But it was Sean . . . who shocked us all that day.

Sean looked at Humphrey floating in his own pool of blood, and simply jumped into the red water. Without thinking to put on a wetsuit, or flippers, or even a mask. He swam through the blood, the bits of flesh and bone, and he gently turned Humphrey's maimed body over. "At least he can die right-side up," Sean had said.

Then he stayed with the turtle, petting his head, looking into his eyes. Mama jumped in after him, and helped. The two of them attempted to comfort Humphrey, who got his name, right then and there in the water.

"I wanna give him a name, Mama . . ." Sean had said.

"What a good idea, darling. What do you think?"

"Mmmm," Sean had said. He looked at the turtle and rubbed him on his head. "What is your name Mr. Turtle . . . ?"

"I had a friend in college named Humphrey," Mama said.

"Yeah?" Sean replied.

"Yes. Humphrey was studying to be a . . . turtle saver . . . Sean, just like me . . . and like Papa. He was a special friend because he had a disability. He was in a special chair called a, *wheel chair,* my love, do you know what that is?"

"Um . . . I think I saw a man in one, one time . . . at the library," Sean said.

"Yes, well that was Humphrey, he was a very brave man who had had an accident, an accident that was not his fault. But, he lost the use of his legs."

"Oh . . . that's sad."

"Well, it is but it also is happy, too," Mama said.

"Why, Mama?"

"Because Humphrey also had another thing happen to him, a thing even stronger than legs."

"What!" Sean said.

"Humphrey had courage."

"Courage . . ." Sean repeated.

"Yes, Humphrey had the courage to use his wheel chair as his legs from the moment he sat down in that chair. And for the rest of his life, he worked hard for the sea turtles. Maybe, he even worked harder for them because he had learned the lesson of loss. He had felt loss, and he knew the sea turtles had loss too . . ."

"Because the turtles have accidents sometimes. With boats."

"Yes, Sean. Like that."

Sean looked at Mama and then at Humphrey and said, "your name is Humphrey, because you have courage, Humphrey . . . okay? You need to be strong now and Papa will help you."

"Okay, ready—got it all here," called Papa from the deck, his steps making loud banging noises on the stairs. He had the emergency supplies from the boat, in his arms. I ran to untie the roping that held the dingy.

"We're losing him," Mama said softly, as we threw the supplies into the dingy, leaping from the deck to the tiny rubber raft. Sean took Humphrey's face in his hands, and just kept staring into the turtle's eyes. Somehow—the eyes didn't close. Humphrey's eyes stayed open, blinking as they fixed on Sean's face.

Papa's hands moved so quickly, it was hard to see what he was doing, but in a moment, he had Humphrey's bleeding stump tightly bandaged, the flimsy oxygen mask secured on his face, the tank attached to it—flipped to high. He had me administer the large syringe into Humphrey's side. As the powerful painkiller took effect, I saw Humphrey's face relax a little. His eyelids lowered. Papa's stethoscope against the turtle's chest read a flickering, but existent heartbeat.

We stayed like that, with Humphrey, for twenty minutes, in the water. Mama examined Humphrey, and nodded at Papa. Very gently, Papa put Humphrey into the dingy, and we got him back on board Mama's boat. "Boys . . . Kauila may have to call Humphrey home. He will be safe with her. She is waiting for him now, in case he needs to go with her. But I love my two boys, who showed such courage and compassion today," and she hugged us for a long time.

Humphrey didn't go with Kauila. He went home with us, instead. He stayed at Honu Hospital, and Papa and a bunch of other people designed his new fake flipper. It was a slow thing to happen . . . about a year, with all the try-outs. Fittings, Papa called it. But the day Humphrey swam laps in the big hospital salt pool . . . oh, that was a wonderful day. He was faster than the average turtle! Many, many people came from everywhere in the world to film Humphrey. Humphrey got real famous. Almost as famous as Mama and Papa.

As I follow Sean now in the deep, I think I must help Humphrey with whatever he needs.

# Sean

Humphrey stops.

I am glad, because I realize . . . I am tired. I also realize I have followed the turtle without knowing where I am. I glance up at the bright water above me. Still close to the surface, I could surface and take a look.

I look back at Liam. He looks upset. He is thinking the same thing. He is my twin, so this happens often. But this time, I know it is my fault, I am the one who led him here, led my brother on this journey. Papa said twins are special. They know deep down inside, what the other is thinking. Papa said there is a big responsibility in this. *"Sean, Liam, you boys are one half of the other. That means you are one-half responsible for the other. And half a boy can't do very well, can he? Nope. Half a boy needs his other half to be a full boy. So, I expect you both to respect that. Watch out for each other, it is like watching out for yourselves."* I am not sure if I have done this today. My heart pounds at the error I may have made. I look at Humphrey. He is resting, flippers hanging down easily, head lolling. I decide to be smart and at least do this. I motion to Liam before I do of course, and he follows my actions.

Fifteen minutes later, I check my tank. Only an hour left of air. I look up to the surface through the current. We could switch to snorkeling, if the air runs out. But of course, we don't know how far we have gone. I decide not to surface to find out just yet. I don't want to freak out. Boys know about freaking out. That feeling when electricity rages through your body, causing you to lose all sense.

Like when a boy at school dared me to surf a storm wave after the hurricane. He dared me, calling me a bad name if I didn't. I wanted to do it, I was going to do it, I even told him so. But then, I didn't. I remembered Mama. She warns us about this all the time. *"When you live in nature, boys, when you live as we do, you must be smarter. You must learn to respect nature. You must read the signs. You must learn to obey what is said to you, Hina will be there to guide you, but you must be able to hear her."* I saw the waves were fifty feet. I knew I might be crushed in them. So, I didn't do the dare. The boy did. And he broke his arms in a fall. His surfboard was destroyed. Mama was right. She was right then, and now. I stay submerged and rest myself.

Then Humphrey starts to move again. We follow. Then—he slows. He slows because there is something floating in the water in front of him. It is bright red. It has a square shape. Then another thing floats next to the first. It is yellow. A circular shape. Then more objects float into view. Many colors. Many shapes. Then something that looks like a jellyfish. I touch it. It is a sheet of . . . plastic. I hand it to Liam. Humphrey submerges then, deeper. We look down, he wants us to follow him. We do. Then he stops and looks up. We do this as well.

Our mouths fall open.

Up at the surface of the water, as far as we can see, is a mass of . . . objects. Millions of objects. *Zillions, even.* Plastic objects, it looks like, from the many bright colors of it all. We look all the way to the left . . . there is nothing but this stuff. And total darkness beneath it. The stuff is so thick, it blocks out all the light from above. I sense immediate danger and tap Liam hard on the shoulder. We need to swim fast—away from this, toward the light. Away from the current, drifting into the stuff. Toward the surface that is free of the stuff, so we don't get lost in the darkness.

Liam and I kick our flippers hard for a while. We put a good distance between the crazy plastic stuff and us, and then we both give a thumbs-up to each other, signaling it's time to rise. To break the surface. It is time to see what is going on.

Our heads pop up like corks, above, and we push our masks up. We take big gulps of fresh air. We hug and look behind us. At the stuff.

It feels like another planet, another ocean. This planet's ocean is made out of plastic stuff. It is endless. I look and look and look but I cannot see where it ends.

"Trash," says Liam. "It is miles and miles and miles of trash, Sean."

"How can that be, Liam?" I cry. Real tears now fall from my eyes. Who would be so mean, so cruel to dump this much trash into the ocean?"

"It is plastic trash. The worst trash. Plastic trash doesn't . . . dis . . . in . . . teg . . . um, *it doesn't go away.* Melt into the seawater.

"Disintegrate," I correct my brother. "It doesn't disintegrate into the water. It stays on top.

"And kills anything that mistakes it for food. It gets stuck in tummies," says my twin.

"Yep," I reply.

"Humphrey found it. He wanted us to know," Liam says.

"Humphrey's a good turtle, Liam."

"Yes he is, Sean . . . he is grateful for Papa's flipper."

At Papa's name, we both look at each other. Then we simultaneously turn around in the water. We need to see how far the turtle has taken us.

A tiny skinny line of land, that is Maui, is still visible. The current must have taken us this far out. It isn't possible for our little legs to have swum that far.

"The current, Liam," Sean says in a frightened voice, "It did this. It drifted us this far."

"What do we do?" I ask him.

"I don't know, Liam." This is the first time my brother has ever not known what to do. He always has some sort of an idea.

"Where is Humphrey?" I say suddenly. We look around. The turtle is gone.

# Liam

I think and think and think. What would Mama tell me to do? I look up. Mama tells me to follow Hina. In all situations, that Hina will lead me home. But I see that Hina not there! How can this be? Where is Hina, the moon? It is late . . . late afternoon. We should be able to see Hina's outline somewhere?

"Sean . . . where is Hina?"

"Gone. Because . . . it's the . . . wait, what do you call it?" Sean says, his forehead wrinkled.

"NEW MOON!" I exclaim, remembering.

"Oh . . . right. The moon . . . is dark? Something about the sun being in the way?" Sean asks.

"I think so," I say. "All I know is Hina is sleeping tonight."

"So we don't have her help . . ." Sean says.

I think about this. But Mama says Hina is ALWAYS with us? She is always there for us to follow. Nothing is making sense. I am starting to get scared. Sean is scared too. We hug in the ocean, the giant trash pile a few feet away.

"I think we should swim away from the trash while we can see it, Liam."

"Okay," I say. This is bad. This is really, really bad.

We swim for a little while, then, stop. I reach around to my tank and remove a thin object. It is my emergency floatie. I look at my brother and nod. He has the same floatie, he gets his out. We both pull the safety stoppers off and the life preservers inflate into large circles. We put them around our bodies. They are adult-sized so they are like little boats for us.

"Well, we can float at least . . . until . . ."

"Papa find us," I finish.

"But how will he see us in the dark, Liam?"

"I don't know," I say.

I look up at the afternoon sky. At where Hina should be. Was Mama wrong?

# Sean

Twilight will be here in an hour or so, I calculate. Fear is start-ing to gnaw at me. I see the enormous mound of floating plastic garbage behind my brother. We won't be able to see much, soon.

"Liam, where SHOULD Hina be?" I ask, looking up.

"Oh, about there . . ." my brother says, pointing up and to the left.

I look. Nothing. Mama says Hina will always take care of us, guide us. Yet she isn't here tonight. I look at the skinny line of land. I suddenly see something, a teeny-tiny orange speck. A speck so small, that it is almost not there. Then another, and another. They start to dot the edge of the faraway land.

I look up at the sky, wishing Hina was there to help me to see the orange flashes better.

But, she isn't there. I look up and see that she is gone.

I can almost hear her saying, "Yes, Sean, I am sleeping tonight. I know you can't see anything. It will soon be dark for you. But, look up here, at the darkness of where I am usually waiting. You think you can't see, but you can see, you see the darkness. What else do you see, Sean?

I think about Hina's question as I look at the fading orange flecks. *Fire. The flecks are fire* . . . torches being lit on Maui . . . night torches. Hina is asking me to create light, since she cannot.

I look at the orange flecks of fire. I need to create *fire*.

I think of my lighter, in the waterproof emergency bag attached to my tank.

I look over Liam's head to the floating trash. Plastic. *What if . . . ?*

"Liam . . . we need to make *fire*. Look at all that trash. Do you think any of it will burn?"

"I . . . don't think plastic burns, Sean?"

"No. Not plastic. Paper. Wood. I know it is wet. But we could . . . try?"

"I could look . . ." he says.

"Just swim around the edge of it. See what you can see.

"You want to make a fire for Papa to see . . . and find us!" he yells to me.

"Maybe," I say, carefully. "I know it's not likely . . . I mean it is wet trash.

"But you never know?" he says.

He turns and swims to the muck.

# Liam

I am poking at the yucky trash. I find a soda can first. Then a bit of a bicycle tire. Then, a candy wrapper. Then, several soda caps. A lid from a coffee cup, I think. Then I swim around to a new patch of trash. Plastic forks, knives, spoons and straws here. Then bags. Bags! Brown bags . . . I think they are grocery bags. They are wet. Soaked. Mushy with seawater, smushy when I touch them. I grab at them anyway, handfuls of squishy brown stuff, and swim back to Sean.

"Paper!" I cry, shoving the mush at him.

"It's . . . great Sean. It is. Good job. But . . . it's too wet. It will never light."

I test this, just to be sure. I take the lighter out very carefully, and flick the flame upwards. Our faces glow. I touch the flame to the mush. It sizzles. Nothing.

"Let me try again," my brother says.

My heart sinking . . . I nod at him.

I look at the orange flecks, now tracing a line in the twilight, where the land is.

Sean is gone a long time. I start to worry and yell out. "Sean . . . come back, we will just wait here together."

Just then, I feel a bump behind me. I turn. "Humphrey!" I yell.

Humphrey has a something in his mouth. I touch it. It looks like tape. It is tape, it has a little stickiness left in it.

"What is that?" Sean says, swimming up to me, "hi Humphrey," he says to the large turtle.

"Tape," I say.

"Oh. It's long, Liam."

"Yeah . . ." I am pulling on the tape. I feel, a heaviness, all of a sudden. The tape is attached to something. Something heavy. It is beneath me. I pull and pull.

"Sean, help me pull this . . . pull this up," I say.

We both yank on the tape, wrapping it around and around our hands. It takes a really long time. The tape is really long.

But, soon a large item appears beneath our feet.

"What is that?" Sean yells. For a moment I am afraid. But I can see it is a square object . . . as it surfaces, I see it is . . . a box!

"Liam, it's a package . . . it is a box. This tape . . . is wrapped around it.

I run my hands over the brown box, and I see that the tape continues over all the edges. It covers a white paper on the top. In the corner of the paper are the letters, UPS.

"It's mail, Sean."

"Let's . . . open it," my brother says.

"Okay . . ." I say.

"But let's be real careful. Keep the top facing up. Don't get it wet."

I look at Humphrey. I nudge his shell. Then I pull on it a little. Humphrey turns around and I place the box on top of his shell.

"Please stay there, Humphrey," Sean says.

We pull the tape off slowly. The box is mushy and wet, and

starts to fall apart, but not as easily as I would have thought.

"It's new trash," Sean says. It's only half-mushy.

He is right. This box . . . must have . . . fallen off of . . . a ship? A ship. Very recently. It is wet, mushy, but not falling apart in our hands like the mushy stuff Sean found earlier.

We open it, and find a large plastic bag inside. A closed, plastic bag.

"It is sealed shut, Liam," Sean says to me.

"Okay, Humphrey, don't move . . . please . . . stay very still . . ." I whisper to the turtle.

I open the plastic bag. Inside . . . are . . . hundreds . . . thousands of paper strips. Dry paper strips.

"Liam. I know what this is. Remember at Christmas, when Papa ordered the fancy dish for Mama? The dish made out of . . . por . . . porce . . ."

"Porcelain, " I finish.

"Yeah, that stuff. I helped Papa open that box too. These . . . paper things were all over the dish."

"Protecting the dish so it wouldn't break," I say.

"Yeah . . ." Sean says.

"How big is this box, Liam?" he asks.

I look at it. It is almost covering Humphrey's shell. "Three feet high about, same . . . deep," I say.

"That's a lot of paper!" my twin says, smiling.

I look up at Hina's darkening sky.

"Thank you Hina, for telling me to make light since you are asleep tonight," I whisper.

"Yeah, thanks, Hina," Sean says.

"Go get some plastic trash, Sean, a large piece of trash if you can," I say. He does this and returns with a . . . jagged piece of purple plastic. Maybe it used to be a lid. I place it a few feet from us and Humphrey and the box.

Then I scoop some paper strips out of the box and spread them onto the plastic. I look at my brother.

"Here goes . . ." I say. I flick my lighter and touch the lip of the flame to the paper.

It ignites immediately.

It explodes, actually. I splash away wildly. Sean does too. He is so scared that he grabs onto the box for safety. Which is a good thing because Humphrey submerged.

"The fire scares Humphrey!" Sean says.

But I see our turtle resurface and go underneath the box that my brother is holding.

Meanwhile the fire has become a fireball. It is burning furiously and lights up the entire ocean and sky.

It is an orange Hina.

"Coooool!!!!!" screams Sean.

"It IS cool! My boyish heart is totally satisfied with the fireball that *I made!*"

I can see the trash clearly now, in orange glow.

I can see my brother's face, grinning.

I can see the waves lapping at our life preservers.

Then I see Humphrey's face. I see his fake flipper glittering— it is made out of metal and the fire is dancing on it. It looks super duper cool.

Humphrey's face is totally calm. I am shocked. His eyes are

sparkling. I feel calm looking at him.

Calm? I laugh out loud. I am trapped in the open ocean, a sea of garbage floats a few feet away, my twin brother is here with me in this mess, and I have just lit someone's mail on fire.

Yet, I feel strangely calm, after looking at Humphrey.

The fire goes out, soon. And my calm . . . starts to go out too.

"More fire . . ." Sean says. He grabs a handful of paper and hands it to me.

# Sean

I am scared again in the dark.

"Liam, light it . . ." I say.

Liam shakes the lighter and flicks it to light.

"It's about half-filled, Sean," he says. "Quick, look inside the box with your hands . . . feel for whatever is in there . . . you know . . . the thing that this paper is protecting . . ."

"Right! The present! The gift!" I had forgotten about that.

I fish around. I feel nothing, just more paper. Then my hand hits something hard. The present! I feel like I am a discoverer . . . I wonder what it could be?

My hand touches an edge. I close my fingers around it. I pull on it. It won't budge.

"Liam, I found something . . . it is . . . pointy," I say.

"Really! What does it feel like?"

"It . . . it has . . . wait, another point! And . . . more . . . Liam, it is . . . wait, wait . . . it feels . . . like a another box?"

Liam swims to me. He jams his hand into the box. Soon our hands touch.

"Here, Sean, let's pull this out . . . GENTLY . . ." he says to me.

We start to yank on the thing, pulling upwards. Paper strips start flying all over the water . . .

"Wait!" yells my brother.

"We must conserve our kindling! For the fire," he says.

I push all the paper strips to the side of the box. It takes a few moments.

"Okay. Liam . . . wanna try again?"

"Yes . . . here we go, slowly now."

We get a good section of the thing out of the box, it is a little heavy but not really . . . which is strange 'cause it's big.

Then Liam lights some more paper on the plastic tray.

Immediately the object comes to life.

It is a castle. A large castle with a pointed roof and jagged walls.

"It is a toy castle," my brother says.

"It is made of wood. Thin . . . light-weight wood," he says, touching it.

"Dry wood?" I say, excited.

We both look at each other. We look up at the sky.

I hug Humphrey, Liam hugs me.

We place the wooden castle on the plastic tray and light it.

It is way, way, way beyond cool. It burns slowly . . . because the wood is in layers . . . whomever built this toy . . . made it with outer walls and inner walls . . . and used light weight wood, probably on purpose for a small child.

We take a piece of tape and stick it to the plastic tray . . . then we unroll the tape to several feet and hold onto the end. We watch our castle burn.

The pointy tops burn first . . . then the flames make their way down the sides.

I look at my brother and at the sea. Everything is orange . . . orange sparkle.

Liam is looking at the line of orange that is the land. It is the same orange.

"It will burn for a while Sean . . ." he says.

We float, hold hands and watch.

"Liam! Sean! Boys—we see you! Stay there . . . I am coming!" a familiar voice yells, then. It is faraway. But we recognize it.

"Papa!!!!" we both yell back, into the darkness. A tiny white light appears then . . . it is Papa's boat. He has found us.

Our castle's walls are now burning. Papa's boat gets close, I see Mama on the deck. She is crying.

"Mama!" I yell.

Papa pulls the boat next to our burning castle. *The Tess* letters appear in the flames.

"We saw the fire from the shore . . . we followed it . . ." Mama cries out, as Papa dives into the water.

"You followed it?" Liam says.

"Yes, darling, we followed your fire. It is a dark night . . . we have been so scared . . . then . . . we saw your fire . . . out of the blackness . . . and we followed it to you."

"I asked Hina what to do but she was sleeping Mama . . . so she told me that since she was sleeping, I should make new light. Since her light is asleep tonight. Then we found this box and . . . we used Papa's lighter . . . and we lit the toy inside . . ." I say to Mama. She continues to cry.

"You did well, my son . . ." she says to me.

"Boys . . . what on earth brought you out here . . . how did this happen?" Papa asks, the wrinkles in his face look deep, his silver hair is sparkling in the flames from the castle.

Just then Humphrey's head pops out of the dark water. It is

outlined in orange flicker.

"Him . . ." Liam tells Papa.

"Humphrey!" Papa cries. He hasn't seen his patient in a year. "How . . . ?"

"Papa, tell Mama to turn on the big lights in the boat," I whisper.

"Love, we are coming aboard, but . . . could you go to the flood lights . . . the emergency ones . . . flip 'em on for me?" Papa yells up to Mama.

She looks worried, and Papa says again, "we're coming up love, right now."

He paddles us both to the ladder hanging over the side of the Tess, each of us under his left arm. Then he hoists himself and us—up the ladder. Papa is strong.

We hear the big flood lights click, on.

Mama wraps us both in towels, though the night is warm as always. She gives us water, she holds a cup for us, like when we were very little.

"We can do it, Mama," we say, taking our cups. But Liam stands up with his cup.

"Come see what Humphrey took us to see," he says to Papa.

I get up too, and Mama takes my hand.

We walk to the back of the boat. The floodlights are shining outward.

There, as far as our eyes could see, was trash. Lumpy, ugly, plastic trash.

Papa and Mama are silent.

Then they take each other's hands. They turn to us.

"This has a name, boys. It is called, ***The Great Pacific Garbage Patch,***" Papa said, his voice low and serious.

"We have never seen it before, because it has never come this close to Maui . . . we had heard of it, of course. It is a terrible thing," he added.

"Ohhhh . . ." Liam and I say together.

"But, you boys . . . and Humphrey . . ." Mama says, looking over the side of the boat then, "have alerted us to this . . . that it is coming . . . and heading to our shores. Now we can alert the authorities . . . before the trash has a chance to kill all our turtles . . . and other sea life."

"Thank you Humphrey, dear boy," Papa says, looking down at the turtle by the boat.

"Tess, I'm gonna get him. We can move him to the other side of the island for now."

We watch Papa pull the cables that lift turtles aboard the boat so that they drape over Humphrey's shell, then he dives into the water and adjusts them comfortably. Soon Humphrey is aboard. Mama goes to the hull and finds fresh algae for him.

Papa fills a plastic tub with sea water, using a special hose.

"Good boy, Humphrey," Papa says softly, stroking the turtle's head. He looks at the flipper closely. It is easy to do in the floodlights.

"Looks terrific . . . Tess, have a look . . . it's as good as new. Wonderful."

Mama bends her silvery head and inspects the flipper. Then she looks into Humphrey's eyes.

"Thank you Humphrey, she says. "Thank you for bringing my boys home."

"And for warning us to the garbage patch!" adds Papa.

Then Mama looks up, at where Hina should be. "Thank you Hina, once again. Thank you."

www.ingramcontent.com/pod-product-compliance
Lightning Source LLC
Chambersburg PA
CBHW072106270326
41931CB00010B/1467